Praise for This Book

"Evaluation quality and use depend on evaluation management. That makes this book essential for all evaluation professionals and commissioners of evaluations."

—Michael Quinn Patton, *Utilization-Focused Evaluation*

"This is a comprehensive 'one-stop shop' guide for evaluation practitioners and evaluation managers: practical, succinct, and full of commonsense advice and wisdom. It shows that the authors speak from experience and expertise."

—Huilan Krenn, W.K. Kellogg Foundation

"A savvy introduction to evaluation management by authors who had, independently from each other and almost alone in the community, provided insight on this topic. Evaluation will look more significant and worthwhile if managed the way it is suggested in this book."

—Nicoletta Stame, Sapienza University of Roma, Italy

"Catsambas and Davidson provide a practical, easy-to-read overview of how to manage program evaluations."

—Marcus Galeste, Arizona State University

Evaluation Management

To our clients who keep trusting us,
our colleagues who make us shine,
and our families who support us when we prioritize the work we love.
Tessie and Jane

Sara Miller McCune founded Sage Publishing in 1965 to support the dissemination of usable knowledge and educate a global community. Sage publishes more than 1,000 journals and over 600 new books each year, spanning a wide range of subject areas. Our growing selection of library products includes archives, data, case studies, and video. Sage remains majority owned by our founder and after her lifetime will become owned by a charitable trust that secures the company's continued independence.

Los Angeles | London | New Delhi | Singapore | Washington DC | Melbourne

Evaluation Management

How to Commission and Conduct Evaluations that Matter

Tessie Tzavaras Catsambas

EnCompass LLC

E. Jane Davidson

Real Evaluation Consulting

Sage

Sage

FOR INFORMATION:

2455 Teller Road
Thousand Oaks, California 91320
Email: order@sagepub.com

1 Oliver's Yard
55 City Road
London, EC1Y 1SP
United Kingdom

Unit No. 323-333, Third Floor, F-Block
International Trade Tower
Nehru Place, New Delhi – 110 019
India

18 Cross Street #10-10/11/12
China Square Central
Singapore 048423

Printed and bound by CPI Group (UK) Ltd, Croydon, CR0 4YY

Library of Congress Control Number: 2023051539

ISBN: 978-1-5443-5312-8

This book is printed on acid-free paper.

FSC www.fsc.org MIX Paper | Supporting responsible forestry FSC® C013604

Acquisitions Editor: Helen Salmon

Editorial Assistant: Sarah Oehlerking

Production Editor: Vijayakumar

Copy Editor: Erin Livingston

Typesetter: TNQ Technologies Pvt. Ltd

Indexer: TNQ Technologies Pvt. Ltd

Cover Designer: Candice Harman

Marketing Manager: Victoria Velasquez

24 25 26 27 28 10 9 8 7 6 5 4 3 2 1

BRIEF CONTENTS

Preface **xv**

About the Authors **xix**

Chapter 1	Overview of Evaluation Management	1
Chapter 2	Commissioning Great Evaluations	19
Chapter 3	Pre–Start-Up: Analyzing the Evaluation Requirements	43
Chapter 4	Managing the Evaluation Contract Start-Up	55
Chapter 5	Managing the Evaluation Team	71
Chapter 6	Managing Data Collection	83
Chapter 7	Managing Data Analysis	97
Chapter 8	Managing Evaluation Reporting	105
Chapter 9	Managing Evaluation Use and Influence	121
Chapter 10	Building Evaluation Management Capacity for Evaluation Commissioners	137

References **157**

Index **161**

DETAILED CONTENTS

Preface **xv**

About the Authors **xix**

Chapter 1 Overview of Evaluation Management **1**

1.1 What Is Evaluation Management? 3

1.2 Whose Job Is Evaluation Management? 5

1.3 What Tasks Does the Evaluation Management Job Entail? 14

1.4 What Are the Key Evaluation Management Competencies? 17

1.5 Conclusion 18

Chapter 2 Commissioning Great Evaluations **19**

2.1 Deciding Whether and What to Evaluate 20

2.2 Evaluation Criteria and Scoping 23

2.2.1 Evaluation Boundaries: What Is In and What Is Out of Scope 23

2.2.2 Clarity—But Not Overspecification—About What Kind of Evaluation Is Needed 24

2.2.3 Purpose and Use: Identifying the Purposes and Uses of the Evaluation 25

2.2.4 Values 27

2.3 Determining the Best Way to Contract an External Evaluation 27

2.4 Getting Practical: The Process of Writing an Evaluation Terms of Reference 28

2.4.1 Content of the Evaluation Terms of Reference 28

2.4.2 Pitfalls to Avoid in Evaluation Terms of Reference 29

Pitfall #1: The Boilerplate Problem 29

Pitfall #2: The Internal Contradiction Problem 30

Pitfall #3: Being Vague About the Budget 30

Pitfall #4: Procurement Inflexibility 30

Pitfall #5: The Methodology Directive Trap 31

Pitfall #6: Making the Proposal Process Too Burdensome for Smaller Evaluation Firms or Those Representing Marginalized Communities 32

2.4.3 Good Practices in Writing Evaluation Terms of Reference 32

Practice #1: Help Your Organization Clarify Its Needs and Convey Them in the Terms of Reference 32

Practice #2: Know When to Remain Open and Flexible 33

Practice #3: Clarify Your Values About Who Should Be Involved and the Implications 33

Practice #4: Develop Realistic Budgets 34

Practice #5: Include Evaluation Competencies in Criteria for Assessing Evaluators 34

2.5 Selecting a Strong Evaluation Team (or Sole Evaluators) 35

2.5.1 Avoid Pitfalls in Evaluator Competency Specifications 35
Pitfall #1: Hiring Researchers to Conduct Evaluation 35
Pitfall #2: Valuing Subject Matter Expertise Over Evaluation Expertise 35
Pitfall #3: Devaluing Context Expertise 36
2.5.2 Strategies for Selecting an Evaluation Team with the Right Competencies 36
Practice #1: Emphasize the Relevant Evaluation Competency Domains 36
Practice #2: Ask the Evaluators to Provide an Example from Their Experience That Demonstrates the Top Competency Requirement for Your Evaluation 37
Practice #3: Hold Oral Interviews as Part of Your Competitive Process 37
Practice #4: Check References 37

2.6 Selecting the Best Evaluation Implementor 38
2.6.1 Competitive Selection 38
Pitfall #1. A Selection Committee That Does Not Represent Key Stakeholders 38
Pitfall #2. Favoring People and Organizations You Like 39
Pitfall #3. Manipulating the Questions to Bidders 39
Pitfall #4. The Points Contradicting Your Intuition 39
2.6.2 Competing Among a Preselected Group 39
2.6.3 Internal Evaluation Teams 41

2.7 Building Capacity in Commissioning Evaluation 41

Chapter 3 Pre–Start-Up: Analyzing the Evaluation Requirements 43

3.1 Pre-Proposal: Understanding the Terms of Reference 44
3.2 Responding to the Terms of Reference 47
3.2.1 Developing a Timeline 49
3.2.2 Staffing 49
3.2.3 The Budget 52
3.3 Clarifying, Negotiating, and Selection 53
3.4 Upon Evaluation Contract Award 54

Chapter 4 Managing the Evaluation Contract Start-Up 55

4.1 Evaluation Management Structure 56
4.1.1 United Nations 57
4.1.2 United States Federal Government 58
4.1.3 Foundations 59
4.1.4 Nonprofit Organizations 59
4.1.5 Investing in Evaluation Planning 60
4.2 Goals of Evaluation Start-Up 61
4.3 Starting in the Middle 63
4.4 Key Evaluation Start-Up Tasks 64
4.4.1 Analysis of the Evaluation Requirements and Preparation 64
4.4.2 Kick-Off Meeting with the Evaluation Commissioning Manager and Evaluation Implementing Manager 65
Evaluation Implementation Manager (EIM) 65
Evaluation Commissioning Manager (ECM) 66
Internal Evaluator (ECM and EIM) 67

4.4.3 Stakeholder Kick-Off Process (Either Group Meeting or Interviews) 68
4.4.4 Submission and Approval of the Evaluation Plan 68

Chapter 5 Managing the Evaluation Team 71

5.1 Goals of Team Management in Evaluation 71
5.2 Configurations of Evaluation Teams 72
5.2.1 Issues That Arise from Evaluation Team Composition 74
5.2.2 Selecting the Evaluation Team 75
5.3 Managing Team Performance 75
5.3.1 Orientation and Team Planning 76
5.3.2 Communication 77
5.3.3 Assignments and Time Management 77
5.3.4 Issues That Arise Within the Evaluation Team 78
5.3.5 Teamwork 79
5.4 Managing Multiple Evaluation Teams at the Same Time 81

Chapter 6 Managing Data Collection 83

6.1 Prior to Initiating Data Collection 83
6.2 Early in Data Collection 84
6.3 Active Data Collection 86
6.4 Managing and Archiving Data 87
6.4.1 File-Naming Protocols 92
6.5 Communication 92
6.6 Good Monitoring Practices 92
6.7 Addressing the Unexpected 93
6.7.1 False Data 93
6.7.2 Incomplete Data 94

Chapter 7 Managing Data Analysis 97

7.1 Role and Scope of Data Analysis in an Evaluation 98
7.2 Important Questions in Data Analysis 98
7.3 The Cost of Skipping Data Analysis 99
7.4 The Role of the Evaluation Manager in Data Analysis 100
7.4.1 Protect Time and Budget for Data Analysis 100
7.4.2 Ensure a Data Analysis Plan Exists and Monitor Progress 101
7.4.3 Managing Different Data Streams 101
7.4.4 Framing and Integrating Findings—the Data Analysis, Integration, and Synthesis Session 101
7.4.5 Protect Evaluation Independence 102

Chapter 8 Managing Evaluation Reporting 105

8.1 Principles and Practices of Good Reporting 105
8.1.1 You Have Questions; We Have Answers 106
8.1.2 Weave the Evidence and Values into a Coherent Performance Story 107
8.1.3 No Surprises 107
8.1.4 Reporting Is a Process, Not a Product 109

8.1.5 No One Should Feel Stupid When They Read, Watch, or Listen to an Evaluation Report 109
8.1.6 Structure Reports for Actionable Answers 111
8.1.7 One Size Does Not Fit All 111
8.1.8 Co-Constructed Next Steps Are Better Than Recommendations from Afar 111

8.2 Written Reports 112
8.2.1 Reporting Structures That Work 112
8.2.2 Creating a Skeleton Report Early On 114
8.2.3 Reviewing and Revising the Report Outline 114
8.2.4 Planning and Making Assignments 114
8.2.5 Substantive Reviews and Collaboration 115
8.2.6 Data Visualization 116
8.2.7 Synthesizing, Editing, and Quality Management 116

8.3 The Debriefing Meeting 118

8.4 Reviews and Approval 119

Chapter 9 Managing Evaluation Use and Influence 121

9.1 No, Evaluation Use and Influence Is Not Only About Implementing Recommendations! 122

9.2 What Is the Evaluation Manager's Job in Evaluation Use and Influence? 123

9.3 What Drives Evaluation Use and Influence 125

9.4 Managing Context and Politics 125

9.5 Managing the Process and Stakeholder Engagement 126

9.6 Developing an Evaluation Use and Influence Strategy 127

9.7 Involving Key Influencers in Evaluation 129
9.7.1 How Do We Identify the Key Influencers? 130
9.7.2 Where and How Should We Involve Key Influencers? 132

9.8 Strengthening Evaluation Culture and Capacity While Facilitating Evaluation Use 134

Chapter 10 Building Evaluation Management Capacity for Evaluation Commissioners 137

10.1 Building a Strong Evaluation System 138
10.1.1 Where Should the Evaluation Function Be Positioned, Ideally? 138
Foundations and Nonprofit Organizations 139
United Nations (UN) Agencies 139
Government 140
10.1.2 The Hybrid Decentralized Model of Evaluation 143
10.1.3 Evaluation Values, Vision, and Philosophy 144

10.2 Evaluation Culture 145
10.2.1 Commitment from the Top 145
10.2.2 Transparency and Shared Meaning Using Evaluation 146
10.2.3 A Robust Learning Agenda 146
10.2.4 Learning About Evaluation 147

10.3 Evaluation Competencies for Commissioners of Evaluation 147
10.3.1 Everyone in the Organization Needs to Understand Why an Evaluation Is Undertaken, What High-Level Questions It Is Asking, and What Decisions or Thinking It Will Inform 148
10.3.2 Evaluation-Competent Leadership Is a Must 148
10.3.3 Program Staff Must Be Able to Articulate Their Program's Theory of Change, Standards of Program Excellence, and Assumptions and Risks 149
10.3.4 Evaluation Competence in the Evaluation Unit 150
10.4 The Operational Level of Evaluation 151
10.4.1 Developing an Evaluation Strategic Plan 151
10.4.2 Monitoring Evaluation Quality 152
10.4.3 Developing Evaluation Learning Plans 153

References **157**

Index **161**

PREFACE

We wrote this book to fill a gap in the literature about one of the five domains of evaluation competencies: management. Tessie had been teaching the evaluation management course for some time and had not been able to find a satisfactory text to recommend to participants who wanted to manage evaluations that facilitate both technical rigor and evaluation use, are honest and constructive, and are guided ethically and efficiently to successful completion. Tessie found herself continually writing new material for the course and thought that evaluators would benefit from a text that helped them plan and manage better evaluations. In her evaluation work, Jane had been advising evaluation commissioners on how to strengthen their evaluation functions; wishing she could give them a text to support their efforts to manage better evaluations, she had started writing extensive notes she hoped to turn into a book. The godfather of the evaluation management book you are holding is our dear friend and fellow evaluator Thomaz Chianca, who, upon hearing about our respective ideas and plans, brought us together to explore a possible collaboration, which we both embraced enthusiastically.

We wrote a book that guides evaluation teams and commissioners of evaluation to work more effectively together to make an evaluation go smoothly and hit the mark from a utilization and an organizational learning perspective. Everything starts with a vision of evaluation excellence, and we then unpack all the things you need to do as a manager to fulfill that vision. How do you make sure things do not fall between the cracks? How do you keep an eye on all the moving parts and not forget the big picture? And how do you shepherd the evaluation home to completion?

In the book, we have included guidance that can be used inside evaluation firms (and for solo evaluators) for how to manage complex evaluation contracts, validating those experiences and giving additional insights. We zoom in on specifics (practical tools, checklists, questions to use, do's and don'ts)—we call this the *tactical* level of evaluation management. Then we zoom out to see the big picture by inviting the reader to step back, reflect, and learn—we call this the *strategic* level of evaluation management. For example, we explore the central role of evaluation in government and many foundations and nonprofits, the range of options for positioning and staffing evaluation, and the implications for organizational effectiveness and learning.

We also wanted to demonstrate how the intentionality of the evaluation manager for equity, sustainability, and culturally responsive practices can make a big difference in the kinds of evaluations we commission and conduct. When the evaluation manager keeps the most important values front and center, they do not get lost in the methodological and logistical soup.

Over our many years' experience managing evaluations, we learned that to do a good job, we needed to use approaches and skills from a range of disciplines: project management, administration and logistics, budgeting, team management, leadership development, communication, coaching, systems thinking, and negotiation. Borrowing from these many disciplines, evaluation managers must hone their judgment; they need to know when to intervene and how as well as when to leave evaluators alone to get their work done. In this book, we have translated and applied these approaches and skills to evaluation specifically enabling the evaluation management task to be fulfilled in the best way.

WHO THIS BOOK IS FOR

In writing this book, we questioned the boundaries of evaluation management and the locus of responsibility for it and considered the wide range of professionals who perform evaluation management functions and would benefit from stronger evaluation management competencies.

This book is for anyone who has a role in evaluation management, including the following:

- staff in organizations that commission evaluation who are assigned to select an evaluation team and then manage or coordinate an evaluation
- team leaders in charge of an evaluation team implementing an evaluation (external or internal to the commissioning organization)
- staff in evaluation consulting organizations who are not evaluators but are assigned to manage or coordinate evaluations
- solo evaluators (external or internal to the commissioning organization)
- program managers whose programs are part of an evaluation
- senior managers in commissioner organizations who oversee an evaluation function or have responsibility for the use of evaluation in the organization
- senior managers in government offices or evaluation consulting firms who are structuring an evaluation or conducting an organizational audit of their evaluation
- proposal writers who are writing up how to organize, staff, and fund an evaluation
- evaluation instructors who wish to round out their courses on any methodology with an understanding of the role evaluation management plays in the success of evaluation
- new and emerging evaluators who wish to bring a wider perspective and understanding to each evaluation task they are assigned and who wish to develop to higher levels of authority and responsibility in evaluation

How This Book Is Organized

Chapter 1 dives into what we understand to be evaluation management, its boundaries, who has responsibility for it, and the key competencies that relate to it.

Chapters 2 through 8 follow the life cycle of evaluation contracts: development of specifications (terms of reference, request for proposal) and selection of evaluation team on the commissioning organization side (Chapter 2), evaluation proposal development on the responding organization side (Chapter 3), start-up of the evaluation contract (Chapter 4), managing evaluation teams (Chapter 5), managing data collection (Chapter 6), managing data analysis (Chapter 7), and evaluation reporting (Chapter 8).

Chapters 9 and 10 address a higher level of leadership in evaluation. Chapter 9 explores managing the use and influence of evaluation, focusing on strategic choices evaluation managers make throughout the evaluation and effective stakeholder engagement processes they might employ. In Chapter 10, we zoom out to consider the implications on the structure and staffing of the evaluation function in evaluation commissioning organizations as well as the overall strategic evaluation plan, including evaluation capacity building for individuals and organizations.

How to Read This Book

To make it easy to navigate, each chapter starts with a short note on how the chapter is relevant to different types of readers. Thus, you can read this book in two ways.

First, you can read chapters that specifically address issues relevant to your interests. Chapters are self-contained in that they cover the evaluation management aspect of the topic, including how to avoid traps and engage in good evaluation management practices. In reading these chapters, think about how to strengthen your evaluation management competencies and how to make sure your evaluation methods and activities incorporate good management practices.

Second, you can read the chapters that relate to your counterpart (the commissioner, if you are part of an external evaluation team, and the evaluation team, if you are on the commissioner side and responsible for liaising with the evaluation team). In reading these chapters, think about how you manage the areas of collaboration and overlap with those on the other side of your role. Evaluation management is frequently shared by those who commission and those who conduct evaluation. The magic of great evaluation management happens when you both manage the logistics of your role well and work effectively with those who share the evaluation management function in another organization or unit.

We promise that, after reading this book, you will

- have a deeper appreciation of the complexity of the evaluation management job,
- be ready to apply practices that will improve your evaluation management, and
- feel more confident about your own development and learning path in evaluation management.

WHO HELPED US

In addition to our friend Thomaz Chianca, the godfather of our book, we owe our gratitude to many colleagues who openly shared insights and ideas from their experiences to help us bring into the book the richness of variation in evaluation management practices from different countries and different evaluation commissioner organizations: Ian Goldman, Patricia Rogers, Marco Segone, Asela Kalugampitiya, Andrea Cook, Julie Thoulouzan, Alexandra Chambel, Anne Bateman, Huilan Kren, and Veronica Olazabal. Special thanks go to Tessie's organization, EnCompass, for its support:

Lynne Franco, who managed EnCompass' evaluation practice for 10 years, contributed her deep evaluation experience and competence to the content of the book; Jonathan Jones, who oversees the evaluation function, shared valuable insights; and more than 50 EnCompass evaluators tested, refined, and documented evaluation management approaches over the years. EnCompass colleague Maeve Tobin helped us to stay organized over the years it has taken to bring this book to completion. Finally, we are grateful to our Sage editor Helen Salmon, who gave us latitude to write the first book on evaluation management and nudged us along when we became distracted. Helen and her editorial team make Sage a vibrant and active learning hub for evaluation.

We are also grateful for the feedback from the following (previously anonymous) reviewers during the development of the manuscript:

- Joanne Carman, *University of North Carolina at Charlotte*
- Marcus Galeste, *Arizona State University*
- Huilan Krenn, *W.K. Kellogg Foundation*
- Michael Quinn Patton, *Utilization-Focused Evaluation*
- Nicoletta Stame, *Sapienza University of Roma, Italy*

As we look back on our collaboration as co-authors, we can honestly say that this book is 100% better because of it. It has been a joy to talk things through and co-create. We were blessed with a writing partnership where we could trust and rely on one another. We hope you enjoy reading and using this book as much as we enjoyed writing it.

The world is facing serious problems, and evaluation is in a position to help inform and guide how well they are solved. Evaluation management can help bring together the expertise we need: the glue that holds together what we need to inform our decisions, grow our confidence, and create positive change. Through this book, we hope to contribute to commissioning and conducting evaluations that matter.

ABOUT THE AUTHORS

TESSIE TZAVARAS CATSAMBAS

Anastasia (Tessie) Tzavaras Catsambas is the co-founder and CEO/CFO of EnCompass LLC, an organization of about 250 staff that provides services in evaluation, learning, leadership, and organizational development. Tessie is a seasoned evaluation manager of large and complex evaluations and a speaker and trainer in a range of evaluation topics. She is an innovator and practitioner in appreciative evaluation, a methodology that incorporates the systematic study of successful experiences in evaluation, which the evaluators in her firm include in their evaluation practice.

Tessie is a past president of the American Evaluation Association. She was a founding member of the EvalPartners Coalition, a global initiative to promote the use of evaluation to inform policy and program decisions. In 2015, she received the International EvalPartners Award in recognition of her "leadership, creativity and exceptional contributions to the global evaluation community." She holds a master's degree in public policy from the Kennedy School of Government at Harvard University.

E. JANE DAVIDSON

Dr. Jane Davidson is an internationally recognized evaluation specialist, best known for developing evaluation rubrics as a methodology for drawing conclusions about quality and value. She has also made significant contributions in the areas of causal inference for qualitative and mixed methods and in synthesis methodologies for evaluation.

Jane is sought after internationally as a speaker and workshop presenter for her signature approach of methodologically robust but refreshingly practical evaluation with breathtaking clarity. She has presented keynotes and invited workshops in the United States, Canada, the United Kingdom, Sweden, Denmark, Singapore, Brazil, South Africa, Australia, and New Zealand.

Jane is a former associate director of the internationally recognized Evaluation Center at Western Michigan University, where she launched and directed the world's first fully interdisciplinary PhD in evaluation. She was the 2019 recipient of the American Evaluation Association's prestigious Paul F. Lazarsfeld Evaluation Theory Award.

1 OVERVIEW OF EVALUATION MANAGEMENT

The goal of evaluation management is to ensure a high-quality evaluation that addresses client and other stakeholder needs, including the needs of social groups and communities who are supposed to receive services and benefits from the programs and policies being evaluated. Evaluation and evaluative work—whether it be an actual evaluation, evaluative contributions to program design, evaluation capacity building, or a combination—needs to be actively managed to ensure that it meets the needs of those who will use it. An evaluation may be an external project typically conducted under a contract or an internal project with a funding source, a commissioner, a stated purpose, participants and stakeholders, a budget, a timeline, and so on. Evaluation management is the job of managing an evaluation project and includes responsibilities for both those commissioning and those implementing the evaluation. The job of evaluation management requires keeping an eye on the evaluation contract while also managing factors that may be well outside the evaluation's scope but affect its credibility and value.

Regardless of size and duration, evaluation takes place in a broader context of complexity. While an evaluation might be focused on a specific policy, project, program, initiative, organization, network, or system, the evaluand itself (i.e., the thing we are evaluating) is typically one of many interventions attempting to influence change in complex, dynamic systems. Many of these systems are coupled, which means they affect each other in a multitude of ways. For this reason, it is important to consider how these systems and their dynamics affect the success of the evaluand as well as how the evaluand might be influencing changes or ripple effects in adjacent systems. Crucially, as we approach 2030 and numerous irreversible environmental tipping points, this includes natural systems, which are often inadvertently damaged by side impacts of efforts to improve human systems (e.g., the economy). Good evaluation will ensure that decision makers are aware of these effects—or their likelihood—so they can fix problems quickly.

Let us give you an example of how projects sit within and are affected by complex systems. In the project depicted by the winding river in Figure 1.1, an evaluation could be commissioned and take place at various times (e.g., at Points A, B, or C in the life of this project shown in the graphic). Even as the evaluation manager focuses on managing within the boundaries of the evaluation, it is important to zoom out and consider the broader context of relevant forces both inside and outside the project, even if these forces are not explicitly part of the evaluation, the project being evaluated, or even the organization commissioning the evaluation. For example, in an evaluation taking place early on in a project's life (at Point A), communities not included in the project might be receiving fewer services (e.g., education, health, civic engagement) than those in the project, resulting in the unintended consequence of economic and social decline in

FIGURE 1.1 ■ Placing Evaluation at a Point in Time in the "Project River" Within Complexity

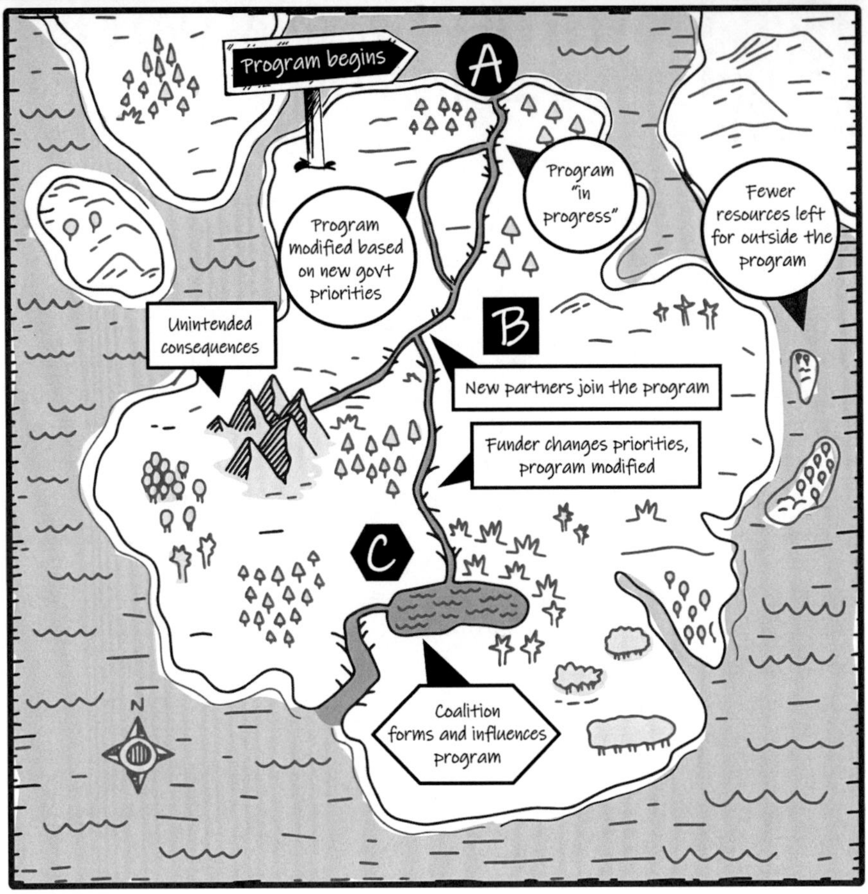

non-project communities. In an evaluation at Point B, a change in funder priorities that might have nothing to do with the project itself may influence the performance, direction, and even survival of the project. In an evaluation at Point C, political change and civil society action outside the project might have resulted in wide coalitions that are pushing the project in new directions.

Thus, using systems and complexity concepts and approaches, evaluation managers must artfully work within an evaluation contract and budget and a limited timeline to ensure that the primary intended users of the evaluation receive the most important insights in the timeliest and most cost-effective way. This book will help you proactively manage evaluations to do just that.

Zooming in to the evaluation contract, the life of the evaluation will begin with a commissioning process and the development of specifications (internal evaluation might start directly with the development of specifications); at pre–start-up, the selection of the evaluation implementor(s) may involve posting a request for proposals, proposal submissions and review, negotiation, and award; the start-up phase of the evaluation contract will involve orientation and planning followed by evidence gathering, analysis and evaluative reasoning, reporting, and exit (which might include responsibility for facilitating use, follow-up, etc.). For evaluation implementors, the goal posts of start-up and exit are typically the boundaries of the evaluation management job.

In this book, we refer to this view of evaluation within a broader context and at a point in time as a *strategic* view: As evaluation managers, we use systems thinking to bring a complexity-aware view to a particular evaluation. In many cases, the evaluation explicitly asks for such a perspective; for example, an evaluation might require incorporating environmental sustainability and biodiversity considerations in evaluation, conducting an evaluation led by Indigenous people, or taking a sustainable development goals lens to an evaluation. We refer to the administrative and logistics management as requiring a *tactical* view necessary for the evaluation manager to "keep the trains running on time" and to get the evaluation done within its scope and budget. Therefore, within a dynamic and political context, evaluation management has both *strategic* and *tactical* goals: At the strategic level, evaluation management aims to design and staff evaluations that add value by asking and answering relevant and useful questions about what key users need to know; at the tactical level, evaluation management aims to implement complex and multifaceted technical requirements within available resources, budget, and time; produce valid and useful findings and conclusions; and ensure the quality of the process, products, and services included in the evaluation.

The purpose of this book is threefold:

1. Create a deeper appreciation of the role of evaluation management in delivering high-quality, value-for-money evaluations.
2. Analyze the roles of commissioning and implementation evaluation managers and the competencies of good evaluation managers.
3. Offer experienced evaluation professionals and funders strategies and tools for managing better and more useful evaluations for adaptive management, organizational learning, informed strategic decisions, and stronger leadership.

This chapter addresses the following questions:

What is evaluation management? How is it different from evaluation design and implementation? How is it different from managing any other project?

Whose job is evaluation management and who plays the role of evaluation manager?

What does the evaluation management job entail at each phase of the evaluation process?

What are the key competencies for evaluation management?

1.1 WHAT IS EVALUATION MANAGEMENT?

Many texts about evaluation equate evaluation management with "doing evaluation tasks" (e.g., evaluation design, evaluation implementation, and stakeholder engagement). Evaluation books often cover aspects of evaluation management in sections where they discuss how to design and implement an evaluation that meets certain requirements. For example, in *RealWorld Evaluation: Working Under Budget, Time, Data, and Political Constraints*, Bamberger et al. (2012) describe four constraints that affect evaluators and outline a seven-step approach, detailing each in subsequent chapters. While one section is devoted to evaluation management, addressing the constraints and challenges presented throughout the book also requires action by the evaluation manager. Similarly, in *The Road to Results: Designing and Conducting Effective Development Evaluations*, Morra Imas and Rist (2009) dedicate a section highlighting the key drivers of successful evaluations as planning and management. In these texts, the boundaries of evaluation management and conducting evaluation are blurred, possibly because the primary audience for these texts are evaluators who must do both the management and implementation of evaluations. Indeed, understanding a program's inherent design and context, building monitoring and evaluation systems, and ensuring a robust methodological approach may also be the responsibility of evaluation managers. . . . But not always.

Evaluation management is, in fact, distinct from "doing evaluation tasks" and yet must support the successful design, conduct, and completion of the evaluation. Evaluation management entails preparing evaluations that matter and that add value to the organizations that commission them and to those who the projects and programs seek to serve. Evaluation management provides oversight and decisions to make sure that all tasks and resources are managed effectively so that the evaluation's goals are met in a technically sound, ethical fashion that is appropriately responsive to client and stakeholder needs. To illustrate, here are three examples of the boundaries between the management and implementation of an evaluation:

- Management and methodology. The evaluation manager may or may not be responsible for designing an evaluation (an evaluation implementor's task), and yet all evaluation managers should be familiar with evaluation design. The evaluation manager needs to understand the budgetary and logistical implications of a particular design and to obtain the necessary agreements to implement that design from those who control the resources for the evaluation.
- Stakeholder engagement. Knowing good techniques for engaging stakeholders in an evaluation (an evaluation implementor's task) is distinct from knowing good techniques for engaging decision makers to negotiate timeline, budget, and methodological adjustments if the need arises (an evaluation manager's task).
- Managing teams and technical direction. Managing evaluation teams and ensuring productive collaboration in an evaluation is an area typically not emphasized in evaluation, but it is very important in evaluation management where several professionals are involved. This is particularly true when working with complexity and coupled systems, where multiple "knowledges" are required to design the evaluation and to make sense of its findings from several vantage points and disciplinary angles.

Evaluation management is therefore a distinct function in evaluation that significantly contributes to the conduct of evaluation and is an integral part of ensuring high-quality, useful evaluations. Distinguishing evaluation management from conducting evaluations will help both those who truly need to remain in the realm of managing rather than conducting evaluations and evaluators and team leaders who will benefit from focusing on how to perform well on the evaluation management aspect of their job.

Evaluations are projects with a timeline and budget, which means that effective project management strategies should be applied when managing evaluations. Project management helps to structure the evaluation, making it more systematic and responsive. Evaluation managers need essential knowledge and skills in planning, budgeting, scheduling, project staffing, managing teams, monitoring, negotiation, communication, procurement, and risk assessment (Yarbrough et al., 2011). The management of evaluations, however, still requires proficiency in evaluation principles, methods, and processes. This is because every management decision has methodological implications and every methodological decision has management implications (Bamberger et al., 2012; Morra Imas & Rist, 2009). For example, a manager looking for a shortcut in the timeline may cut out a key evidence-gathering activity or truncate the time for data analysis, leaving no time for proper triangulation, evidence synthesis, and evaluative reasoning—all of which would compromise the quality of the evaluation. Therefore, both strong project management skills and proficiency in evaluation are needed to manage an evaluation effectively. Evaluations should not be managed by project management specialists who are not also familiar with evaluation.

In addition to managing time, budget, and people as well as strong evaluation methods and quality, the context of evaluation typically presents additional challenges. The evaluation manager may have little formal authority over the evaluation team (besides a contract) and no authority over most of the stakeholders who participate in the evaluation. And yet, the evaluation manager must negotiate agreements on evaluation questions and ensure adherence to standards for evaluation methods and processes, even in cases where stakeholders may not understand that need. Evaluation managers who are internal staff typically take an external or independent stance vis-à-vis the program or organization being evaluated and must contend with the same issues of limited authority and high responsibility for engaging with others as needed for the evaluation.

Furthermore, since evaluation reporting is generally shared among stakeholders beyond the implementers of a program or members of the organization being evaluated or even shared publicly, the judgments about the program or organization inherent in the findings, conclusions, and recommendations of the evaluation may be contextually sensitive and at risk of producing unintended consequences. Evaluation is inherently an assessment of the value of the program or project being evaluated; all evaluation stakeholders want to see their issues understood and prioritized and no individual or organization wants to be criticized, especially if that may have negative implications such as reductions in budget, staff, or program scope. Therefore, evaluations can bring high stress and polarizing views on important issues to all those involved. It is the evaluation manager's responsibility to allay any stresses and manage the politics of the evaluation.

1.2 WHOSE JOB IS EVALUATION MANAGEMENT?

Most definitions of the role of the evaluation manager focus on their operational role (Bamberger et al., 2012; Morra Imas & Rist, 2009; United Nations Evaluation Group [UNEG], 2016) while some definitions add responsibility for alignment with an organization's broader policy and compliance with its standards (World Food Programme [WFP] 2015, 2016). What is less clearly defined in evaluation texts, however, is the *diversity* in the placement of people who may hold the role of evaluation manager, the *shifts and changes* over the life of an evaluation of the people who influence key evaluation decisions, the *shared management* responsibilities for that evaluation, and how this may vary depending on the overall evaluation approach the commissioner requests or the evaluation implementing manager (EIM) proposes.

Tessie has been teaching a course on evaluation management at The EnCompass Learning Center that attracts a wide range of people, including evaluation managers in commissioning organizations such as foundations, government or international agencies, and nonprofit organizations; evaluators looking to move up the ranks to becoming team leaders; internal evaluators managing a portfolio of evaluations; and solo external evaluators looking to improve the management of their evaluations. Less-expected participants have been auditors, proposal writers, agency staff involved in monitoring who wish to understand how best to link monitoring to evaluation, and managers who want to improve how best to collaborate with evaluators in their organizations. This book is useful for a wide range of readers, but it is explicitly focused on professionals identifying as evaluation managers who may work for funders or commissioners of evaluation or who may be team leaders of evaluation teams, solo evaluators, internal evaluators, or even senior managers involved in or using evaluation. Figure 1.2 describes the range of people who may identify with the role of evaluation manager by organizational affiliation, and the box below describes the main groups in more detail.

This book focuses primarily on the evaluation management roles of the evaluation commissioning manager (ECM) and the EIM, and they come in a variety of organizational affiliations.

The ECM is the one who develops the evaluation specification and selects the evaluation team. The ECM may or may not be the funder of the evaluation; sometimes large programs commission their own outside evaluations, so the commissioner may be part of the organization implementing the program being evaluated—for example, Save the Children received funds from The Bill and Melinda Gates Foundation to implement the Saving Newborn Lives (SNL) program, and Save the Children also acted as the ECM for an evaluation of the SNL program that EnCompass was selected to conduct (so Save the Children was the ECM and also the program implementer).

The EIM is the one who is responsible for conducting the evaluation. We typically think of EIMs as part of evaluation consulting firms or team leaders of evaluations. In fact, EIMs could also work for the commissioning organization itself (an internal evaluator), be a solo evaluator, or be a non-evaluator with management responsibility from the contracting organization that is fielding the evaluation team. There are others who

FIGURE 1.2 ■ Types of Evaluation Management Roles by Organizational Affiliation

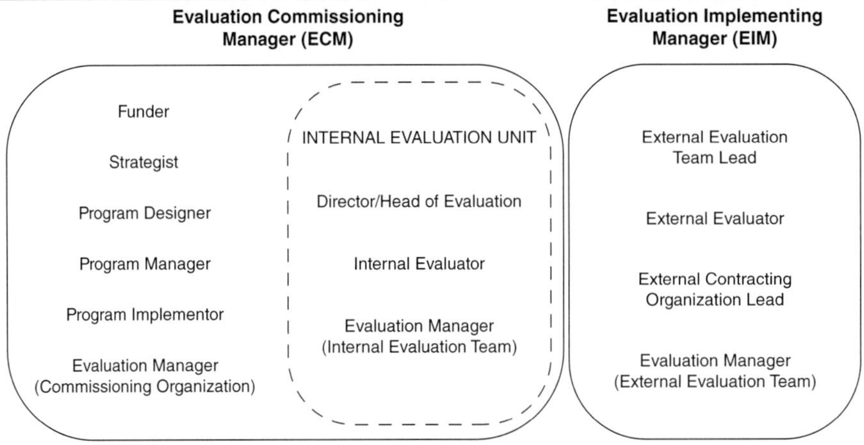

can influence management decisions besides the ECM and the EIM; these stakeholders include funders, project or program implementing partners, those with an interest in the project or program process or results, and those served by the project or program. How big a role these other actors have will depend on the evaluation approach and the circumstances of the evaluation.

EVALUATION MANAGEMENT ROLES

Evaluation Commissioning Manager (ECM)

The role of the ECM is critical in developing the terms of reference. This is an internal process that typically includes understanding and formulating the purposes of the evaluation, evaluation questions, and other guidance around the expectations of the commissioning organization or group. General expectations may include the values the evaluation must adhere to, important criteria to be covered, the type of evaluation, key stakeholders, timeline, and other logistics. The ECM also plays a key role in the next phase—the selection of the winning proposal, contracted either to a solo evaluator or to an organization fielding the evaluation team.

After this phase, the ECM collaborates with the EIM on ensuring a feasible evaluation design that meets stakeholder needs and adheres to the commissioning organization's values, managing data collection, analysis, reporting, and sharing findings. The ECM frequently takes on a more active role in the reporting and use phases, approving the evaluation's final products, ensuring adequate stakeholder engagement, and facilitating data use and follow-up.

Evaluation Implementing Manager (EIM) (External Evaluator Manager)

The external EIM typically manages and implements an evaluation that has been commissioned, contracted, and funded by one or more organizations, whether they are a solo evaluator, an evaluation team leader directly managing an evaluation team, or a manager from the organization contracted to do the evaluation who works with the team leader. The commissioning organization will expect the EIM to deliver on time and in compliance to contract requirements, and the evaluation team (if there is one) seeks the evaluation EIM's guidance, support, and troubleshooting skills.

The external EIM oversees the evaluation process, including evaluation activities and budgets, as well as safeguards the integrity of the methodology. Additionally, evaluation managers must manage people—including clients, stakeholders, and possibly other evaluation team members. They effectively collaborate with ECMs throughout the evaluation, reporting to them regularly and negotiating any needed changes. In cases of highly participatory evaluations (e.g., in developmental, equitable, or Indigenous evaluation methods), the EIM must have strong facilitation and organizational development skills to ensure appropriate engagement of all stakeholders. In the end, the EIM shoulders the responsibility for the success of the evaluation, frequently dealing with unexpected challenges and making decisions that influence the quality and usefulness of the evaluation.

In some cases, by the time the external EIM is appointed, a great deal has already taken place—the proposal has been written and the contract negotiated. In fact, the EIM might not have written the winning proposal, as many organizations have proposal writers to take care of that job. In these cases, the EIM will need to catch up and engage in a productive start-up phase in which aspects of the proposal may be renegotiated as they now begin to understand requirements, promises, agreements, methodology appropriateness, timeline, team competencies, level of effort (person hours devoted to each task), and budget.

Internal Evaluator (ECM and EIM at the Same Time)

The internal evaluator is generally part of an organization's evaluation unit and is responsible for conducting evaluations for the organization's programs. In some organizations, the internal evaluator may be one person working alone; in others, there may be several people who belong to an internal evaluation unit. The role of the internal evaluator or unit may be combined with that of the ECM and EIM in cases when the unit is responsible for commissioning and managing the evaluation. In other cases, the internal evaluation unit may play a monitoring role in the organization. While internal evaluators usually know more about the program being evaluated and its context, organization, culture, or policy than outsiders, they face various internal political challenges (Morra Imas & Rist, 2009). In cases where the evaluation function of the organization is weak (see Chapter 10 for more on evaluation capacity-building), the internal evaluator frequently has trouble engaging internal stakeholders and is in the uncomfortable position of having to maintain a level of independence despite opposition from colleagues. In addition to maintaining this internal-yet-outsider position, they may also face discomfort in their ability to surface weaknesses in the organization's programs. Whether the role of the internal evaluator or unit is combined with commissioning and managing the evaluation or simply monitoring it, it is important to tailor the approach to evaluation management to the circumstances of each office.

To better understand the range of people who influence or who are directly responsible for evaluation management, it is useful to review the life cycle of an evaluation. Evaluation management begins when the evaluation is conceptualized, which typically takes place when someone is appointed to oversee the development of the terms of reference or request for proposal for the evaluation. This person has to engage colleagues and other stakeholders in a meaningful way to determine the purpose, boundaries, and plan for the evaluation; internal evaluators are frequently in a position to draft their own terms of reference and plans but may still face the challenge of engaging stakeholders in thinking about the evaluation's purpose and use. The next step may involve hiring outside evaluators or internally organizing to conduct or implement the evaluation. The endpoint for evaluation management involves managing the activities that follow the completion of an evaluation, possibly including a management response, public meetings, or other evaluation uses.

Finally, anyone can be the evaluation manager. Evaluation managers range a gamut of experiences and can come from diverse backgrounds; they may be novices in evaluation or evaluation experts and anything in between. They may work in the organization commissioning the evaluation, the organization implementing it, or for no organization at all; and their employers may be a governmental, nonprofit, or for-profit organization. In fact, the title *evaluation manager* is used for several different jobs, including the person assigned administratively inside an organization that will commission an evaluation, the person who is selected through a competitive process to implement an evaluation and who may or may not be managing a team, or the internal person assigned to conduct evaluations within an organization (Morra Imas & Rist, 2009). UNEG (2016) says that "the role of evaluation management may be subsumed by other roles, such as that of an evaluator, evaluation commissioner or the evaluation unit head, for example, depending on organizational context and arrangements."

Why is it important to appreciate the shifts and shared nature of the evaluation management role, the shifts in responsibilities, and the diversity in the type of people who play that role?

Understanding the shifts and shared nature of evaluation management is critical because it helps us to dispel a belief that "evaluation is someone else's job": a belief that can threaten the success of an evaluation. For commissioners, it is very easy to think that developing the terms of reference is external to the evaluation and to see it as an administrative task, thus missing the strategic role they need to play during that time. Commissioners may also erroneously believe that once an evaluation team is selected, evaluation management is the job of the team leader. For evaluation teams, the danger is either that they see their team leader as the sole evaluation manager (thus ignoring the important role of the commissioner of evaluation) or that they see the commissioner as the evaluation manager (thus stepping down too easily from their role of educating the commissioner and standing up for evaluation quality, independence, inclusion, resources needed, etc.). For an internal evaluator, the danger is in seeing themselves as an administrator and allowing the evaluation to be marginalized, thus minimizing its use and utility. Understanding the shared responsibility of evaluation management means that those in charge see the evaluation as an essential part of learning and shared accountability and take responsibility for actions that make that evaluation a worthwhile investment for the client, for the organization, and for society.

Diversity is important, because having such a wide range of people identifying with the evaluation manager role means that their needs are quite diverse. Evaluators may need to dust off their management skills and managers overseeing an evaluation would benefit from a deeper understanding of evaluation to prepare for the job. Meanwhile, internal evaluators will need to address issues unique to their insider-yet-outsider position. Ultimately, managing evaluations successfully requires a combination of management and evaluation skills as well as an understanding of the intersection of methodological choices with planning, budgeting, and management decisions—they are inextricably interwoven. In addition, evaluation managers need to rely on their interpersonal competencies to manage stakeholders and encourage the use of the evaluation they are managing.

Figure 1.3 outlines the major responsibilities of ECMs and EIMs in the various phases of the evaluation process. Figure 1.3 highlights key roles, and Table 1.1

FIGURE 1.3 ■ Evaluation Management Roles Throughout the Evaluation Process

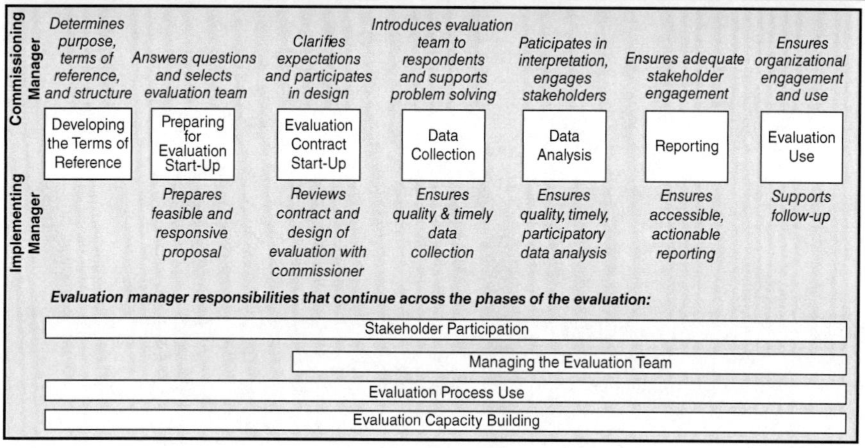

TABLE 1.1 ■ Evaluation Management Roles in Various Evaluation Phases

Evaluation Tasks/Phase	Evaluation Commissioning Manager	Evaluation Implementing Managers		
		Evaluation Team Leader	Solo Evaluator	Internal Evaluator
Needs assessment	Conducts	Conducts	Conducts	Conducts regularly
Define evaluation purpose	Facilitates	Interprets and facilitates	Interprets and facilitates	Facilitates and sets
Terms of reference or scope of work	Develops	Interprets and negotiates	Interprets and negotiates	Develops
Evaluation plan, inception report, or design	Develops preliminary, high-level plan and evaluation parameters	Develops and negotiates a detailed plan, including finalizing methods, sample, sites, and roles of stakeholders throughout the evaluation	Develops and negotiates a detailed plan, including finalizing methods, sample, sites, and roles of stakeholders throughout the evaluation	Develops and negotiates a detailed plan, including finalizing methods, sample, sites, and roles of stakeholders throughout the evaluation
Evaluation oversight and implementation structure	May set up or be appointed to manage the evaluation from the client side Leads evaluation steering committee or planning group Appoints or makes requests to set up any additional groups that might advise the evaluation progress (e.g., a reference group of representative stakeholders) May appoint a technical advisory group of well-known experts in the field to provide guidance to the evaluation	Recruits or is given the members of the evaluation team May request a reference group In consultation with the client representative, may appoint a technical advisory group of well-known experts to provide guidance and feedback to the evaluation Coordinates and negotiates evaluation matters with commissioner throughout the evaluation	May request a reference group In consultation with the client representative, may appoint a technical advisory group of well-known experts to provide guidance and feedback to the evaluation Coordinates and negotiates evaluation matters with commissioner throughout the evaluation	Recruits or is given the members of the evaluation team or may be left alone in conducting the evaluation Coordinates and negotiates

TABLE 1.1 ■ Evaluation Management Roles in Various Evaluation Phases *(Continued)*

Evaluation Tasks/Phase	Evaluation Commissioning Manager	Evaluation Implementing Managers		
		Evaluation Team Leader	Solo Evaluator	Internal Evaluator
Evaluation team	May play a role in orienting the evaluation team	Orients and actively manages the team (scheduling, role clarification, individual and team performance)	Not applicable	May play a role in orienting the evaluation team
Data collection	Introduces the evaluation team to evaluation participants Resolves any issues evaluation participants may bring up or issues that challenge the evaluation team in accessing evaluation participants	Manages the completion and approval of method tools (e.g., interview guides, survey instruments, etc.) Monitors and troubleshoots timely access and completion of data collection elements Resolves issues and negotiates adjustments as needed Monitors emerging findings and negotiates adjustments if needed	Develops tools, gets client approval, and collects data	Develops tools and collects data
Data analysis	Monitors any issues around emerging findings Supports evaluation team by protecting space for this task	Facilitates or arranges for facilitation of data analysis session and triangulation of data types, sources, and evaluators Facilitates session with reference group, other stakeholders or those served by the project or program to ground truth and interpret findings and preliminary recommendations	Protects space for data analysis and triangulation May engage a peer in a data analysis session	Conducts data analysis

(Continued)

TABLE 1.1 ■ Evaluation Management Roles in Various Evaluation Phases (Continued)

Evaluation Tasks/Phase	Evaluation Commissioning Manager	Evaluation Implementing Managers		
		Evaluation Team Leader	Solo Evaluator	Internal Evaluator
Evaluation report writing	Responds to any draft sections, especially around verification of facts, if requested May get involved in supporting consultations in the development of recommendations	Manages the report writing process Plans ahead for additional support in data visualization, editing, and so on	Writes the report	Writes the report
Managing stakeholder feedback	Develops a system for soliciting, tracking, and responding to stakeholder feedback Liaises with the evaluator(s) to ensure timely and comprehensive receipt and response to feedback	Liaises with the evaluation team to ensure timely and comprehensive receipt and response to feedback and integration as agreed in the report Troubleshoots delays	Tracks and responds to stakeholder feedback Troubleshoots delays	Tracks and responds to stakeholder feedback Troubleshoots lack of engagement
Monitors progress (throughout data collection, analysis, and report writing)	Liaises and coordinates with the evaluation team or evaluator Solicits feedback from the evaluation stakeholders, including the evaluand, funder, implementer(s), beneficiaries, or participants	Monitors progress on all evaluation tasks with all evaluation team members Monitors feedback from evaluation participants during data collection Regularly reports to ECM or funder or implementer on progress and negotiates needed adjustments in the plan	Not applicable	If working with a team, monitors progress on all evaluation tasks with evaluation team members Monitors feedback from evaluation participants during data collection

TABLE 1.1 ■ Evaluation Management Roles in Various Evaluation Phases *(Continued)*

Evaluation Tasks/Phase	Evaluation Commissioning Manager	Evaluation Implementing Managers		
		Evaluation Team Leader	Solo Evaluator	Internal Evaluator
Manages dissemination of evaluation reporting	Implements dissemination plan agreed in the contract Supports evaluation team to make arrangements, introduce the evaluation report, and so on	Ensures development of additional dissemination products, including coordinating with the videographer if a video is planned, preparing PowerPoint slides or other products, and scheduling a briefing of key stakeholder groups	Ensures development of additional dissemination products, including coordinating with the videographer if a video is planned, preparing PowerPoint slides or other products, and scheduling a briefing of key stakeholder groups	Ensures development of additional dissemination products, including coordinating with the videographer if a video is planned, preparing PowerPoint slides or other products, and scheduling a briefing of key stakeholder groups
Facilitates use of evaluation, including recommendations	May organize a formal response from those who would implement evaluation recommendations as to how they interpret the recommendations and what they plan to do in response May insert evaluation components in deliberations for decisions the evaluation informs May engage in wider dissemination of evaluation results as another form of evaluation use	May facilitate or arrange the facilitation of a follow-up deliberation meeting May be present at a future deliberation on issues relevant to the evaluation	May facilitate or arrange the facilitation of a follow-up deliberation meeting May be present at a future deliberation on issues relevant to the evaluation	May facilitate or arrange the facilitation of a follow-up deliberation meeting May be present at a future deliberation on issues relevant to the evaluation

(Continued)

TABLE 1.1 ■ Evaluation Management Roles in Various Evaluation Phases (Continued)

Evaluation Tasks/Phase	Evaluation Commissioning Manager	Evaluation Implementing Managers		
		Evaluation Team Leader	Solo Evaluator	Internal Evaluator
Assesses evaluation quality	Solicits feedback on the evaluation process from key stakeholders Holds a debriefing session with the evaluator(s)	Solicits feedback on the evaluation process from clients Participates in a debriefing session	Solicits feedback on the evaluation process from clients Participates in a debriefing session	Solicits feedback on the evaluation process from the program being evaluated Participates in a debriefing session

provides more detail by type of evaluation manager. Later chapters in this book cover evaluation management tasks by evaluation phase in depth and address the different roles ECMs and EIMs play in each phase of the evaluation as well as the different challenges they might face. As the evaluation management role may be shared by different people, having a common vision of what evaluation management is and how to do it well will contribute to managing better evaluations. When funders, commissioners, implementers of evaluation, and those served by the project/program are on the same page about the job of evaluation, it is more likely that they will engage in a constructive endeavor that supports the advancement of useful knowledge and better-informed decisions.

1.3 WHAT TASKS DOES THE EVALUATION MANAGEMENT JOB ENTAIL?

The role of evaluation managers entails the following major elements:

1. *Ensure clear vision and realistic evaluation plans (both ECMs and EIMs).* Evaluation reporting may be well-written, rigorous, on time, and within budget, but it will be a waste if it is not relevant. Because of the time that elapses in the development of the terms of reference and planning phase of an evaluation, it is critical for the ECM and EIM to review the purpose of the evaluation and the evaluation questions in light of its expected use and to ensure the relevance of the evaluation. Once there is a clear and shared vision of the evaluation's use, the values and evaluation criteria, and the evaluation questions, the EIM can formulate an operational evaluation plan. In fact, evaluations have strict timeline parameters (e.g., data collection should not be scheduled in schools during summer break, or evaluation reports must be submitted prior to the programmatic decision they are intended to inform). Evaluation plans must include tasks, subtasks, and deliverables as well as who is responsible for each one.

2. *Organize and manage evaluation teams, stakeholders, and participants.* Managing teams means dealing with people's individual issues—competence, confidence, potential conflict of interest—as well as facilitating the dynamics between people. Besides the evaluation team, which is the responsibility of the EIM, both the ECM and EIM must work with planning groups, steering committees, or reference groups that provide oversight and/or input as well as the evaluand and other stakeholders. Doing this part of the job well is critical for the credibility of the evaluation, a goal that Bustelo describes as "neither simple nor straightforward"(United Nations Development Programme [UNDP], 2013).

3. *Monitor evaluation activities, budgets, and people.* There are many fast-moving, time-sensitive parts in an evaluation. The EIM needs not only to stay current but to stay ahead. For example, finding out that there have been too few survey respondents two days before the survey ends is too late; figuring out that site visits failed to address a key emerging question after all site visits are completed is also too late. The EIM must have a clear sense of when to check in and on what issues while avoiding interfering inappropriately in the progress of colleagues because it may compromise the evaluation's independence and may become counterproductive. The ECM also has a role in monitoring the evaluation process to help troubleshoot when necessary.

4. *Negotiate needed adjustments when issues arise.* Even with the best plans, the need to make adjustments during evaluation implementation is almost inevitable. ECMs and EIMs have a joint responsibility to negotiate and come to mutual agreements with all parties involved. These changes may include adjustments to the timeline and rearranging of the budget, pushback on controversial findings, or modification to the scope of the evaluation to pursue an interesting emerging finding that makes the evaluation more relevant.

5. *Protect evaluation independence and rigor while responding to commissioner and stakeholder needs.* Evaluation stakeholders may have strong points of view about who should be involved, how things should be presented, and other aspects of the evaluation. The evaluation manager has to encourage participation but also protect the boundaries of influence by each stakeholder. This is a fine line, and it may involve some risk to the evaluation manager's own relationships, future employment opportunities, political standing, and so on. Both ECMs and EIMs have a role to play in maintaining appropriate boundaries. While the evaluation managers may wish to accommodate a practical consideration or stakeholder request, they may have to disappoint evaluation participants by standing firm on issues that have ethical implications or compromise the evaluation's rigor and independence. This requires vigilance and continual education of stakeholders about the implications of their requests for the evaluation. It also calls for the evaluation manager to be self-aware of pressures and stresses related to this role.

6. *Ensure the quality and usefulness of evaluation products and briefings.* An important part of the role of both the ECMs and EIMs is ensuring that the evaluation is accessible, understood, and used by key stakeholders. The content

of evaluation reports must be easy to access, clear, easy to understand, and ensure transparency of the methodology. From the implementation side, this may require access to professionals with strong communications skills such as editors, writers, graphic artists, data visualization experts, and videographers. The EIM must plan and budget appropriately for the type of communication needed for the evaluation, including making it accessible to evaluation participants who might not easily have access to the evaluation report (e.g., in communities and sites visited). The ECM must respond to internal and external stakeholder needs about communication and facilitate evaluation use.

The depth of evaluation and management skills needed by evaluation managers to perform these roles varies depending on the size and context of the evaluation. Managing a multiyear, multisite evaluation differs in several ways from managing a small, school-based program evaluation. In their book, *RealWorld Evaluation*, the authors outline the different requirements between "simple projects, complicated programs and complex development interventions," although they recognize the overlap between these categories; they define "simple" projects as of limited scope and definition with few layers of institutional structure involved; "complicated" programs are those that involve several components and layers of institutional structure and actors; and "complex" projects seem to be harder to define but generally involve national programs, multiple funding levels, and less-clear definitions of the intervention (Bamberger et al., 2012). Michael Quinn Patton's developmental evaluation model offers a more granular definition of complex programs as ones where the level of certainty about the evidence supporting a program theory and the level of agreement about the intervention and its desired outcomes is low (Patton, 2011). Thus, when managing "simple" or "complicated" projects, the evaluation manager might focus mostly on managing budgets, timelines, and quality, while in a more complex evaluation, the evaluation manager must also facilitate negotiations among stakeholders even to agree on what is being evaluated and the core evaluation criteria.

Naturally, the manager of a larger, more complex evaluation may have access to management systems and resources not available to the smaller one, such as a coordinator assigned to support evaluation management tasks or a central system that produces status reports and timeline updates. The manager of a smaller evaluation still has challenges in organizing and negotiating the evaluation journey, but the requirements and boundaries of what can be done with a smaller budget are going to be fewer and narrower than for larger ones. No matter the program and evaluation size, however, all evaluation managers will need to adjust to fit the culture and context of the stakeholders where an evaluation is taking place. For example, the manager of an evaluation in an Indigenous community may have to employ an Indigenous evaluator and add time for respectful permissions and entry into those communities before the evaluation is allowed to take place. Thus, the core tasks of evaluation management will need to be adapted for different circumstances.

Managing stakeholder engagement and participation is a key responsibility of both ECMs and EIMs. Figure 1.4 shows how, whether internal or external, evaluation managers need to decide on the appropriate extent of participation and share in decisions that influence the evaluation's success. This figure demonstrates once again the shared responsibility of evaluation commissioners and evaluation implementors in a key aspect of evaluation.

1.4 WHAT ARE THE KEY EVALUATION MANAGEMENT COMPETENCIES?

With the rise of evaluation competency models in recent years such as from the American Evaluation Association (AEA, 2018), International Development Evaluation Association (IDEAS, 2012), the Canadian Evaluation Society (CES, 2010), and the UNEG (2016), it is interesting that there is a convergence of competency domains between several of these models. Figure 1.5 presents four competency models that emerged between 2010 and 2018 demonstrating the synergies between them and their agreement in naming evaluation management as one of the five core domains.

Within the evaluation management domain, these models include skills valid for both ECMs and EIMs related to planning, budgeting, monitoring, ensuring quality, managing people, coaching, mentoring, establishing relationships, leadership,

FIGURE 1.4 ■ Evaluation Management Roles in Stakeholder Engagement over the Life of an Evaluation

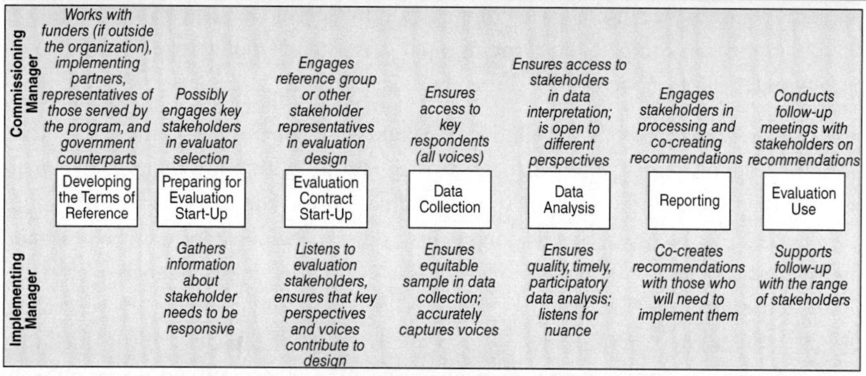

FIGURE 1.5 ■ Domains of Four Evaluation Competency Models

Competency Domain Category	American Evaluation Association (2018)	Canadian Evaluation Society (2010)	United Nations Evaluation Group (2016)	International Development Evaluation Association (2012)
Values **Culture** **Added value of evaluation**	Professional practice	Reflective practice	Personal attributes	Professional foundations Promoting a culture of learning
Methods and technical skills for conducting evaluation	Methodology	Technical practice	Technical and professional skills	Evaluation planning/design Conducting the evaluation Communicating
Context	Context	Situational practice	Knowledge of the United Nations	Monitoring systems
Management	***Planning and management***	***Management practice***	***Management skills***	***Managing the evaluation***
Interpersonal skills	Interpersonal	Interpersonal practice	Interpersonal skills	*Not included*

and administration. Evaluation managers need to have competencies in the management domain in addition to competencies in the other core domains such as the ability to understand and incorporate context; respect culture; perform in an ethical, self-reflective manner; and support high-quality, methodologically sound evaluations. In *RealWorld Evaluation*, Bamberger et al. (2012) included a section titled, "Greater Attention Must Be Given to the Management of Evaluations," recognizing the central role that strong evaluation management has for the success of an evaluation.

1.5 CONCLUSION

Evaluation management is the job of managing an evaluation project within a budget and timeline to inform specific evaluation questions. Evaluation management is connected to but distinct from evaluation design and implementation. The role of evaluation manager can be played by more than one person at any phase of the evaluation and by different people throughout the life of the evaluation. The professionals that play the role of evaluation manager may come from a range of backgrounds and may have a great deal of experience in evaluation or not at all. Evaluation management is one of the five core evaluation competency domains in all competency models of evaluation associations and societies as well as the United Nations.

When managing an evaluation well, the ECM and the EIM each see to their individual and joint responsibilities for ensuring that they end up with an evaluation that matters. The ECM communicates the vision of evaluation use and can provide clear guidance to the EIM, secure access to documents and stakeholders, and ensure provision of valid and accurate data while protecting the evaluators' independence to do their job. Concurrently, the EIM is a partner in getting honest and complete answers to key questions, helps to frame findings in constructive ways, facilitates fruitful meetings that clarify purpose, and generates excitement as well as meaningful participation from stakeholders while managing the process and budget, guiding team members in productive participation, forecasting and troubleshooting challenges effectively, and producing clear and accessible reports and other outputs for decision making. Ultimately, evaluation commissioning organizations as well as internal and external evaluators want their evaluations to be relevant to important decisions and to be valued and used by their stakeholders; good evaluation management makes that possible.

PRACTICE

Study Question: What strategies would you use to understand the context for a particular evaluation, and how would that inform your evaluation planning process?

Exercise: How would your understanding of context influence your approach in managing an evaluation in New Zealand versus if you were working for the United States General Accountability Office (GAO)? Hint: Review the mission, values, and standards for evaluation of the Aotearoa New Zealand Evaluation Association (ANZEA, 2015) and the United States GAO (2018).

Self-Reflection: What role(s) do you or will you play in evaluation, and how would you define success in those roles?

2 COMMISSIONING GREAT EVALUATIONS

WHO SHOULD USE THIS CHAPTER

This chapter focuses on what an evaluation commissioning manager (ECM) as defined in Chapter 1 needs to do to ensure a great basis for the evaluation. However, evaluation implementing managers (EIMs) can benefit from this chapter by understanding what the ECM should do or has done and what additional questions they may want to ask. Remember, internal evaluation managers frequently play both roles of ECM and EIM. Finally, sometimes ECMs hire evaluators to help in this process.

A senior person in a large nongovernmental organization recently confided in Jane that their organization had spent tens of millions of dollars on evaluations over the years. *Every single one* had been a disappointment, some even downright embarrassing.

This experience is far from unique. Over the years, we have heard similar stories from government agencies, philanthropic organizations, educational institutions, businesses, and many evaluators who work with them.

While some of the responsibility for evaluation gone awry must rest with the EIMs, an important theme of this book is that it takes two to tango. If a client organization does a poor job of scoping an evaluation, writing the terms of reference, or finding the right team for the job, even the most skilled and conscientious evaluation team will find it impossible to deliver what is truly needed. This is the role of the ECM in setting the stage for a great evaluation—one that matters.

A few years ago, Jane published a tongue-in-cheek blog post titled *9 Golden Rules for Commissioning a Waste-of-Money Evaluation* (Davidson, 2010) on the Genuine Evaluation blog. That post generated more engagement than anything else she and co-blogger Patricia Rogers had published. Evaluators from nearly every continent, working in virtually every sector you can imagine, chimed in to share a myriad of ways in which they had seen the investment in evaluation being wasted due to serious flaws on the commissioning side.

How prevalent is this problem? Although we are not aware of any systematic research that might answer this question, our discussions with a wide range of clients and fellow evaluators certainly suggests that it is widespread, although there is variation depending on sector, country, and so forth. Whatever the prevalence really is, there are lessons to be learned that can make a huge difference to the quality and value of evaluation.

Different language used to describe scoping:

Terms of reference (TOR) set out the purpose(s) of the evaluation and its key evaluation questions, a timeline (and possibly the available budget and existing data resources), and any direction related to staffing the evaluation; for external evaluations, this can include contractual arrangements. In some cases, the TOR includes an evaluation plan setting out the methodology.

Scope of work (SOW) is a plan for conducting an evaluation that outlines the work that is to be performed by the evaluation team. This can be included in the request for proposal.

Request for proposal (RFP), sometimes referred to as *request for application* or *request for quotation*, is a formal request for evaluators to prepare a response to a planned evaluation and is generally used to select the final evaluator for the evaluation. An RFP would include a SOW, staffing requirements, budget and contractual information, information on how evaluators will be selected, and instructions for the proposal.

In this chapter, we take a careful look at where the slippage most often happens and what ECMs can do at the front end to develop the scope, commission the kind of evaluation they truly need, and find the right team to bring it to life. We will also explore how commissioning organizations have different requirements and levels of flexibility in how they scope the evaluation and the implications for commissioning evaluations. Before we begin, let us define some of the terms used by various commissioning organizations—*terms of reference, scope of work*, and *request for proposals* (see above box)—and how they relate to the ultimate evaluation contract awarded.

Some commissioning organizations use the *request for proposal* (RFP) and *scope of work* (SOW) terminology while others use *terms of reference* (TOR). Figure 2.1 shows the overlaps and what is ultimately included in the evaluation contract for external evaluations. Internal evaluations will generally only need TOR since there is no competition for the evaluation. For simplicity, we will use *terms of reference* (TOR) throughout this chapter because it includes all the main points for commissioning a great evaluation: the work to be done, the requirements for an evaluation team, and the resources available.

2.1 DECIDING WHETHER AND WHAT TO EVALUATE

How do we decide whether to and what to evaluate? This might sound like strange advice coming from a couple of evaluators, but one thing you should seriously consider before even getting started is whether to evaluate a particular initiative *at all*. Yes, really!

Evaluation is an investment that will require not only the funds set aside to pay evaluators but also the time and effort of the leaders and staff whose program or policy is being evaluated and the other stakeholders expected to participate in the evaluation. Before investing in evaluation, make sure it will give you a good return—that it is likely to be a "value-for-money evaluation," as described in a 2014 blog by Dr. Caroline Heider, then director of the World Bank Independent Evaluation Group. John Wholey (1987) called this an *evaluability assessment.*

Under what circumstances might an evaluation be a bad idea? Sometimes it is blindingly obvious that an evaluation is unsafe, impossible, or highly inadvisable. Reasons

FIGURE 2.1 ■ Relationship Among Terms of Reference, Scope of Work, Request for Proposal, and the Evaluation Contract

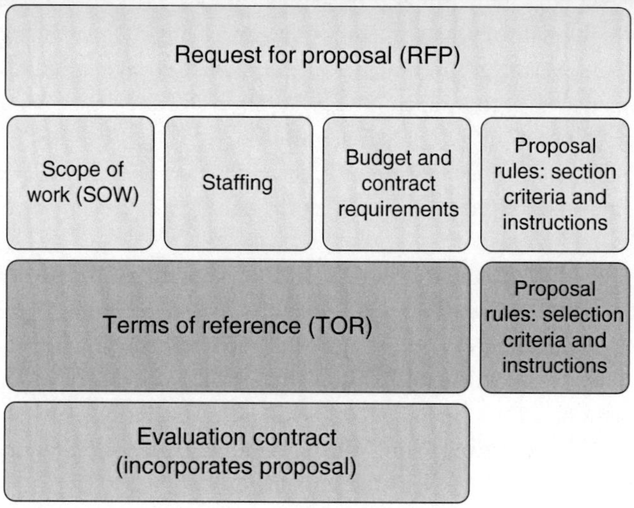

include an unsafe context (e.g., in an active war zone) or total unavailability of a crucial type of evidence (Dershem et al., 2018). These extreme circumstances aside, it is still important to ask whether a feasible evaluation would in fact deliver insights valuable enough to justify the needed investment of time, effort, money, and other resources. "Programs with sparse data and other challenges will require a higher level of expertise and a greater intensity of effort, both of which can be costly" (Dershem et al., 2018, p. iii).

The other part of the story is to ensure that whatever is being evaluated is the right thing to evaluate. This may seem like an obvious point, but we have been surprised over the years to see many organizations commission evaluations that were only ever going to tell them things they already knew or things that were academically interesting but not particularly useful or actionable. Some of this is due to asking the wrong evaluation questions (we will explore that later), but sometimes the mistake is deciding to evaluate something that simply cannot provide the insights needed to inform thinking, design, and/or decisions. For example, Tessie found out in a kick-off meeting of an evaluation with a foundation that the key aspect of a program to be evaluated had been evaluated by a different team six months prior asking the same questions. The reason? It was in the agreement of the funding partners, and the foundation was going ahead with the plan that had been agreed upon two years prior. (You can find out what Tessie did and what happened in Chapter 4.) Who should be part of deciding what to evaluate when commissioning an evaluation? Do not keep this important conversation between an external evaluation adviser and the in-house evaluation specialists. Instead, make the most of the opportunity by involving your organizational leaders and decision makers in the conversation. Why? Because the true value of evaluation—and the numerator of its return on investment—lies in its eventual use and influence. Evaluation directors contribute most when they succeed in linking the work program of evaluation to key strategic questions, needs, and goals of the organization. There is nothing more potent for evaluation than organizational leaders waiting with bated breath for its results and then folding them into strategic discussions for the organization and its programs. Well, actually, there is one thing that can be more potent—in fact, galvanizing—for evaluators: engaged *public* anticipation for an evaluation's results. Of course, many evaluations are completed without such level of engagement and anticipation, but a strong level of interest by decision makers and intended users of the evaluation is critical for value-for-money evaluation. A high-quality evaluation languishing in a filing cabinet is a major waste of resources. The only way to get use and influence right is to engage early and deeply with primary intended users of the evaluation (see Patton, 2008, and Figure 1.4 in Chapter 1 on engaging stakeholders in the evaluation process).

What should we ask when deciding whether and what to evaluate? Here are a few questions to guide the conversation.

1. **When we look across our entire portfolio, what do we already know and what great unanswered questions remain, even after having completed several evaluations over the years?** What do we already know and definitely do not need to ask yet again? What is already answered by our monitoring system? What are we frustrated about still not knowing? Who would use these answers if we could find them? What insights and understandings might usefully inform our thinking and action?
2. **If we genuinely want to find answers to those great unanswered questions, what would be most fruitful to evaluate?** Sometimes the best *evaluand* (what is being evaluated) is not yet another program. It may be more valuable to bring the focus up a level to conduct a more strategic evaluation of a portfolio of initiatives, policy instruments, or even the organization's entire strategy itself.
3. **Is there a more cost-effective way to get the answers we need, other than a full evaluation?** Options might include a synthesis of existing evaluations, a piece of nonevaluative research to fill a gap and answer some important nonevaluative questions, or a more in-depth assessment of the aspects of a program or policy that are the least well understood (e.g., because program evaluations never have the resources to go deep on that part). Or are we better off investing in evaluation capacity in our programs so they can undertake narrower, more locally relevant evaluations? Sometimes the best option is a mix of complementary pieces of work rather than a single evaluation or research project.
4. **How would we use the results of this evaluation?** Imagine the evaluation is complete, and it is wildly successful, *exactly* what you needed, useful, credible, and influential. What happened to achieve this result? What does it look like? How do you know it is a raging success? What made it so successful? How was it different? What was its breakthrough?

Once you identify the key primary intended users of the evaluation in the commissioning organization (and outside) and fundamental questions to guide a conversation with them, how do you engage them? A question we often hear, especially from internal evaluators, is, "It is so hard to get stakeholders to evaluation meetings. Do you have any tips?" Yes, we do! One reason why evaluators often do not get good engagement is that they may not be speaking at the level and in the language that resonates with their non-evaluator audiences, especially more senior managers. Internal evaluators in particular will find that these strategic conversations are powerful for building the visibility and credibility of evaluation and evaluative thinking among non-evaluator colleagues and stakeholders. Another trusted strategy is to "talk money." People are frequently surprised by seeing the investment that goes into evaluations: direct expense for consultants but also time (the person hours and hourly rate) of ECMs in organizing, liaising, responding to, reviewing, and generally interacting with the evaluation. Add to that the probability times the potential cost of an evaluation going awry and having to fix political fallout and the probability times the potential opportunity cost of not using a useful evaluation, and you can develop a convincing case for focused attention to evaluation by leadership right now.

2.2 EVALUATION CRITERIA AND SCOPING

Once you have identified the most fruitful thing to evaluate, the next step is to figure out what the scope and focus of that evaluation should be.

We cover several considerations:

- drawing boundaries for what is in and what is out of the evaluation's scope
- providing enough clarity on what is needed without over-specifying the evaluation approach or methodology
- thinking expansively about the purposes and potential uses of the evaluation
- articulating the values that need to guide the evaluation

2.2.1 Evaluation Boundaries: What Is In and What Is Out of Scope

Clearly defining the boundaries of what is to be evaluated may seem like an obvious point, but there is more to it than meets the eye (Williams & Hummelbrunner, 2010). Every project, program, or policy is part of one or more larger systems, cultures, or policy environments with various contextual factors that influence them. Well-designed change will consider the most important elements of those systems, which include facilitating and enabling factors that can enhance or inhibit change. Similarly, a well-designed evaluation should consider not only how well an initiative contributes to immediate needed change but also how well it creates lasting change, which often means influencing the wider systems in which it operates. For example, efforts to address inequalities in social, educational, and/or economic outcomes should not only be accelerating progress for those who need it and repairing past harm; they should also be addressing the systemic and structural inequities that caused those unequal outcomes in the first place and that will otherwise continue to exacerbate them. Similarly, efforts to restore land, waterways, the air, and the atmosphere should ideally also address how the actions that caused the damage will be prevented in the future.

It is, of course, a delicate balance. Draw the boundaries for an evaluation too wide and the job becomes unwieldy and unfeasible within the budgetary and timeline constraints. Draw the boundaries too narrowly and the evaluation will be myopic and not sufficiently insightful. Add to that the politics of including elements that the initiative might not have been intending to influence but that may be important in hindsight, and you can see we have our work cut out for us! Do go ahead and bite the bullet, though; it is important to have these conversations within the commissioning organization (or with your funder) *before* locking down an evaluation budget and timeline, if possible. This will help avoid getting boxed into a set of constraints that could severely limit the value of the evaluation before it even goes out for bid.

Frequently, in cases where an organization has defined the general budget available for evaluation, the question is one of setting priorities within these budgetary constraints. Is it best to centralize resources in one or a few larger evaluations, or is it best to have a mix of a few larger and a few smaller evaluations that are decided and controlled locally (i.e., at lower levels of the organization or system)?

2.2.2 Clarity—But Not Overspecification—About What Kind of Evaluation Is Needed

An important balance when scoping an evaluation is providing enough clarity about what you are looking for without over-specifying the evaluation approach and methodology. Over the years, we have seen countless RFPs where the required evaluation methodology is spelled out to a level of detail that no longer requires any serious thought by prospective bidding evaluators or organizations about what would be the best fit. For example, we have seen RFPs specifying that the methodology to be used will be surveys and interviews of a specific group of people, using a set of prespecified instruments, and sometimes even specifying the analysis strategies to be used. As experienced evaluators, when we see RFPs like this, our first thought is that this is a paint-by-numbers evaluation job that requires no deep expertise and could be easily conducted by a team of master's students. Pass! That is boring. But in all seriousness, if an organization already knows that this is exactly what it needs, maybe the right team is one of less-experienced evaluators working under an internal evaluator.

It is also very possible to be far too vague about what kind of evaluation you need. It is common to see RFPs asking for an evaluation to be done without much thought given to the kinds of evaluation approaches that might be the best fit. That is often not on purpose; it sometimes means that someone with, say, a policy or research background has been tasked with writing the TOR, and they may not be aware of the range of possible evaluation approaches. Non-evaluators are often surprised that our discipline is so deep and rich, with many different approaches that can be applied depending on the purpose and intended uses of the evaluation.

Many organizations that commission external evaluations or use internal evaluations rely on guidance and documents for how their organization manages evaluation. This is, of course, a good practice and part of building internal evaluation capacity, creating transparency, and enabling more people to become ECMs. Sometimes these rules, however, become too narrow. For example, in the World Food Programme's Decentralized Evaluation Quality Assurance System (DEQAS) that guides country-managed evaluations, data collection in the country is allocated three weeks, which is barely sufficient for secondary data analysis but woefully inadequate for participatory methods, gender analysis, or even engaging seriously in answering more strategic evaluation questions. In fact, the allocation of time for these country-level, country-managed evaluations places emphasis in planning (9 weeks), inception for more planning along with evaluators (7 weeks), and reporting (11 weeks). There may be good institutional reasons and history why this is the case, but it is worth reviewing the implications of such evaluation resource allocation and the expectation that decentralized evaluations will rely mostly on secondary data analysis.

Here is a suggestion: Put someone in charge of writing the RFP who has attended at least half a dozen major evaluation conferences. Don't have one in house? Maybe it is time to invest in a couple of evaluation conferences for your writers of evaluation TOR—or at least send them on a good course! In fact, Tessie's evaluation management course usually includes proposal writers.

While those who *commission* evaluations do not necessarily need to have the kind of rich and deep expertise of those who *conduct* evaluations, they do need enough working knowledge to be informed and discerning purchasers and users of evaluation services. The more you know about the different options you might ask for, the more you can effectively request the kind of evaluation that is going to be most useful to you and your organization—or at least have more productive conversations with evaluators about the pros and cons of what they are proposing.

Here are some helpful tips for getting enough clarity about what kind of evaluation you need:

- **Stop short of building your own preferred design or approach into the TOR.** Instead, lay out some principles for what is going to align best with your goals. Focus on how you would like the evaluation to be used and how it will be influential: by whom, about what, and to what end.
- **Research is *not* evaluation** (or why some of the world's most useless evaluations were conducted by researchers instead of evaluators). If the RFP for the evaluation looks and feels like an RFP for an applied research project, it is probably missing the mark.
- **Do not be limited to formative and summative uses of evaluation**. There are so many more options out there: Developmental evaluation, which walks alongside an emerging policy or project and helps you define and develop it as you go, can be highly actionable in ways that traditional evaluation is not (Patton, 2011; see more on types of evaluation use in Chapter 9).
- **What is the evaluation really for?** Answering this question (as addressed in the next section) will also help clarify the kind of evaluation you need.

2.2.3 Purpose and Use: Identifying the Purposes and Uses of the Evaluation

Clarity about the purposes and uses of the evaluation can make or break any evaluation. Who and what is the evaluation for? If this is not crystal clear, you are in trouble.

Let us start with the primary intended users. Who is the evaluation for? Who *should* it be for? This is a powerful question that can drive strategy considerations (How do organizational leaders wish to engage colleagues and partners in developing or revising a vision and strategy?), decisions (How can program managers use the evaluation to inform their decisions?), advocacy (Who do we want to influence?), equity considerations (Are we effectively including everyone who should have a say in what gets evaluated and the key questions?), and organizational culture (Is this evaluation emphasizing collaboration, efficiency, audit, support for human rights, etc.?).

Evaluation often needs to consider the needs of a wide range of potential evaluation users:

- the overseeing agency or funding organization(s)
- cabinet, elected, or appointed officials in local, regional, or central government
- organizational providers or implementers
- participants/those impacted and their families
- communities, tribal organizations, and advocacy groups
- employers
- taxpayers and the public

This task—identifying the potential users (and "influencees") of an evaluation—is sometimes confused with the task of identifying all who have a stake in the program. The groups overlap but are not the same. The primary intended users of an evaluation are those who are likely to see or hear the evaluation findings and apply its insights in some way—to inform decisions (e.g., to develop or improve the policy or program) or to feed into their thinking and actions more broadly.

Next, think through what these audiences will be using the evaluation for and what will be most useful for them:

- What do they need to know? For what decisions or purposes?
- When do they need the information?
- What kinds of evidence will be convincing to them? What level of certainty makes sense in this context?
- What need is there for evaluation capacity building (i.e., what skills do they need to be able to make best use of the evaluation)?

By clarifying how the evaluation is likely to be used and by whom, you can scope the evaluation to ensure it delivers, within budget, what the commissioning organization and various stakeholders need, when they need it, and in a form that is credible, convincing, and actionable. In fact, when you do a good job of engaging key stakeholders in responding to the questions above, you will frequently find yourself having to fit the excitement and expectations of these stakeholders within a finite budget. (This is a good problem to have.)

Determining the purpose and intended uses of evaluation should not be a desk exercise or a guessing game. Even a modest investment in consulting with potential users will help the evaluation manager shape a more compelling and useful evaluation as well as create anticipation among key stakeholders. In fact, when we have dug deeper on the question of purpose for an evaluation, a frequent goal is to solidify shared understanding among key stakeholders. This does not mean that everyone shares the same goals but that everyone understands each other's interests and goals and respects them. Engaging those stakeholders from the beginning sets up an evaluation process that is more likely to develop shared understanding and working together toward a shared vision. When an evaluation feels like it is working well and people are engaged, curious, and open, it is frequently because the engagement process has been well managed, constructive, and fruitful, even when people do not agree on everything. Michael Patton calls this "evaluation process use," and it begins here with identifying the purpose and scope of the evaluation (Patton, 2008).

2.2.4 Values

An important contribution of evaluation is that it clarifies the values that are important to the commissioning organization and stakeholders and then applies them systematically to assess programs and organizations; for example, equitable and shared growth, women's equality, human rights, sustainability, antiracism, and so on. When we articulate the values that are important in an evaluation, we enable evaluators to operationalize them and use them as part of the evaluation criteria. Once articulated, these values will inform the evaluation questions and be enacted in the methodology and highlighted in the evaluation report. These values will ultimately drive evaluation design: Who collects data from whom? What data sources and perspectives are included? Such values might include equity, sustainable development, human rights, and transparency. If the commissioning organization is committed to certain values—for example, if you want your evaluators to look like those who the program serves, if you want localization and engagement, if you believe that climate or equity are key—then be ready to articulate these in your TOR.

2.3 DETERMINING THE BEST WAY TO CONTRACT AN EXTERNAL EVALUATION

An important decision in commissioning an external evaluation is determining what kind of contract to use. Some contracts are easier for the commissioning organization, and some are more advantageous for certain kinds of EIMs but not others. The main types of evaluation contracts include the following:

- **Fixed-price contract:** This means the evaluation implementer is paid one negotiated price for tasks and deliverables outlined in the TOR upon completion of work or on a schedule of fixed-price amounts tied to specific deliverables or a group of deliverables. The financial risk lies with the evaluator—if the costs are actually lower, they earn more; if the costs are higher, they still need to produce the deliverables. Fixed-price contracts are simpler for invoicing and payments because they do not require justification of specific expenses. Note that sometimes the fixed portion is only for labor, and travel and other costs are reimbursed at cost.
- **Time and materials contracts:** The evaluator is paid for labor using fixed (negotiated) labor rates and material costs up to a ceiling. This has less risk for both parties because payments are based on what is used, although the commissioner holds the risk of not having enough funds because of decisions made along the way.

Fixed-price contracts are the most common for shorter duration evaluations, while time and material contracts offer advantages for evaluation services that span a longer period or where there is a need for more flexibility in the TOR over time.

2.4 GETTING PRACTICAL: THE PROCESS OF WRITING AN EVALUATION TERMS OF REFERENCE

In addition to the strategic discussion in earlier sections, an ECM will ultimately have to put pen to paper and establish the evaluation parameters in a way that evaluators can understand so they can submit strong proposals to conduct the evaluation. Every commissioning organization has its own requirements, processes, and norms for writing the TOR. The discussion below is designed to sit alongside those requirements rather than replace them. It may also spark some ideas for improving the TOR writing process in your evaluation commissioning organizations.

2.4.1 Content of the Evaluation Terms of Reference

Guidance on what kinds of content a good TOR should include is generally consistent across funders, as can be seen in the sample of evaluation funder guidance shown in Table 2.1.

As you can see, the TOR usually specify the following:

- purpose of the evaluation (including intended use)
- background and context

TABLE 2.1 ■ Examples of Guidance on Evaluation Terms of Reference Content from Three Evaluation Commissioning Organizations

General Topics (Comprehensive List)	United States Agency for International Development (USAID)	World Food Programme (WFP)	World Bank
Purpose Background Evaluation questions Evaluation methodology Expected deliverables Expertise requirements Time frame and budget Requirements for submitting the proposal	Purpose of the evaluation and how it will be used Background and history of the projects or activities being evaluated Questions that must be answered and how they might be answered Expected deliverables Expertise needed to do the job Time frame and budget available to support the task	Background Reasons for the evaluation Subject for the evaluation Evaluation approach, methodology, and ethical considerations Organization of the evaluation	Background information and rationale Specific objectives of the evaluation and evaluation questions Scope of the evaluation Approach and methodology Governance and accountability Guiding principles and values Professional qualifications Deliverables and schedule Budget and payment Structure of the proposal and submission guidelines Additional references or resources

- evaluation questions
- evaluation approach or methodology
- expected deliverables
- expertise requirements
- time frame and budget
- requirements for submitting the proposal

While the general categories in an evaluation scope are similar, there is significant variation in the specificity required by different types of stakeholders. Some commissioners (e.g., United States [U.S.] federal government organizations) have strict requirements because of procurement rules, while others (foundations and nongovernmental organizations) have more flexibility. There will be more discussion about this later in this chapter.

There is ample guidance developed and shared openly on the internet on the mechanics of what to include and how to develop a good TOR for evaluation. In our experience, the art of a strong TOR within these categories hinges on avoiding a few pitfalls and engaging in some good practices.

2.4.2 Pitfalls to Avoid in Evaluation Terms of Reference

Hopefully, the guidance below will go a long way toward avoiding some of the problems we have all encountered in the commissioning of evaluations. You will see that most of the issues with a TOR are not because of bad writing but because of lack of preparation and consultation.

Pitfall #1: The Boilerplate Problem

Have you ever written an evaluation proposal—or waded through a pile of proposals—where the proposals seemed to be little more than large amounts of copy-and-paste boilerplate? Proposal writers and reviewers alike find this exasperating because it is both uninformative and boring! What might be behind that?

Using boilerplate language and copying from another evaluation's TOR may mean that the author does not know what is needed, does not have access to people who can help clarify it, or is not interested in spending the time to figure it out, possibly because the bid seems like a long shot. A common result of boilerplate TOR is poor proposals that sound generic. To the proposal reviewer, this can feel as if the evaluation is not that important to the bidders. If the evaluation is important and worth submitting a proposal for, it is worth investing time to figure out what is needed, and if it is not important, it is best not to waste time and money on it.

If you are an ECM and this happens to you a lot, ask yourself—or ask some of your evaluation contractors—whether you are giving them sufficient information to be able to write an intelligent proposal. Some procurement processes forbid any interaction between bidders and the commissioner beyond a timed submission of questions and responses going to all bidders, leaving proposal writers flying completely blind on many of the essential details. In the absence of a nuanced understanding of what you need, they fill the white space with their "tried-and-true" formula and hope it looks impressive enough to get them on the shortlist so they can actually talk with you.

Pitfall #2: The Internal Contradiction Problem

Imagine how confusing it is being asked to implement a participatory approach to an evaluation with only two weeks for data collection or imagine being asked for a culturally responsive evaluation that prescribes a methodology of only a survey using an existing survey instrument. Such contradictions typically show up in a TOR when a draft is circulated, different people provide their edits, and those edits are accepted without any follow-up discussion among editors or consideration of the implications.

Pitfall #3: Being Vague About the Budget

Sometimes a TOR, especially for newer commissioners of evaluation, does not provide cost guidance and budget expectations. The motivation is frequently to ensure cost competition and pay the lowest price they can for the evaluation. This silence on the budget might also be motivated by shifts toward evaluation procurement that appear to be designed to mimic the purchasing of products. The broad intent behind the competitive bidding approach does make sense, given the need to ensure that taxpayers' or donors' money is spent wisely. However, it is often highly problematic in practice.

In the early 2000s, when a U.S. federal health agency first expanded its international programs that included evaluations, it repeatedly canceled contract competitions because it consistently underestimated the cost required to implement the scope of the work. After the sixth such cancellation under its contractual mechanism Global AIDS Program: Technical Support Services, all six eligible contractors wrote a joint letter that they would cease bidding and wasting their proposal funds on competitions that went nowhere. Eventually, the commissioning health agency increased its costing capacity and established realistic expectations, and the bidding resumed.

Clear budget and time parameters need to drive the number and scope of evaluation questions and evaluation requirements. When there is not even a ballpark budget given, it is extremely difficult for prospective evaluators and evaluation teams to figure out what the ECM is seeking. Evaluation questions can be answered in various ways, starting with a lean approach (possibly relying primarily on secondary data already collected) all the way to an extremely thorough, high-quality, and robust evaluation with site visits and extensive primary data collection or something in between. When the budget is vague, the evaluation bidding process becomes a "guess the number in my head" exercise. It is of no use to anyone if many proposals are way off base because they scope and design an evaluation that is either methodologically overkill or far too light.

Pitfall #4: Procurement Inflexibility

Many of the evaluators and clients we speak to feel very constrained by procurement processes. These have been put in place with the best of intentions: to ensure the best possible use of funder or taxpayer money via a competitive bidding process and to ensure fairness and equitable access to all bidders. Makes sense, right?

Here is the problem. Many procurement processes were originally developed for the purchase of products (such as computers) or simple services (such as catering) where the requirements are predictable and can be specified in detail. Suppliers simply need to demonstrate that their product or service will meet all required specifications within the required time frame. The task for the procurement team is to assess track record and qualifications to ensure those claims are plausible and then choose the most cost-competitive offer.

Evaluation, in contrast, is much more complicated and complex. Even with clearly laid out evaluation questions and requirements, there are infinite possibilities for how to approach the job. In addition, it is almost certain that by the time an evaluation is awarded, the requirements will need to change. In some cases, such as for the U.S. federal government, procurement is governed by very strict regulations that leave almost no leeway. For example, some RFPs require an evaluation plan to be submitted two weeks after contact award, which makes any consultation almost impossible.

Best practice here is to include an inception phase in all evaluations, something that is thankfully becoming increasingly common practice. For example, the United Nations' contractual requirements for evaluations include an early product called "the inception report," which includes any revisions to the evaluation questions, requirements, and methodology mutually agreed to by the evaluators and the commissioner to update the evaluation plan based on the current organizational reality and relevant changes to the broader context. Another practice to consider is not including specific evaluation questions but articulating some lines of inquiry and using the inception phase to develop the evaluation questions. This allows additional flexibility to shift or tweak the evaluation questions as you are finalizing the design and getting the input from your evaluators on what questions can be reasonably answered within the evaluation constraints (time, budget).

We have also seen evaluation procurements that include an evaluability assessment/design phase and a separate phase for evaluation implementation based on the design. This lowers the risk for both the commissioning organization and the evaluator. Some foundations conduct a request for qualifications and then invite one or more organizations (who are compensated for their proposal preparation) or require the entire evaluation plan to be developed during the inception phase. Not only does this better serve evaluation commissioners by ensuring the evaluation team has a deep understanding of requirements before the evaluation begins; it is also fairer to the evaluators. Developing an evaluation plan is a significant amount of work and is not something we should be asking people to do for free.

Building a strong inception phase into your TOR allows the important dialogue and collaboration between the ECM and EIM to get the evaluation design right (rather than in the proposal submission phase; see more in Chapter 4).

Pitfall #5: The Methodology Directive Trap

Sometimes a TOR goes overboard and not only specifies requirements but also spells out exactly how to fulfill them. When that is the case, there is no room for evaluators to showcase their thinking and demonstrate their expertise. There may be cases when commissioners do know exactly what they want, in which case, it might be more cost-effective to hire evaluation interns or students with university professor supervision rather than invest in a professional evaluator. Or the TOR writer might have fallen into the "similar to me" trap, lacking imagination for what they do not already know, thus seriously limiting the methodology options.

We can appreciate cases where an organization is devolving the authority to commission evaluation to different parts of the organization, and to compensate for possible lack of capacity, it provides narrow guidance for TOR development and cost. An example of such a heavily directive approach could be seen when the World Food Programme (WFP) initiated its decentralized evaluation practice, moving evaluation commissioning for country evaluations to country level. In parallel, to support the growing of capacity in countries, WFP established a structure of regional evaluation advisers to support groups of countries in each of its regions and an intensive online evaluation training program for staff members when they were first asked to act as ECMs. The specificity of the guidance for decentralized evaluations was comforting to newly minted ECMs in country offices, while it provided time for WFP to invest and expand its evaluation capacity throughout the organization. We have seen similar evolution paths followed by some of our foundation clients.

Pitfall #6: Making the Proposal Process Too Burdensome for Smaller Evaluation Firms or Those Representing Marginalized Communities

If we make the procurement process complicated and time-consuming to prepare and submit a proposal, we will likely prevent the participation of those evaluators we want proposals from in the first place. Requiring a very detailed design in the RFP means we are asking evaluators to do a lot of the evaluation work for free, since they are only paid if and when they have won the contract. Commissioners need to be aware that preparing proposals costs money, and smaller or less-established evaluation firms will be hard-pressed to prepare long, detailed proposals. As mentioned in Pitfall#5, there are ways to address this by lightening the RFP phase and putting most of the design work into the contract itself in an inception phase, where the evaluators can be paid for their design work.

2.4.3 Good Practices in Writing Evaluation Terms of Reference

To avoid the pitfalls discussed above, here are some practices that we have found useful in our experience with writing and responding to evaluation TOR.

Practice #1: Help Your Organization Clarify Its Needs and Convey Them in the Terms of Reference

Begin by imagining that the readers of your TOR are considering whether to submit a curriculum vitae (CV) or proposal and are trying to figure out what they need to include in their proposals. The most important characteristic of a good TOR is clarity and the most important thing you will do is to engage in the discussions needed within your organization to get clarity. Clarity is not simple because frequently there are many stakeholders with different points of view. Furthermore, in some cases, satisfying one requirement will directly contradict another requirement; for example, on the one hand, you wish to ask for a participatory evaluation with extensive consultations while on the other hand, you may wish to minimize the cost and limit the timeline. These are choices TOR authors need to push their colleagues to address so the TOR is clear on expectations and boundaries and reflects an organizational consensus and not only the author's point of view. Consultation within the organization is worth the investment to ensure your TOR will lead to an evaluation that matters—it is relevant to the organizations and key stakeholder needs so that it has the potential to be used.

The bottom line is, ensure that your TOR

- conveys who the evaluation is for, what is it trying to inform, and who will make those decisions and by when;
- includes your draft questions but invite input;

- shares the values that are important for your organization, which should inform the way the evaluation should be conducted and what it needs to cover (such as equity or sustainability);
- comments on methodology but invite the experts to suggest their ideas; and
- provides the budget level and the assumptions you used as well as timeline parameters.

Practice #2: Know When to Remain Open and Flexible

While it is important to be clear on what is required, it is also important to be clear where the TOR invites input and ideas from evaluators. Those areas might include the following:

- What other questions do evaluators think might be important given the purpose and context of this evaluation?
- What considerations (risks and opportunities) are important for designing the evaluation and selecting methods? What do evaluators think is the best methodology?
- How are evaluators planning to engage stakeholders?
- How do evaluators think about ensuring the evaluation reaches and includes all key stakeholders and underserved minorities?
- The TOR can also explicitly invite responders to push back if they think something is unrealistic or ask for reflections on the TOR itself or on how they would go about constructing a learning agenda.

Giving responders areas where they can showcase their thinking, knowledge, expertise, and creativity will serve you in the selection process and is likely to be helpful no matter who is selected. Therefore, within the procurement rules of the commissioner, consider being explicit about the values that are important for the organization and program and specifying the required approach rather than the methodologies needed.

Practice #3: Clarify Your Values About Who Should Be Involved and the Implications

Evaluators need information on who you consider important to include in the evaluation. This will provide a more culturally and contextually responsive proposal and a more realistic budget. While the TOR will not specify all methods, the extent of the stakeholder consultation required should be reflected in the timeline and be adequately budgeted. Here are some questions to help guide our thinking:

- Who needs—and has the right—to be engaged and informed directly, and who can be represented in different ways? For example, if several stakeholder groups have recently produced analysis that represents their point of view on key questions, these do not need to be repeated.
- If stakeholders are dispersed, will you require travel or online consultations?

- How might the evaluation engage representatives of some key groups (to limit the numbers) and then, after data collection, consult with a wider number of stakeholders to engage in evaluative sensemaking, validate findings, and develop recommendations or action plans?
- If the evaluation will require deep engagement across distances or in different languages, the budget must enable it. We have seen examples of RFPs calling for a participatory approach for people in rural communities with an expectation of one-week visits when it requires two days to get to a site. This is simply untenable.
- If you do not have the resources for meaningful participation but still believe in it, invite responders to suggest strategies for increased participation within your means.

Practice #4: Develop Realistic Budgets

When commissioning an evaluation, the evaluation budget needs to be developed by someone who understands evaluation enough to ensure that the provision for resources is adequate and allocated appropriately. Frequently, procurement regulations make it impossible to share the total budget allocation with bidders because it is assumed that cost competition will be most advantageous for the evaluation commissioner. In fact, the result is frequently an inefficient proposal process that focuses on lowballing the competition and under-resourcing the evaluation. A different and more productive way to stimulate competition is to let everyone know how much money is set aside for the evaluation or the cost range expected and focus the competition on the most cost-effective use of the available resources to get the best evaluation possible. Otherwise, the range of assumptions made in different proposals is so wide that they are not comparable. And, if the commissioner selects the lowest-cost proposal, it will either not be done well or the "smart" contractor will later negotiate a cost adjustment to make the budget more realistic. The U.S. Government has a category of proposals where its selection is based on "lowest cost technically acceptable," and we have seen bidders propose unrealistically low prices, which have been later renegotiated and increased. The most respectful and fiscally responsible practice is to conduct cost analysis and aim for cost realism, not lowest cost.

Practice #5: Include Evaluation Competencies in Criteria for Assessing Evaluators

Most of the attention in a TOR is given to background and methods and less on laying out the requirements for evaluator competencies. This might have been partly because evaluation communities have only recently developed competency frameworks and partly because it is assumed that someone who understands this type of program will be the best person to evaluate it. We have seen a TOR that values content expertise the most (perhaps because TOR writers are most familiar with it) while showing little appreciation of the evaluation expertise needed and a devaluing of context and cultural expertise. An evaluation of a transportation program, for example, may ask for a transportation expert (content expertise) and a survey designer (limited evaluation expertise) without mention of expertise in context and relevant stakeholder communities (e.g., remote station travelers, unions, etc.). Overall, we recommend centering evaluation expertise for an evaluation TOR, placing a high priority on contextual and cultural expertise, and placing content expertise in an advisory capacity.

2.5 SELECTING A STRONG EVALUATION TEAM (OR SOLE EVALUATORS)

In developing an evaluation TOR, commissioners of evaluation focus first on the evaluation scope, questions, timeline, and budget, and this sometimes leaves less time to develop the specifications for the type of evaluation team they need. In fact, when the TOR is developed by non-evaluators, it is difficult to provide any kind of specificity about what is needed. And yet, given that evaluation is not generally a standardized product, selecting qualified evaluators who are a good fit for the specific evaluation is critical.

Although the practice of evaluation is millions of years old, our existence as a profession and a discipline is much more recent (Scriven, 1991). One consequence is that clients and people working in other disciplines are often not aware that there is any such thing as specialized evaluation knowledge and know-how.

2.5.1 Avoid Pitfalls in Evaluator Competency Specifications

The following are some frequent pitfalls in developing staffing requirements for an evaluation.

Pitfall #1: Hiring Researchers to Conduct Evaluation

When evaluation emerged as a profession separate from research, the first evaluators were social scientists. Still today, many evaluators get into evaluation through social science research. These researchers need to change their frame of mind to perform well in evaluation.

More typically, research is funded by grants, has longer timelines, and does not have a visible client. We have seen many nonevaluative research studies with the word *evaluation* on the cover but that clearly are not actually evaluations. What do we mean by that? They tend to describe what happened (quantitatively and/or qualitatively) but they are not at all clear about whether whatever happened was significant and/or to what extent. In other words, there are no explicit conclusions about merit, worth, or significance. The reader is supposed to figure that out.

An evaluation typically has a shorter timeline, the people commissioning it need information and lessons from the evaluation to inform upcoming decisions, and stakeholders tend to be more involved in decisions that influence the evaluation. This is why evaluator competency models include management and interpersonal domains alongside methodology and professional behavior and why context has emerged as its own domain rather than receiving an honorable mention under methodology.

Pitfall #2: Valuing Subject Matter Expertise Over Evaluation Expertise

A common related problem is assuming that all one needs to evaluate *X* is a deep knowledge of subject matter *X*. While subject matter expertise certainly needs to be used in evaluation, evaluation expertise is critically important for figuring out how best to weave the subject matter expertise into the evaluative conclusions in a coherent and valid way. In fact, subject matter experts frequently disagree on the standards of performance for a given topic; selecting one expert over another may mean very different evaluation results. Good evaluators are skilled at identifying differing beliefs, assumptions, and values and bringing them to the surface for discussion and consideration. Good evaluation makes such difficult and necessary conversations possible.

Our observation has been that studies performed by researchers with deep subject matter expertise (Pitfalls #1 and #2 together) but little evaluation expertise tend to get lost in the details and sidetracked by questions that are of academic interest to the subject matter expert but of little relevance to decision makers. This is why it is important to commission a team that will have an evaluation specialist as the lead rather than a content expert.

Pitfall #3: Devaluing Context Expertise

TORs will frequently identify content and evaluation expertise but are silent related to context expertise. What do we mean by *context*? If, for example, the evaluation concerns a program that serves incarcerated populations, what should the evaluators know about the context of prison life and the needs of incarcerated people? If the program serves only women, would an evaluation team of all men be adequate? What if the program relates to refugee camps where gender-based violence is a very possible occurrence—do we expect that women program participants will speak openly to men evaluators? When programs serve people of color, including Indigenous groups, how will this be factored into the evaluation team competency requirements? There are other kinds of context knowledge that are important—knowledge about the local systems, the political and economic environment, and cultural and social practices.

In fact, the makeup of the evaluation team both in terms of competencies and in the identities of the evaluators themselves will greatly influence the effectiveness and credibility of the evaluation. And let us be clear, assuming that an evaluation team has sufficient cultural expertise when the only Black or Brown faces on the evaluation team are a couple of research assistants is not OK.

For those evaluators who believe that "value-free" evaluation is desirable or even possible, we assert that there can be no "value-free evaluators." The challenge is often implicitly characterized as a language/translation issue, where it is assumed that the needed outcomes are very straightforward and culture/value-free. Instead of asking for value-free evaluation, it is best to specify the values implied in that request; in our experience, *value-free* might mean prioritizing efficiency, not taking sides/considering all sides, using the same standards across the board regardless of location or stakeholder group, and so on. Unpacking the concept of a value-free or objective evaluation will help clarify the values and standards that are being prioritized by this evaluation.

2.5.2 Strategies for Selecting an Evaluation Team with the Right Competencies

Screening people on paper is difficult, but here are some practices that can be helpful.

Practice #1: Emphasize the Relevant Evaluation Competency Domains

One of the lessons from the pitfalls mentioned above is that evaluation expertise should be prioritized. How do we achieve that? The emergent global consensus on evaluation competencies (see Figure 1.5 in Chapter 1) is making a significant contribution to developing great clarity in how to seek the right evaluators for each evaluation. So, decide on the evaluation competency model that best fits your organizational context and include a reference in the TOR asking respondents to address how their team meets these qualifications. Also, use the evaluation competencies as a checklist to see what you need to emphasize for your particular evaluation. For example, a large and complex evaluation should include some language under the evaluation management competency domain; an evaluation that emphasizes high engagement of stakeholders might include language under the methodology/qualitative and the interpersonal domains—and so forth.

Practice #2: Ask the Evaluators to Provide an Example from Their Experience That Demonstrates the Top Competency Requirement for Your Evaluation

Let us say you need to keep track of and organize findings in an easy-to-access database of evaluation sources and methods because you will repurpose the data in the future. Ask candidates to give you an example of an evaluation where they had to work with big data sets and where indexing and retrieval of data were well done. If you need to have evaluators who have managed a politically charged issue, ask for an example of that. The personality of the respondent and their experience will come through more clearly than reading their CV.

Practice #3: Hold Oral Interviews as Part of Your Competitive Process

You will be working closely with your selected team and you will want to trust them with sensitive information and access to your people and data as well as your thoughts for the future. When you think of the potential benefit of a strong evaluation team and the risks of hiring the wrong one, you will see that including an oral part to the competition will give you valuable information and allow you to consider how well you would work with this group of people.

Practice #4: Check References

Never skip this step. Check references for team members and for the organization. We have found ourselves acting as members of evaluation commissioning groups, and we are grateful for this practice every time. In one case, a reference check of the work of a well-known evaluation organization (and one that the whole commissioning team thought was a shoo-in for the work) revealed that the organization was overstretched, changed its personnel frequently, and was sloppy in keeping track of the data and demonstrating the inference path of the findings, conclusions, and recommendations. In contrast, the reference checks of the team selected (that was less well known) revealed that a weakness of the team was that they needed to be encouraged to speak up because they were very insightful and methodical and had great instincts. We were very glad to select the second team, and they did a fabulous job in the evaluation.

Ultimately, you want an evaluation team that is flexible, attentive, and respectful. You want to trust the team to handle your sensitive issues and information responsibly. You want them to act with integrity and to hold to the path of independence and impartiality with empathy and understanding, and with a commitment to leaving your organization and programs better off for having intervened with high-quality evaluation. Picking a good team is worth your time.

2.6 SELECTING THE BEST EVALUATION IMPLEMENTOR

If you have done a good job with the TOR, this step will be much easier because you will have all the information you need. Selecting a person or team to conduct the evaluation may take place by competing the evaluation widely, to a preselected group of individuals or organizations, or through a sole-source process. We discuss these processes below.

2.6.1 Competitive Selection

Evaluations (especially large ones) are competitive, with some exceptions. Managing the selection process well is critical. There is a final section in your TOR that is essential for the selection, and that is the evaluation criteria for your evaluation and a scoring sheet that includes the maximum points that can be awarded for good performance in each criterion and the weight of each criterion (see the following, for example):

- Technical approach: 25 points
- Organizational track record: 25 points
- Evaluation team expertise: 50 points
- Cost ceiling (published in the proposal): *X* amount (if exceeded, the organization is disqualified)
- Total points: 100

Under each criterion, you need to specify what elements are needed for a high score, and this should be aligned with the TOR and be quite detailed. Also, each criterion should have a "bar"—a minimum level of acceptable performance. This is critically important for ensuring that exceptionally high scores in one area cannot make up for inadequate performance in another.

In some cases, the ECM might select the evaluation team without consulting others, but for most evaluations, some consultation is preferred or required. In public and international organizations, the selection process is usually more formal. It involves appointing an evaluation selection committee (about five people including the ECM who developed the TOR) and having the members of the selection committee review and score all or subsets of the proposals independently. A good practice mentioned above is the ability to ask questions of clarification to the proposing teams to make a better-informed decision. After the scoring is compiled and shared in the group, the committee members meet together to discuss the results and make a recommendation. In some cases, the recommendation is informed by a reference check conducted during the review; sometimes, the reference check is conducted only for the two or three finalists.

In theory, if you have done a good job with your TOR, this decision should be easy—and sometimes, it is. Next are some pitfalls we have seen in the selection process and how to avoid them.

Pitfall #1. A Selection Committee That Does Not Represent Key Stakeholders

If the composition of the selection committee seems biased, the risk of opposition and sabotage of the evaluation is high, even if the selection committee does a good job at applying the criteria fairly. Our suggestion is to lean into the discomfort of potential conflict and include those who may have a different view of what is important in selection. In one of Tessie's experiences, an international organization experienced conflict between the perspectives of its headquarters and its regional office for a contract that would take place in the region. The headquarters manager, adept in this dangerous political nuance, created a more elaborate selection process than what he had originally intended: He included regional representatives in the selection committee and assigned Tessie's company (as a neutral partner) to conduct site visits and lead the scoring process, thus protecting the integrity of the selection process through transparency and negotiation.

Pitfall #2. Favoring People and Organizations You Like

If members of your selection committee express predictions about which they expect to be the best proposal, admonish them about the cost of this bias. In one such case, Tessie (who was leading an evaluation steering committee) saw the selection committee evaluate a proposal (that was mostly boilerplate) higher because the members knew the team leader personally. These committee members were so sure in their choice that they refused to conduct reference checks, so Tessie (a firm believer in reference checks) undertook them herself. To Tessie's shock, the committee's higher assessment of this weak proposal persisted even after the reference checks came out quite negative for this favorite team leader. The problem here was twofold: (1) Favoritism did not result in the selection of the best evaluation implementor and (2) Prejudging based on prior knowledge was unfair to those who submitted proposals and unethical on the part of the steering committee. Now, Tessie uses this story in preparing selection committees.

Pitfall #3. Manipulating the Questions to Bidders

This is another manifestation of Pitfall #2. In this case, selection committee members pose questions to their favorite bidder to give them a chance to strengthen their bid. In cases where you ask for an elaboration, a fairer strategy is to ask all bidders to elaborate on that same aspect of the proposal or to provide all bidders with the top weakness in their proposal and give them a chance to elaborate. U.S. federal government proposal processes require transparency in questions and answers prior to proposal submission and require any elaboration requests by the government to be shared with all bidders until they enter negotiations with a selected organization.

Pitfall #4. The Points Contradicting Your Intuition

When points and intuition are not aligned, more discussion is warranted. Ask yourself and the selection committee, *What would happen if I went against the point selection? What am I concerned about?* In responding to these questions, you may either come up with an insight that influences the points awarded, which would update and improve the scores, or you might identify a personal positive bias that you have based on friendship or a negative bias that you have based on past experience that you may have to let go. You might also articulate a criterion that should have been identified but was not or an elaboration to an existing criterion that was unclear. The answer is not straightforward and, in the end, you will have to make an ethical decision about fair decision making and your responsibility to the stakeholders.

2.6.2 Competing Among a Preselected Group

In the interest of efficiency, commissioners might share an RFP with a smaller group of potential evaluation implementers who have been prequalified for different types of evaluation. The prequalification process may be informal or formal. Some foundations or nonprofits, for example, create a roster of consultants by word of mouth or simply reach out to consultants or organizations that have worked with the commissioner before. In the U.S. federal government, the prequalification process is a competition that results in a prequalification contract, usually called an indefinite quantity contract (IQC) or an indefinite delivery indefinite quantity (IDIQ) contract.

The ultimate type of preselection is awarding a sole-source contract to an evaluation implementor without competition, which is typically done with a justification that it is more efficient than conducting a wider competition.

We empathize with commissioners' efforts to use their resources more efficiently and shorten the process through preselection or prequalification. However, there are two important pitfalls to manage in a preselection process: favoritism and barriers to entry for smaller or less-resourced candidates.

Favoritism falls under Pitfall #2 (Favoring People and Organizations You Like). Over time, the favored evaluation team might stop being independent or impartial and become an extension of the hiring unit of the evaluation.

Barriers to entry are erected because small evaluation firms or some evaluators may not have the networks or resources to become known to decision makers or to pursue opportunities that require investment. If being considered requires being already in the network, how do you enter? Or, if you need to win a prequalification contract to be considered, that may represent a significant endeavor that a small evaluation firm cannot afford.

So, what should a commissioner do to make a process fair, inclusive, and efficient? Let us start by recognizing that commissioners must make realistic decisions that fit their own values and goals and do their best to establish fair and inclusive processes within their own resource constraints. Good evaluation management means value-for-money evaluation decisions, so commissioners must do their best within their means. Having said that, a lot can be done, and we have seen many creative solutions on the part of ECMs:

- Commissioners might include requirements to show preference to small firms, minority evaluators, or minority-run evaluation organizations. In the U.S. federal government, this can be seen in evaluation contracts reserved for competition only among small businesses in qualified minority-run businesses through the Small Business Administration's 8A program or other programs. In foundations and nonprofits, this could be an explicit criterion for selection.

- Commissioners might create a less intensive prequalification process through a short expression of interest and then reimburse a portion of the proposal development process for two or three finalists.

- Commissioners might develop intentional plans to encourage entry and placement of minority evaluators; for example, the American Evaluation Association's Graduate Evaluation Diversity Initiative (GEDI) hosted by different universities and initially supported by The Kellogg Foundation or internship programs being developed by United Nations agencies in different countries to support candidates through EvalYouth, the global network of young and emerging evaluators.

So here is what we are saying: We know our standards of independence, impartiality, fairness, and inclusion are high, and we work in the real world of limited budgets and time. We accept that we all carry our own biases and blind spots. Within this reality, we commit to being thoughtful, not always taking the most expedient path but intentionally including ethical considerations and decisions in our selection process.

2.6.3 Internal Evaluation Teams

In internal evaluation, there is more limited choice. Internal evaluation teams may be small and constant or only one person; in a larger internal evaluation office, there is a selection process usually made by the evaluation office supervisor. Internal teams might be supplemented with outside consultants depending on the evaluation budget, and their selection would fall under one of the categories discussed above. The way to enact impartiality, fairness, and inclusion for internal teams is through their staffing decisions and their evaluation process.

2.7 BUILDING CAPACITY IN COMMISSIONING EVALUATION

Building capacity in commissioning evaluations has a good return on investment by ensuring that more useful and reliable evaluations are commissioned that help the organization learn and grow its programming in more productive directions that serve the public good. Simultaneously, competencies in commissioning better evaluations bring about more strategic thinking and coherent programming because of the questions that ECMs ask of their leaders and colleagues. There is more discussion on this in Chapter 10.

CASE EXAMPLE

Review the distribution of time for a decentralized evaluation by the WFP DEQAS. List possible reasons why it makes sense and the challenges it might create. Based on your analysis, what would be your recommended time distribution allocation if the evaluation were still to take 34 weeks (see Figure 2.2)?

FIGURE 2.2 ■ Recommended Duration of a Decentralized Evaluation

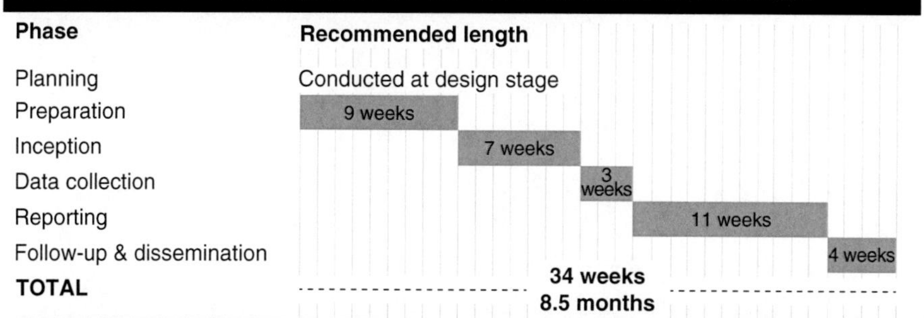

Source: World Food Programme. (2021, April). *Decentralized evaluation—guidance for process and content.* https://docs.wfp.org/api/documents/9f13fcec2d6f45f6915beade8e542024/download/

3 PRE–START-UP: ANALYZING THE EVALUATION REQUIREMENTS

WHO SHOULD USE THIS CHAPTER

This chapter focuses on what an evaluation implementing manager (EIM) needs to do in response to seeing the evaluation's terms of reference (TOR), because the way a proposal is written has management implications. Evaluation commissioning managers (ECMs) can benefit from reviewing this chapter; understanding what the evaluation teams are trying to navigate will help commissioners write better evaluation scopes of work and TOR. For internal evaluators, the writing of the TOR, preparation, and start-up phases may be integrated into a continuum. This chapter is useful for internal evaluators as they consider how to be responsive to the needs and requirements of their internal clients and how to organize the evaluation.

In Chapter 2, we discussed the importance of writing good TOR for actionable evaluations, highlighting the need for evaluation commissioners to integrate evaluation planning with strategy development. In this chapter, we are suggesting that EIMs share the responsibility of designing and managing actionable evaluations—evaluations that matter—by the way they interpret and respond to the TOR. The interpretation of the TOR begins with a phase we call *pre–start-up*, which may include two separate tasks: first, the proposal development task (if a proposal is required) and then, after the award of the evaluation contract, the task of reviewing the contract and getting ready to meet with the client.

But why review the proposal development process for an evaluation in a book about evaluation management? Well, evaluation proposals shape the path of the evaluation by providing an initial framework. You cannot imagine how frequently evaluators in evaluation firms celebrate winning an evaluation proposal and immediately exclaim, "Who wrote this?!" The trouble is, they are now contractually obligated to deliver whatever is in that imperfect proposal.

When done well, upon analysis of the TOR requirements, the evaluator can understand what enables and constrains the evaluation, creating parameters within which evaluation management must take place. In other words, the proposal stage is not merely an administrative step but a first key part of a responsive and creative evaluation design that requires deep listening, interpretation of client needs, and critical choices about how to ensure and manage an actionable evaluation.

As discussed in Chapter 2, many evaluations are commissioned through a competitive process. Sometimes, evaluation commissioners select evaluators by reviewing curriculum vitaes (CVs), but often, candidate evaluators, teams, or organizations are required to submit proposals in response to a TOR by the commissioning body (also called a *request for proposal* or *RFP*). These competitive proposals outline how the candidate(s) would approach the evaluation and provide a rationale regarding their specific qualifications for it. Proposals can be prepared by evaluators, proposal writers, or a collaboration of both. Proposal writers are usually a part of the business development staff of consulting firms, who may or may not have deep technical evaluation expertise. It is best to have a qualified evaluator participate in the proposal when responding to the TOR, bringing technical knowledge and realism to the response.

This chapter demonstrates the critical choices EIMs or proposal writers make at the pre–start-up phase that influence all aspects of the evaluation; we will also explore the responsibility of the evaluators to own the evaluation design they are proposing as well as manage it, and we offer suggestions for how to develop successful proposals for actionable evaluations.

3.1 PRE-PROPOSAL: UNDERSTANDING THE TERMS OF REFERENCE

Evaluators and proposal writers need to review the TOR through two different lenses that are essential to developing a good response: a strategic lens and a tactical lens. At the strategic level, the goal is multifold: to understand the evaluation context, the political landscape and pressures, the purpose of the evaluation in the broader strategy of the funder and the evaluand (organization, project, program being evaluated), the history of past programming and evaluations in this arena, and client and stakeholder expectations and concerns. At the tactical level, evaluators and/or proposal writers need to understand the specific guidelines and requirements set out in the TOR, such as relevant dates and timeline, staffing requirements, proposal outline, methodology and implementation specifications, specific deliverables (including communication products), and any contractual and budgetary requirements.

When applying these two lenses (strategic and tactical), the initial step in understanding the TOR begins with reading with intention and for the explicit purpose of understanding it. Secondly, it requires silencing your inner critical voice that will hamper your understanding such as when your keen eye calls out the potential errors and inconsistencies in the TOR. Reading with the intention to understand involves minimizing anything that would reduce your ability to do that. Simply stop imagining how the TOR could have been better written, lest the urge to criticize hamper your understanding. Here are some practices that can be helpful:

- <u>Get comfortable and organized</u>. Choose your modality to fit your reading preferences as well as your note-taking method, whether on screen or on paper. Some people prefer to write on the TOR document using small Post-it flags to enable them to go back to important sections and points. Ensure that you have both the TOR and your preferred note-taking method on hand before you begin. This step may seem obvious, but you might be surprised how many people think they can simply remember important information, and later they cannot find it.

- Get in a mindset to understand. Before you begin to read, focus your mind and awareness on the evaluation commissioner, the prospective client. Imagine that the TOR document may be a result of a consultative process of people trying to negotiate, writing the TOR amid busy schedules and possible political pressures. Appreciate that they are on the front lines in this TOR formation, while you are not. Remind yourself that the TOR is written by the commissioner and reflects both client language and culture. Imagine how great it would be to develop an outstanding proposal, be selected, and serve the client and its key stakeholders in conducting an excellent evaluation. Now, with that mindset, suspend judgment and begin to read.
- Read the TOR three times. Read the TOR three times and focus on something different each time. This will slow down the urgency to respond before you think, enabling you to give understanding a real shot. In the first reading, read through it like a story, reflecting on what this client is telling you. Note your first impressions: What confirms your expectations? What is surprising? What is noteworthy? What values are prioritized in this TOR? How prescriptive is the TOR—is it giving you the design or providing the purpose and questions and asking you to propose design and staffing? Remember, the TOR is written in the lens and language of the client, thus you should pay attention to the references to context, evaluation questions, scope, guidance on methodology, timeline, staffing, and so forth. It may be helpful to jot these things down. During your second reading, take notes on information that is important for your response to the TOR; for example, the duration of the evaluation, requirements for a particular methodology, location(s) where the evaluation will take place, key stakeholders, deliverables, key dates, and so on. You might use a form such as the one in Figure 3.1. In the third reading, begin to note the elements required for the written response, including any specifications and guidance embedded in the TOR (e.g., guidance on structure of response, page limits, fonts, required forms, etc.).
- Getting clarification on the TOR. During your three readings above, imagine actually conducting the evaluation as you read. List any questions that the TOR raised for you. Remember, the key to understanding the TOR is powerful questioning. What guidance is missing? Is there any seemingly contradictory guidance? How can you get clarification? Some clients allow for an informal consultation in the response to the TOR; some allow a more formal and transparent consultation; in other cases, no consultation is allowed. Commissioners of evaluations from foundations and nonprofit organizations tend to be most consultative; some government or international organization commissioners have a formal process for answering questions (usually one round with a strict deadline); and other government commissioners merely select proposals with no negotiation.

  In the case that consultations are allowed, think strategically about what questions to ask. Asking the right questions is important in developing your response and approach to the TOR. Make sure that your questions are not already explained in the TOR, as that signals you have not been reading carefully. Usually, a formal and transparent process means that your questions

FIGURE 3.1 ■ Reading the Terms of Reference (TOR) Checklist Form

General

1. Title: ______________________________
2. Location: ______________________________
3. Site visits: ______________________________
4. Timeline: ______________________________
5. Staffing: ______________________________
6. Budget: ______________________________
7. Questions: ______________________________
8. Submission: ______________________________
9. Response/proposal structure: ______________________________

Methodology

10. Type of evaluation: ______________________________
11. Methods requirements:

Questions:

1. Title: Write the title of the evaluation or project to be evaluated.
2. Location: Where will the evaluation take place? If there are multiple locations, say so.
3. Site visits: Will there be site visits? How many? Are the locations known? Where? What might be needed (cars, hotel, translators, local consultants)?
4. Timeline: When is this evaluation supposed to begin and end? How many months is it supposed to last? Are there any events driving this timeline (for example, conference key for data collection or presentation of preliminary results, decisions that need to be informed by the evaluation)?
5. Staffing: How many staff are envisioned? What are their roles and required competencies?
6. Budget: What information is given for the available budget? Is there any guidance on what they will pay and what the contractor is supposed to pay? Will travel be required?
7. Questions: Is asking questions allowed? Is there a deadline by which questions must be submitted?
8. Submission: On what date and time does the proposal need to be submitted and to whom (write the name, address, etc.)?
9. Response/proposal structure: What are the requirements of the proposal? Is there a page limit? Are exhibits and graphs included in the page limit? Is there a preferred font type and size, a required outline, or guidance on the response?
10. Type of evaluation:

and the commissioner's responses will be shared with all respondents. Therefore, you should think about which questions to ask and which to withhold. If your question gives good hints about considerations others might have missed, you may choose not to ask it. Formulate your questions in a way that does not imply a criticism of the TOR.

You may also choose to ask questions that reveal information about your point of view and test whether there is potential alignment between your values and the commissioner's perspective. For example, if the TOR does not call out key values—inclusion, human rights, combating human trafficking, sustainability, equity—and you consider these important to build into the criteria and methodology, you might want to ask a question that helps reveal whether the commissioner prioritizes these values or not. If the commissioner shares these values, this is an early signal that a responder is sensitive to them as well. If the commissioner does not share these values and answers accordingly, an evaluation implementer can decide whether it is worth it to make the case for those key values in the proposal or to not submit a proposal at all.

- Reflecting on the TOR. Now pause and reflect. What do you already know about the context of this commissioner and the program being evaluated? What are their core values and guiding principles? Who might have more information about the context of this evaluation—for example, a staff member or consultant who has worked there before or someone with expertise on the context and issues? Do the rules allow you to speak with a staff member from the commissioning organization? As much as possible, it is useful to reach out for more information.

3.2 RESPONDING TO THE TERMS OF REFERENCE

From an evaluation management perspective, it is your job to think about how to propose a plan that is responsive to what the client is asking for and that can be completed within the time and budget of the TOR—or if you do not have a budget, then within a budget you presume will be both sufficient and competitive. Here are some good practices for organizing an evaluation proposal.

- Develop a proposal outline. The first step in responding to the TOR is to develop an outline that follows relevant guidance such as naming of sections, page allocation, and so forth. This will keep you disciplined and responsive. United States government proposals can be very strict—for example, proposal reviewers will not read any pages that exceed the required page limit. However, even when there is not a page limitation to the proposal, it is respectful to the reviewers to provide them with a clear and concise proposal. Your ability to be succinct and to the point in your proposal will signal to them that you will be clear and concise in their evaluation.
- Postpone innovation(s). Just as it is important to resist the temptation to criticize the TOR quality, proposal writers should also resist any immediate temptation to innovate and propose alternatives to what is being asked for. In fact, the best guide for a proposal layout and what to emphasize is the evaluation criteria section, if it is listed in the TOR. In this section, the client lists how it will allocate points to evaluate your proposal and thus it is important to keep that section front and center when preparing the proposal.
- Remember, it is not about you. Proposal writers may be tempted to showcase how great their company or team is, but the readers first want to see that

you understand the client, what is being evaluated, and their needs. Do not merely repeat what is in the TOR; it is boring and uninformative. Find ways to communicate that you are listening and thinking about their issues and the work to be done. And, when you convey the strengths of your team, be humble but clear. This is a delicate balance: Find a way to talk about what makes your team different and well-suited for this evaluation without coming across as though you are speaking negatively about every other evaluator on this Earth.

- Focus on implementation. Proposal writers frequently spend a lot of time on the general approach, the philosophy of evaluation their team brings, and the way they think about an evaluation. While this is certainly important to include, the readers are also looking for what you will do to implement this evaluation. Be open about the values that guide your proposal so commissioners can know where you are coming from, but also tell them how you imagine the work will get done. For example, proposal writers frequently write that they will "use mixed methods" but are unclear about how they will synthesize what they learn from different sources and types of evidence (not merely report them out separately as unrelated facts). If you are implementing a policy evaluation or an evaluation with a sustainability lens that requires analysis beyond the boundaries of a program and wish to explore unintended consequences, the convenings and space for such reflection needs to be in the plan. Linking evaluation philosophy, approach, methodology, and timeline requires critical thinking, where you create parameters and commitments that will guide how the evaluation will be designed and managed if you are selected. If the proposal writer is not an evaluator, this is where it is most useful to seek an evaluator's input.

- Define shared responsibilities. Proposal writers frequently assert that they will work collaboratively with clients and stakeholders. While this is great, develop it further and define what that shared responsibility would look like. To define shared responsibility, imagine that you are developing a memorandum of understanding with the client regarding the evaluators' expectations of what they need to do to implement an actionable evaluation. Inclusion of such a section in your proposal honors the shared responsibility for the evaluation, and if you are selected, the proposal will inform the evaluation contract, in which case, specific requirements of commissioner input and collaboration will be helpful to the EIM. Table 3.1 presents an example of how to lay out shared responsibility expectations related to the design of a survey. It is not necessary to include every task but rather the areas where collaboration is important to highlight. In an evaluation that is implemented in accompaniment with program and community members, the memorandum concept should be expanded to include them as well.

- Decide how much detail to include in a proposal. Although writing the proposal should not include a completed design of an evaluation, the proposal should include the scaffolding of the design. As mentioned above, the proposal frequently serves as part of the evaluation contract, and as such, it is an opportunity to put forth your understanding, assumptions, and expectations as a first step in your dialogue with the client.

TABLE 3.1 ■ Example of a Shared Responsibility Table

Task	Evaluator's Responsibility	Commissioner's Responsibility	Comments
Site Selection	• Develop sampling strategy for site selection • Incorporate client feedback • Apply sampling strategy	• Provide input on site selection in a timely way • Approve site selection	
Conducting Site Visits	• Draft guidance for sites on what to expect during site visits • Follow up with site personnel to develop site visit schedules	• Introduce the evaluator and provide guidance to sites • Resolve any issues that arise in scheduling and conducting site visits	
Develop Survey	• Draft survey questions • Test the survey	• Provide feedback on survey questions • Approve final survey	

3.2.1 Developing a Timeline

Developing the timeline is a crucial part of planning but can be tricky—you do not want to develop the full-fledged design, but you do need to show you understand what they are asking for and to assess whether it is even feasible. To get started, first list all the required evaluation tasks and deliverables in the TOR and add any timing information. For example, the TOR might indicate you have 30 days to submit the evaluation matrix to the client, that site visits should be one week each, or that the final debriefing at the end of the evaluation must take place in an already planned stakeholder meeting—all of which should be included in your timeline. For internal evaluations, there is usually an overall workplan for the year and expectations for when evaluations must be completed and final reports submitted.

Once these larger categories of tasks and deliverables are added to the timeline, you can identify intermediate actions and products you need to complete them. These intermediate actions and products might include input from stakeholders (where you need to leave time for review and comments), organizing the work of others (e.g., your team or stakeholder staff gathering information for the evaluation), conducting data analysis, writing the report, and so on.

Table 3.2 presents an illustrative set of key tasks and deliverables for generating a timeline, while Figure 3.2 presents a timeline that could be shared in the proposal with the client.

Figure 3.2 lists sample tasks for an evaluation timeline that is disaggregated by months (denoted by letters). This can be further developed to detail weeks.

3.2.2 Staffing

Once the timeline is developed with tasks and deliverables, a staffing section that names key people to be involved in the evaluation is usually included in the proposal. The TOR

TABLE 3.2 ■ Key Activities, Tasks, and Deliverables

Tasks and Subtasks	Interim Products/Deliverables
1. Project Management	
Administration Logistics Coordination Quality control	Monthly progress reports
2. Development of Study Methodology	
Work with client on revising evaluation plan Prepare data collection plans Prepare data analysis plan Finalize data collection schedule	Evaluation plan that includes the following: • Evaluation questions • Plan for documenting progress • List of data elements • Data collection plan • Data collection instruments and procedures • Data analysis plan • Schedule and timeline

FIGURE 3.2 ■ Illustrative Evaluation Timeline

	2022												2023												2024					
	J	F	M	A	M	J	J	A	S	O	N	D	J	F	M	A	M	J	J	A	S	O	N	D	J	F	M	A	M	J
Develop methodology																														
Develop core data elements																														
Data collection																														
Site visits																														
Periodic memoranda																														
Stakeholder consultations																														
Analysis and reporting																														

may have specifications for staffing, but there may also be room for the proposal writer to propose a staffing strategy and staffing specifications. Sometimes a TOR specifies the number and type of staff, the educational background and degree, years of experience, and so forth, while a different TOR allows the evaluators to specify what is needed. Generally, driven by the TOR requirements and depending on the size and complexity of the evaluation, the proposed staff may include competencies in the following:

- knowledge and experience in evaluation
- experience in conducting and leading similar evaluations

- knowledge of the subject matter (if required)
- understanding of the client's system and context
- writing and communication skills

It is usually not expected that each competency will be covered by a different person but rather that the overall team will have the required competencies (i.e., the same person may cover more than one set of competencies). Also, several competencies may be addressed by staff who work in the evaluation on an as-needed basis at different stages of the process (e.g., a writer-editor might be involved at the end to review and improve the evaluation report).

Many clients check references, and therefore it is important to ensure that the proposed staff have strong references (i.e., not only have experience in doing the work but also in doing it well). Even if clients do not check references, the EIM (if not involved in preparing the proposal) will be grateful to the proposal team for checking references.

Figure 3.3 presents a framework for developing and presenting the staffing strategy.

FIGURE 3.3 ■ Staffing Strategy

The shaded area provides an example of how to develop the evaluation staffing matrix with sample technical qualifications, substantive qualifications, and operational skills. In the biographical section, you should also include relevant diverse characteristics such as language skills, gender, and context-relevant experience.

BACKGROUND INFO				EXPERTISE AND EXPERIENCE																	
Biographical Information				Technical Qualifications						Substantive Qualifications						Operational Skills					
Name	Degrees	Project Role/Position	Staff/Consultant	Evaluation	Quantitative Analysis	Qualitative Analysis				Community Development	Civil Society	Marginalized Populations				Communications	Report Writing	Project Management			
MG	PhD	Project Director, Task Leader Languages: Gender:	S	X	X	X				X		X					X	X			
CT	PhD	Principle Investigator, Task Leader Languages: Gender:	S	X	X	X				X	X	X				X	X	X			
		Task Leader A																			
		Task Leader B																			
		Team Member																			
		Team Member																			
		Team Member																			
		Team Member																			
		Team Member																			

3.2.3 The Budget

Now with your completed timeline and staffing section, it is time to build the budget. As shown in Figure 3.4, list each proposal task down the left column and the people across the top horizontally and determine how many hours (or days) each task requires of each member of the proposal team. Once completed, this table presents the level of effort (LOE) for the evaluation (i.e., the number of "person hours" required by different types of staff to complete the evaluation). Based on the LOE, the remuneration for each type of staff can be used to develop the budget for the labor cost of the evaluation. Then, by adding expenses for other costs such as travel, the proposal budget can be developed.

Using this strategy, you build the budget from the bottom up—systematically thinking through all the details, figuring out what each task will cost, and then aggregating those costs to a total proposal budget. Now, it is time to cross-check this draft

FIGURE 3.4 ■ Evaluation Budget

The shaded area provides an example of a task with associated subtasks underneath.

TASKS & SUBTASKS	Project Director				Principal Investigator				Task Leader A				Task Leader B				Team Member			
	Yr 1	Yr 2	Yr 3	Total	Yr 1	Yr 2	Yr 3	Total	Yr 1	Yr 2	Yr 3	Total	Yr 1	Yr 2	Yr 3	Total	Yr 1	Yr 2	Yr 3	Total
TASK: Methodology/ Evaluation Plan																				
Plans for timeline, data analysis/collection																				
Data collection instruments																				
TASK SUBTOTAL	*0*	*0*	*0*		*0*	*0*	*0*		*0*	*0*	*0*		*0*	*0*	*0*		*0*	*0*	*0*	
TASK 1																				
Subtask 1																				
Subtask 2																				
Subtask 3																				
TASK SUBTOTAL																				
TASK 2																				
Subtask 1																				
Subtask 2																				
Subtask 3																				
TASK SUBTOTAL																				
TASK 3																				
Subtask 1																				
Subtask 2																				
Subtask 3																				
TASK SUBTOTAL																				
Task 4																				
Subtask 1																				
Subtask 2																				
Subtask 3																				
TASK SUBTOTAL																				
Task 5																				
Subtask 1																				
Subtask 2																				
Subtask 3																				
TASK SUBTOTAL																				

total budget cost with any information about the budget the client has allocated for this evaluation and how the plan and budget laid out in the proposal compares. If a budget limit is provided, it contains information about the client's expectations regarding how extensive this evaluation needs to be. Even if no amount has been specified, past experience with this client or other evaluations of similar size may inform a sense of what a reasonable budget should be. Review the budget for realism, and if you have to reduce it, consider whether you are trimming fat and doing things more efficiently or whether you need to simplify the evaluation plan to reduce the required time or to eliminate steps from the proposal plan. Strategies for budget reduction may include the following:

- assigning fewer people to complete key tasks so there are fewer people attending relevant meetings and reviewing documents
- reducing the number of reviews for input by the client
- reducing the number of meetings anticipated with the client (e.g., from weekly to every two weeks)
- reducing the number of questions in a survey

As you make changes, note the assumptions you are using to make them so if your proposal is selected, the EIM can easily see how you planned to implement the evaluation within that budget.

When you are done cutting the budget, pause and consider whether the evaluation can be completed within the pared-down budget, given what you know about what is needed. If you have concerns about budget realism, you may decide to ask the commissioner about it, you may propose an alternative budget with an explanation, or you may choose to not submit a bid altogether. Tessie's company had two experiences where two different commissioners were systematically demanding very low prices. One commissioner used a "lowest cost, acceptable quality" selection rule and kept selecting evaluation companies that would ask for budget increases within a few months; Tessie decided not to bid on any more of that commissioner's evaluations. Another commissioner, who was newer in evaluation, kept publishing budgets that were 50%–60% of what was needed. Tessie's company joined five other companies that invited a discussion with the leadership of the commissioner's evaluation office and provided joint feedback on cost realism.

3.3 CLARIFYING, NEGOTIATING, AND SELECTION

Once a proposal is submitted, commissioners go through their selection process (see Chapter 2). During the selection process, commissioners may decide to ask questions of the individuals or firms that submitted bids.

Questions from a commissioner provide useful information about areas that are important and need correction or elaboration and are also an opportunity to improve the submitted proposal.

If you are prone to feeling defensive when reading commissioner questions, stop. No matter how clear you think your writing is, it is not clear enough if it is not understood. Consider instead your good luck in being in the running and having an opportunity to improve your proposal in the eyes of the decision makers. Really consider the questions you received and what information they are imparting to you. If a section is questioned, take the opportunity to strengthen your response by making it clearer and more compelling.

Commissioners should note the intensity of the competition for evaluators and strive for respectful, clear, and timely communication.

If your organization is invited to a final evaluation contract negotiation, this is a new opportunity for you to ask questions and raise issues about expectations, timing, requirements, and so forth. Prioritize your issues, know your boundaries, and be ready to compromise. In the end, if you are selected, assemble your team and celebrate. If you are not selected, then request a debriefing and listen closely to the commissioner's feedback. This is not about one proposal but about an important relationship you are building. If you know who was selected, congratulate them and signal that you are part of a larger professional community of evaluators.

3.4 UPON EVALUATION CONTRACT AWARD

By the time a team is selected to implement an evaluation, it is quite possible that significant progress has been made toward evaluation design during the proposal. This may be helpful or hindering, depending on the quality of thinking that went into the proposal. Upon award of an evaluation contract, the EIM needs to review the TOR from the beginning to understand what was originally requested and then review the proposal to understand what has been promised. Furthermore, the EIM needs to consider any known implications of the time between proposal submission and selection; for example, if the date for evaluation commencement listed in the TOR has now slipped, then the evaluation timeline needs to be adjusted. Or if a major change has taken place for the commissioner or evaluand—such as a reorganization or the adoption of a new piece of relevant legislation—then this is an item that must be discussed with the client.

If the evaluation contract was awarded based on a broad concept note or on CVs only, the EIM will need to go through the detailed analysis described in the proposal process to prepare for the first meeting with the client (see Chapter 4).

In addition to the above documents and analysis, the EIM must also become familiar with the evaluation contract, as this is the legal document that needs to be followed during the evaluation.

The EIM is now ready to plan and implement the start-up phase of the evaluation.

EXERCISE

Imagine that you are developing an evaluation proposal but do not know much about the context beyond the RFP.

- What questions would you ask?
- How might you build flexibility in the proposal you are writing to allow the evaluation manager to make adjustments after the contract is awarded?

4 MANAGING THE EVALUATION CONTRACT START-UP

WHO SHOULD USE THIS CHAPTER

This chapter is crucial both for evaluation commissioning managers (ECMs) and evaluation implementing managers (EIMs). This is the starting point for their relationship and provides the foundation for the evaluation. For internal evaluators, the evaluation start-up does not involve a contract but still requires planning and coordination with the implementors of the programs being evaluated. This chapter contains useful ways to organize this initial phase of the evaluation and the relationship being established with counterpart program implementers.

The evaluation literature focuses on evaluation planning, but we see this start-up phase as much more; planning is an important subset of start-up. In our experience, the start-up phase involves establishing a relationship between the evaluation commissioner and the evaluation implementor and engaging in co-creation of the evaluation with a wider set of actors, including evaluation team members, program implementors, and other key stakeholders.

You may be feeling some impatience to get to planning the evaluation, but you will circumvent other aspects of start-up at your own peril. Remember the story we shared in Chapter 2? Tessie found out in the kick-off meeting that the ECM had completed an evaluation of the same program only six months prior. As EIM, Tessie negotiated with the ECM to redirect the focus of the evaluation on newer and more complex components of the program, which resulted in an engaging and useful evaluation. Initially, the ECM resisted, but by having the strategic conversation suggested in this chapter, a way forward that satisfied all parties became possible.

When the contract for the evaluation is awarded to the selected contractor/evaluation team, both the ECM and the EIM have key responsibilities and goals. This includes keeping evaluation goals and objectives clear, monitoring the work and providing timely feedback, to name a few (Morra Imas & Rist, 2009). Both the ECM and the EIM have two primary sets of goals for the start-up phase of the evaluation: tactical goals and strategic goals (two lenses the evaluation manager needs to use, as defined in Chapter 1). This chapter reviews how the ECM and the EIM can start an evaluation on its best foot and mindfully organize, negotiate, and plan the evaluation right from the start.

At this phase of an evaluation, a lot of thinking and consideration has already gone into the commissioning organization's shaping of the evaluation requirements

(Chapter 2) and preparing its high-level design and planning in the proposal phase (Chapter 3). It may feel as though the evaluation has already started with the considerable time it has taken to prepare for this phase—and in many ways, it has. As EIM, you have been awarded the evaluation contract, so what now? Let us review the evaluation's journey so far:

- The terms of reference (TOR) are released by the evaluation commissioner and shaped by the mandate that enabled it (whether internal or external to the commissioning organization).
- You have scoped the evaluation, analyzed its requirements, and gotten clarification that led to the specifications in the TOR with the commissioner.
- If a proposal was required, the proposal writer(s) presented an approach and outlined a high-level evaluation plan in the proposal.
- You have been awarded the evaluation contract.

Now, the EIM, whether a team leader or a solo evaluator, is ready to take over to begin the implementation of the evaluation contract. This is the first time in the life cycle of the evaluation that the evaluation needs to follow the contract with its requirements and specifications. It is a great time to pause and seek greater clarity about what needs to be done. The EIM and the evaluation team stepping in to implement the evaluation may be new, and things may have changed since the development of the TOR or since proposal submission. It can often take six to eight months between publishing a request for proposal and an award. The EIM must lead a purposeful and well-organized start-up phase in order to set the stage for a successful evaluation.

In this chapter, we discuss the start-up phase of an evaluation that is guided by a newly awarded evaluation contract. We will cover the EIM's responsibilities related to the preparation and negotiation between the ECM and EIM, clarifying roles and responsibilities, effective stakeholder engagement during the start-up phase, and finalizing the evaluation design. While they are technically held as a part of the start-up phase, team planning meetings are covered in Chapter 5.

> If internal evaluators are part of a larger evaluation unit, the activities covered in this chapter will be relevant, except that the internal evaluation team may report to a unit supervisor rather than an outside client. If the internal evaluator is part of a smaller unit, the start-up phase may be solitary. In those cases, engaging stakeholders can be more difficult.

4.1 EVALUATION MANAGEMENT STRUCTURE

Now that we have a contract in place, it is important to recognize the individuals who play a role in influencing and approving the evaluation including its work plan, timeline, and deliverables. The management structure of the evaluation depends on the evaluation funder and commissioner. It is important for the EIM to seek clarity (and the ECM to provide it) about the decision-making authority and hierarchy under which the contract will be managed. Why? Well, because there are a myriad of decisions and forks in the road throughout the course of the evaluation that may dramatically alter it (i.e., results, costs, and time) and how and who makes those decisions is extremely important. Here are some questions that we need to clarify:

- Funding versus commissioning. Who is funding the evaluation, and if this entity is different from the organization that is commissioning and managing the evaluation, what is their role? Sometimes, the funders of an evaluation are silent partners and all the authority rests with the commissioning organization; other times, the funders need to be consulted and informed.
- Approvals. Who is directing decisions and approvals related to the day-to-day evaluation design, implementation, and reporting decisions? In some cases, the day-to-day approvals rest with the ECM while larger decisions on findings and conclusions are made at a higher level. It is important to understand the commissioner stakeholder landscape that the ECM is facilitating.
- Contractual accountability. Who approves decisions that change the requirements in the scope of work and what constitutes a change in the requirements (e.g., is it duration, staffing, budget, sites to be visited, methods, number and type of reports, etc.)? When is a contract modification required? Does the EIM have a direct relationship with the contracts office of the organization?

Lack of role clarity affects quality decision making, can slow down the evaluation plan and timeline, and can place the evaluation team at risk for breach of contract if proper approvals are not secured in a timely way. For example, if the evaluation manager reduces the number of sites visited in exchange for an increase in the number of interviews per site and does not have approval from the right body in the right format, the contract may be found to be in noncompliance, and there may be a financial cost and negative ratings of the evaluation contract performance. These structures are unique to each type of commissioning organization and they change over time, so it is worth pausing and clarifying who oversees what and the right process for administering the contract. Additionally, it is important for the evaluation team to be looped into these management and reporting structures. A good EIM builds a solid organizational structure on key areas of communication flow, including aligning management and reporting structures and processes to the evaluation team. Internal evaluators or internal evaluation units are part of the organization and have firsthand knowledge of its policies, procedures, personnel, and management, since they are part of the overall organization (Love, 1991).

Be careful not to make any generalizations or assumptions regarding management structures. Figure 4.1 outlines differences for typical evaluation management structures in the United Nations (UN) and the United States (U.S.) federal government. Additionally, we detail some of the key elements of these evaluation management structures for the United Nations, U.S. federal government, and foundations below.

4.1.1 United Nations

In the United Nations, an individual is appointed as the evaluation manager (with a possible back up, depending on the size and importance of the evaluation). The ECM

FIGURE 4.1 ■ Sample Evaluation Management Structure Bodies

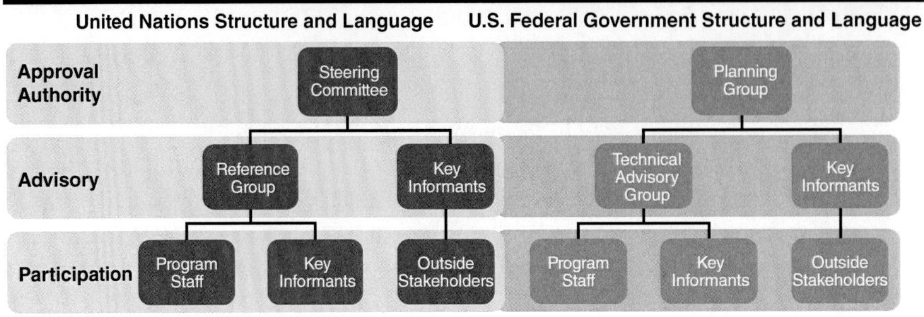

is the go-to person for day-to-day decisions for the contracted evaluation. That person reports to a *steering committee*, a formally appointed group that represents the headquarters evaluation office for global or corporate evaluations or the country evaluation office for country-level evaluations. The steering committee is comprised of formal representatives of key stakeholders whose job is to convey their organizational perspectives. For headquarters-led evaluations (also called *corporate evaluations*), the steering committee typically includes evaluation office representatives, representatives of other key departments, and country leadership representatives. For country-level evaluations, the steering committee will typically include the commissioning UN agency, the country's government counterparts involved in the implementation of the program being evaluated, other UN agencies involved, other program funders, and key implementing partners. The steering committee provides official guidance and feedback to the evaluation and has the authority to accept and approve the final evaluation report.

Typically, UN evaluations also have a *reference group* in their management structure. The reference group is comprised of members of key groups being evaluated who do not have any formal authority over the evaluation but are there to inform the external evaluation team on the context and to act as a built-in focus group. They provide insight to the evaluators with their reactions to different elements of the evaluation, such as the language and questions in interview guides and interpretation of preliminary findings. The reference group is an invaluable support to the evaluation team, and even when not required by non–UN clients, it is always a good idea to put one together. Even though the reference group does not have formal authority, it can have a significant influence on how the evaluation is perceived by stakeholders. This is a good practice even for small or internal evaluations; a reference group widens the visibility and credibility of the evaluation and frequently helps to avoid interpretation and communication errors.

The ECM, steering committee, and reference group provide useful guidance and input to the EIM and evaluation team, but only the contracts office can approve any changes in the TOR listed in the contract. In other words, time extensions, changes in the budget, and modifications in the number and types of deliverables may require a contract modification to be implemented and approved by the contracts office.

4.1.2 United States Federal Government

Similar to the United Nations, in the U.S. federal government, an individual ECM is typically the day-to-day contact with the authority to steer the evaluation. Typically, this person works with a planning group in the commissioner's organization, and the ECM knows when to check with the internal hierarchy. The planning group may be two to five people and will typically be comprised of staff from the federal agency's evaluation unit and the unit that oversees the project or program being evaluated. The evaluation might be managed out of the agency's office of evaluation, policy/planning office, or the program office.

Large, U.S. federal government evaluations may also have a technical advisory group (TAG), a small group of experts (usually three to five) in evaluation and/or in the specific topic of the evaluation. This group may be convened twice in the life of an evaluation contract—in the beginning to review the evaluation design and provide feedback and after the draft report is completed. Feedback from the TAG is shared with the commissioning agency, including the planning group and possibly some key stakeholders. Their opinions are very valuable and carry influence. The evaluation team must address their concerns and advice; the gravitas of a TAG lends credibility to the evaluation results.

The role of the contracts office is key, just as in UN evaluations. Typically, the TOR in UN evaluations leaves room for some modifications (e.g., after award, the design can be modified as long as the budget is not changed). In federal evaluations, things can be stricter; if significant changes are required, the contracts officer may require that the evaluation contract be recompeted. Why? If the evaluation scope changes significantly, firms that were not selected for the originally competed evaluation may protest that they were not given a chance to submit plans and capabilities for this modified evaluation and that they should be given a chance under the open competition rules.

4.1.3 Foundations

Foundations are varied in how they structure the management of their evaluations, and so outside evaluators should suspend their assumptions (even from working with other foundations) and get clarification on the expectations of the foundation they are working with. First off, the placement of the evaluation function can be anywhere from the policy unit to programs to knowledge management or the leadership team. Furthermore, the evaluation function might be central or peripheral.

In some cases, the ECM within the foundation may have little power. For example, in some foundations, the ECM's job is to convey the feelings of a broader group (e.g., program team, senior management), and the EIM cannot rely on that one person's feedback on a deliverable unless it is representing the decisionmakers' views. This can make it difficult to know when a decision is actually made or approved on the foundation's side or to understand the guidance received. The flexibility embedded in the way foundations manage their evaluations can be a blessing that allows evaluation team leaders to make sensible decisions for the evaluation, while at other times, it takes patience to understand what the foundation really wants out of the evaluation. Because of this kind of flexibility, EIMs should be especially careful with scope creep in foundation-led evaluations, especially when foundation colleagues get excited about early findings and want the evaluation to explore a few more questions not originally in the TOR . . . but do not increase the budget to cover the additional work.

4.1.4 Nonprofit Organizations

When nonprofit organizations commission evaluation, it typically means that the nonprofit organization is the implementor of a program funded by the government or by a foundation, and it is entrusted with the responsibility of managing the evaluation of that program with an expectation that it will report to the funder. Our experience with larger nonprofits is similar to that of foundations. Small nonprofits present their own set of challenges. Nonprofits with low to no evaluation capacity may need significant education to go alongside evaluation implementation so they can be effective evaluation partners and get the most out of evaluation. Nonprofits with some evaluation knowledge and enthusiasm for evaluation may need help agreeing to and sticking with evaluation scope boundaries; as the evaluation evolves or their needs change, they are more likely to ask for new things that are beyond the scope of the current evaluation and to feel misled if the evaluation implementor has not educated them about their choices and trade-offs along the way.

4.1.5 Investing in Evaluation Planning

ECMs define the start-up process and place an emphasis on evaluation planning in different ways. For example, federal government evaluations frequently envision a short and rapid start-up in evaluation, with some evaluation timelines and matrixes due within 2–4 weeks of the contract award. Foundations generally take on a more collaborative and flexible approach to start-up and expect to work closely with their selected evaluators in the design and planning of the evaluation. UN agencies rules provide for a formal and longer start-up phase referred to as the *inception phase* of an evaluation, during which it is possible to make modifications to the evaluation TOR based on consultations between the ECM and the EIM. This phase is allotted around seven weeks and requires its own deliverable called *the inception report.* During the inception phase, it is expected that the evaluation team will revisit the evaluation questions, design, methods, timeline, sampling strategy, and the outline of the evaluation report. It is also expected that the evaluation team will review relevant documents and consult with the client and key stakeholders in individual and group interviews, including with the reference group. The inception phase ensures a mutual understanding between the commissioner and the evaluation team of the plan of action and timeline for conducting the evaluation. It also provides an additional guarantee of adherence to and interpretation of the TOR.

There is a significant variation in how different evaluation commissioners invest in the start-up phase and the extent to which they collaborate, review, and revise the evaluation plan. It is evident that the United Nations allots more time—up to four times more—than the U.S. federal government. Let us take a pause and consider this for a second. Why is that? The U.S. federal government is constrained by the rules that safeguard a fair process in the selection of individuals and firms to implement evaluations. In some cases, U.S. government agencies have come up with creative solutions. For example, when the U.S. Agency for International Development's evaluation office in the Policy, Planning, and Learning Bureau (USAID/PPL) commissioned an evaluation of its program cycle and several key policies, it wanted to have a significant say in the evaluation design and plan. To resolve the need to protect the competitive process, it released two separate contracts: one for the design and a separate one for the implementation for the evaluation. This strategy gave USAID/PPL flexibility to co-create the evaluation's design.

Let us take a closer look at how the World Food Programme (WFP) approaches the inception phase of country-level evaluations as outlined in their guide. For WFP, the inception phase of an evaluation is allotted seven weeks and has two main purposes: (1) to ensure that the commissioning office, the evaluation team, and the stakeholders involved in the evaluation have a common, in-depth understanding of the evaluation TOR and (2) to develop an agreed operational plan (indicating the approach, methodology, team work plan, and field work schedule) for the evaluation. Guidance for the inception meeting alone includes 22 separate items covering the goals of the meeting, technical aspects that should be discussed, and who should be included.[1]

The distinct variation between this UN agency and the U.S. federal government prompts us to reflect on the potential impact of an up-front investment in the start-up phase. When an outside evaluation team is selected, a deliberate investment in thoughtful planning during start-up will contribute significantly to the success of the evaluation.

4.2 GOALS OF EVALUATION START-UP

All evaluation managers should be mindful of two sets of goals for the start-up phase of the evaluation: immediate/tactical goals and strategic goals. We encourage both ECMs and EIMs to review and reflect on the detailed attention to the goals and process envisioned for this phase (see Figure 4.2).

At the tactical level, the ECM and EIM need to achieve three things:

1. Clarify requirements. Review and clarify the purpose of the evaluation, review the intended use of the evaluation, and identify the key stakeholders whose perspective the commissioner wishes to include in the evaluation. These items may sound basic to the reader, but experienced evaluation managers know how critical it is to develop a clear and deep understanding about these fundamental issues. This will also provide an opportunity for updates and for an understanding of the personal perspective of the person who represents the funder or client in this evaluation.

FIGURE 4.2 ■ Tactical and Strategic Goals of Evaluation Start-Up

[1] This can be found at https://docs.wfp.org/api/documents/9f13fcec2d6f45f6915beade8e542024/download/

2. Agree on roles. Agree on roles and expectations on who guides the evaluation. Is there an appointed group (such as some of the groups noted above) or will it be done by an individual? Who approves evaluation plans and products? What role will the client play in facilitating data collection?

3. Develop ground rules. Agree on boundaries and ground rules. For an effective and actionable evaluation, it is important to develop conditions for its success, including key events in the evaluation timeline (e.g., a planned key stakeholder gathering), reviews, communication or coordination plans, reasonable time to review drafts for the commissioner, contingency margins, regularly planned check-ins, and so on.

In arriving at these agreements and clarifications, ECMs and EIMs may need to renegotiate different aspects of the contract within the boundaries of what is permissible. As the EIM, you must establish clear boundaries of the evaluation, the perspectives that the client expects you to include, and the ways in which you will interact with evaluation stakeholders, including the client and the evaluation team. So, use your judgment about what you will put forward and what you will address using your independent authority as EIM. Of course, you are bound by the contract, but you should consider elements of uncertainty in the interpretation of parts of the contract and the unpredictability in the evaluation life cycle. As the ECM, you are responsible for orienting the evaluation team and bringing everyone up to speed about recent pertinent developments that may influence the evaluation. If changes need to be made, you need to be prepared to negotiate them and to make any needed adjustments to the contract.

EIMs should not be surprised if the commissioner brings up a list of things that need to be renegotiated because of new developments. ECMs should not be surprised if the evaluation team leader has issues that need to be clarified and renegotiated. Internal evaluators who act as ECMs and EIMs simultaneously and usually do not supervise their evaluands will also likely need to renegotiate their evaluation plans.

In parallel with the tactical goals, at the strategic level, ECMs and EIMs aim to do the following:

1. Develop a joint vision of the evaluation's success. Let us admit that evaluation may feel, at best, like an unwelcome imposition to the evaluand (the organization[s] and program[s] being evaluated). An evaluation is an intervention that demands time from busy people, may threaten to expose issues, challenges the status quo, and brings about change that may or may not be desirable to many. It is the joint responsibility of the ECM and EIM to invite everyone to the table and facilitate discussions on evaluation success to ensure that every voice is heard in this evaluation. This type of consultation will help everyone accept that the evaluation is taking place and consider that they will be better served by participating and adding their voice and perspective to it. If this initial consultation process is managed well, it can create a sense of appreciation and positive anticipation of the evaluation. Clarity around how the evaluation will be most useful will help the EIMs prioritize evaluation questions that are most appropriate for the program's needs and future direction.

2. Create mutual commitment to the success of the evaluation. An evaluation is an invitation to engage in multistakeholder conversations and reflections about the merit, worth, and value of the intervention and to build a better future together. This jointly developed vision is beneficial because it invites and makes cooperation of stakeholders more likely and, more importantly, because it will result in a better quality and more useful evaluation. A joint vision of success and a mutual commitment to that success invites everyone sitting at the table to work hard to ensure that collected data is accurate and valid, the evaluation questions are relevant, and the conversations are rich. A joint vision and mutual commitment frequently result in evaluation recommendations being implemented before the evaluation is completed. This is a key element of utilization-focused evaluations, where the primary intended users are engaged at the beginning of the process to ensure that their intended uses can be identified (Patton & Cambell-Patton, 2021).

3. Receive useful advice, including do's and don'ts of the evaluation, and understand political sensitivities of different stakeholders. Evaluation is a form of organization knowledge, and politics are often inherent in the evaluation process since they are carried out in a political context. Evaluators are outsiders—even internal evaluators are considered outsiders—and as outsiders, they greatly benefit from guidance on political sensitivities, appropriate use of language, divisive issues, organizational culture, and other such issues that can hinder building the relationships needed to conduct a good, responsive, and actionable evaluation. So, during start-up, EIMs should keep asking, "What advice do you have for the evaluation team and me to navigate the organizational culture and do a good job in this evaluation?"

4.3 STARTING IN THE MIDDLE

An important perspective for ECMs and especially EIMs is that no matter when they get started with the evaluation, they are actually stepping into the middle of a process that had commenced before them and will continue after they are gone. This image of stepping into the middle of the flowing river (depicted in Figure 1.1) mirrors the nature of evaluation where programs and activities are continuing; an evaluation comes in at a point in time to review how things have gone as the flow of the river continues. The evaluation then unfolds parallel to the work of the program, and when the evaluation ends, it has already been overtaken by events and program work that continue beyond the period covered in the evaluation. Even summative evaluations work within a changing context where, as they produce conclusions and lessons learned, events and perceptions around the subject of their evaluation continue to change.

The evaluation plan and budget give the impression of a bounded and static whole, but ECMs and EIMs need to be aware of the past, present, and future all at once and keep being aware of the dynamic and unstoppable changes in the context. Awareness of ongoing change will help the evaluation manager be more attune to changes that may have significant implications for the evaluation and to the different perspectives that exist and keep changing concerning any aspect of the evaluation and the program being evaluated. Awareness that we are always starting in the middle will help the evaluation managers be flexible, listen deeply, and be able to negotiate and navigate inevitable ongoing changes.

4.4 KEY EVALUATION START-UP TASKS

We have delved into the context behind the start-up phase and acknowledged its significance and objective. So then, what are the key tasks to start up the evaluation? There are four main evaluation management start-up tasks:

1. analysis of evaluation requirements and preparation by the EIM
2. kick-off meeting with between the ECM and EIM or the internal evaluator and the program liaison
3. stakeholder kick-off process—either group meeting or interviews usually facilitated by the EIM with ECM participation or facilitated by the internal evaluator with program liaison participation
4. submission and approval of an evaluation plan or inception report by the EIM to the ECM

4.4.1 Analysis of the Evaluation Requirements and Preparation

At this time, there is usually an evaluation contract or at least a concept note. Both the ECM and EIM should review the contract or concept note to clarify the requirements. In cases where the evaluation involved a proposal, that proposal might have been folded into the contract, which makes it important to review not only the contract but also the attached proposal to make sure the EIM has a clear and comprehensive picture of what has been promised. This review should note the following (see Figure 4.3):

- expected timeline of the evaluation, time dedicated for each task in the evaluation, deliverables envisioned by the contract, and deadlines for intermediate deliverables (e.g., the evaluation plan, data collection protocol, etc.)
- budget and level of effort anticipated, relevant assumptions (e.g., is there a lump sum estimated for site visits? Are there funds for a local evaluator and/or a translator as needed?) and any flexibility in the distribution of budget items

FIGURE 4.3 ■ Reviewing the Evaluation Contract

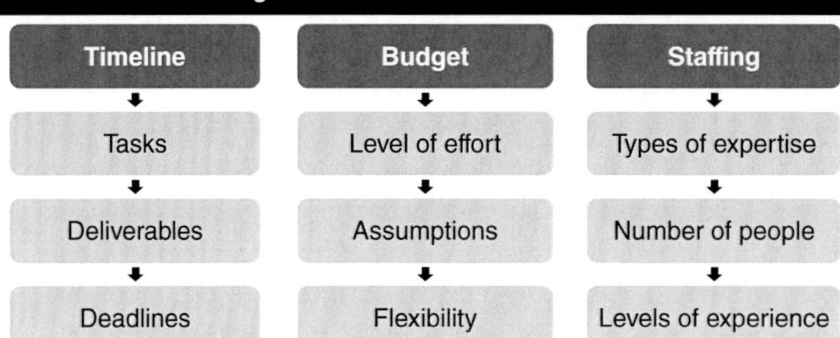

(e.g., if there is a shift in methodology, can funds be redistributed from the survey to site visits?)

- staffing requirements, including types of expertise, number of people, levels of experience, and so on

After reviewing the contract, the EIM should be clear on all evaluation requirements and any commitments made in the proposal that are included in the contract on how the evaluation will be implemented. Now it is time to assess whether the plans embedded in the contract still represent the best way to implement this evaluation and the extent to which the plan is still feasible within the available budget as well as to create a list of any areas of the contract that are unclear. If there are areas of concern—such as an unanticipated increase in costs for travel and/or evaluation staff who were promised but are no longer available—these need to be discussed and negotiated with the ECM. With a list of draft plans to be confirmed, areas for negotiation, and any outstanding questions, the EIM is now ready to hold the first kick-off meeting with the ECM.

In parallel, the ECM should also conduct the same review of contract requirements. The ECM should review any assumptions or expectations listed in the contract that might have changed, consider their influence on plans for the evaluation, and be ready to brief the EIM. For example, there may be new strategic priorities or structure for the commissioner's organization, shifts in stakeholder roles, staffing changes with key persons who may need new briefings, and so on. The ECM needs to communicate these types of changes, help the EIM interpret their implications for the evaluation, and negotiate how these changes might be addressed within the boundaries of the existing contract or initiate a contract amendment, if needed.

At the end of their respective reviews of the evaluation contract, both the ECM and EIM are ready for their first meeting with a list of updates, questions, and potential requests.

4.4.2 Kick-Off Meeting with the Evaluation Commissioning Manager and Evaluation Implementing Manager

The setting of the first kick-off meeting between the ECM and EIM may vary; it might be an informal, face-to-face discussion or a more formal event with a group of people on the commissioner's side. In either case, it is best to touch base informally first, especially if this is the first time you will be working together. Understanding and appreciating each other's perspectives prior to the intense collaboration involved in an evaluation will undoubtedly be helpful in working together, and given the nature of managing short-term contracts, establishing a good working relationship is critical for success. So, let us begin with a reflection of the mindset both evaluation managers bring into that first meeting.

Evaluation Implementation Manager (EIM)

As the EIM, before you enter the meeting, take a moment to examine your own assumptions and biases about the ECM you are about to meet and their organization. If you detect any superiority in your thoughts because of your skills as an evaluator or your position of power to expose wrongs, do your best to shift any such thoughts. Feel your excitement in meeting the ECM(s) who will be your close colleague(s) for the duration of this evaluation and experience gratitude for all the knowledge and access this person has that will help you with the evaluation's success. Remember that this person may be very busy with other things, and be prepared to facilitate a focused conversation, making their life easier in managing this evaluation. With that in mind, you are ready to go into this kick-off meeting. Remember to be open-minded, curious, humble, and eager to do a great job for this organization.

Be clear about your goals for this meeting and organize the agenda to meet those goals. This may seem obvious, but many of us get into technical questions as soon as we introduce ourselves. In Western cultures, we may consider this more efficient and respectful of people's time, but in many other cultures, it is more respectful to spend a little time getting to know each other before diving in.

Table 4.1 includes possible questions to consider asking the client in your initial one-on-one meeting.

Evaluation Commissioning Manager (ECM)

As ECM, you may be excited you finally have a team to take over the evaluation process, or, if you were recently assigned the evaluation, you might be new at it and need

TABLE 4.1 ■ Possible Questions for Evaluation Start-Up

Possible Questions	Why Ask?
Why did you select our team for this evaluation? What in our proposal caught your attention?	Knowing what the client values in what you have to offer will enable you to conduct the evaluation more effectively and increase client satisfaction.
As you think ahead, what are the three major topics/issues that you expect the evaluation to bring up?	You are asking for client expectations and want to make sure you look out for those issues. Follow-up questions can help you understand the mental model and perspective of your client.
Imagine the evaluation is finished and you are pleased with the outcome. What does success in the evaluation look like for you?	You are asking about the client's theory of change of the evaluation. You are getting information about what you need to achieve to get the highest marks from your client.
How do you imagine using the evaluation?	You are exploring both the purpose of the evaluation and the stakeholders that are visible to the client at this time. You want to use this information to make sure the intended users are appropriately engaged in the evaluation.
Who are the key stakeholders to engage in the start-up phase?	Building on the previous question, make sure you have ways to involve people as appropriate.
With whom will I coordinate to get access to documents, arrange interviews, and organize site visits?	The logistics of evaluation management need to be clear when you walk out of this meeting. You may need a special badge that allows you to get into the building, permission to access relevant documents online, introductions to people you will interview, and so forth.
What advice do you have for me to be successful in leading/implementing this evaluation? What are some do's and don'ts?	You are inviting the client to be an advocate for you, showing your humility, and getting some advice on the context.

an orientation. In any case, your role in evaluation management is very important. The evaluation team needs your guidance on who to contact and how, updates that have an impact on the evaluation timeline or scope, and how to engage with your organization and stakeholders appropriately. Before meeting an EIM, the ECM should review the contract, the proposal, and the notes about why they were selected. Make some notes on the evaluation scope and proposal to clarify what is expected and seek updates in the organization or program about aspects that seem relevant to the evaluation—for example, if dates have shifted for a key meeting where the evaluation team is expected to have a role, be prepared to inform them. Updates such as these are important for the evaluation team to know, and you must take the initiative to stay informed and communicate relevant updates throughout the evaluation.

As the ECM, you have a significant role in guiding and supporting the evaluation; you will ensure that the evaluation team is properly introduced and understood by your organization and stakeholders, has access to documents and people in a timely way, and complies with the terms of the evaluation contract. You are also responsible for communicating to the EIM the key organizational values and strategic issues that are important to prioritize in the evaluation (e.g., climate change, community participation, etc.). As commissioner, your relationship with the EIM will be finite and intense, and if successful, you will have facilitated a significant and useful intervention that will enable your organization or team to learn, adapt, do things better, and move more confidently on your path to organizational excellence and social benefit.

As ECM, you must walk a fine line between providing guidance, pushing the evaluation team to do a good job for your organization, and protecting the external evaluation team's independence, advocating for the evaluation for your organization's time, attention, and cooperation—and at times, for more resources. You need to decide when to insist on requirements and restrict the evaluation team's actions and when to let yourself learn and change alongside the evaluation team so you can advocate for the best actionable evaluation the team can deliver within the contract. You are in a key position to facilitate learning and increase your organization's capacity through this evaluation, and you should view your role and the evaluation from this lens.

So, come to the first kick-off meeting prepared, organized, and open to the talent of the evaluation team. Convey why you are excited about this evaluation and how important it is for your organization. Lay out rules, boundaries, and requirements, and stay open to how the evaluation team will fulfill them. Share examples of evaluation reports you appreciated and preferred structures of outputs with the evaluation team—be direct if you already know what you want. If you are not sure of the boundaries, ask your supervisor and colleagues. Ask what you can do to support the team and get yourself organized to be actively involved without micromanaging them.

Internal Evaluator (ECM and EIM)

As the internal evaluation manager, you may feel in control of the evaluation scope and plan, but in terms of stakeholder engagement, you may experience indifference to your work in evaluation or you might be subjected to lobbying by colleagues about a particular evaluation that may involve their work. Depending on the position of evaluation in the organizational chart (close or distant to leadership), the extent to which decisions are influenced by evaluation, and the degree to which evaluation is respected in an organization, the internal evaluator may be either invisible or highly visible at different times. Internal evaluators may have additional issues to consider, such as maintaining long-term relationships with colleagues as they work within the same organizational structure.

Thus, if the internal evaluator has any type of kick-off meeting, it might be internal to the evaluation office to plan the evaluation or with colleagues from departments participating in the evaluation to stimulate their interest in the evaluation and seek their collaboration. For the internal evaluator, any one evaluation is not a one-off activity but part of a larger collaboration. If possible, the internal evaluation would benefit from developing a vision of evaluation success and employ strategies to increase engagement and visibility of a particular evaluation while continuing to clarify a role for the evaluation function as a whole and build evaluation capacity in the organization.

4.4.3 Stakeholder Kick-Off Process (Either Group Meeting or Interviews)

The first stakeholder kick-off meeting creates first impressions and shapes the opinions of stakeholders for this evaluation and the evaluation team. This meeting is the responsibility both of the ECM and EIM, and it is one that should be carefully planned.

For stakeholder kick-off participants, this may be a routine meeting or even one they expect to be boring and unrelated to their work. Some participants may be skeptical about the ability of the evaluation team to understand and do justice to the complexity of their programs or services. Others may enter the meeting anxious about what this evaluation will surface and whether their work (and maybe their careers and livelihood) may be adversely affected by the evaluation. How ECMs and EIMs engage with the evaluation's stakeholders in the beginning is critical for building a healthy and appropriate collaboration that will influence the success of the evaluation. Usually, this meeting is designed and facilitated by the EIM with participation by the ECM.

In this meeting, participants should find themselves talking about the program or services being evaluated in a more systematic way that helps them have deeper, more authentic conversations. We recommend using an appreciative lens (i.e., starting with the assumption that some things work and that this group is proud of some of the things they achieved). Table 4.2 presents an illustrative sequence of questions to use in a multi-stakeholder evaluation start-up meeting.

You can organize the agenda and activities for this meeting based on your own comfort level. You can find good ideas in the appreciative evaluation book (Preskill & Catsambas, 2006) and in Michael Patton's book on facilitation (Patton, 2017).

4.4.4 Submission and Approval of the Evaluation Plan

The final step in the start-up phase is the submission of a final evaluation plan that documents sequential evaluation activities to answer the evaluation questions, your sample selection methodology, key methods and design, a matrix of evaluation questions and sub-questions or annotations, indicators, data sources and methods, and finally, an outline of the evaluation report.

EIMs should document agreements and track updates throughout the evaluation, and the end of start-up is a great place to start. This type of documentation tracks decisions and justifications not only for the client but also for orienting new members of the evaluation team and for creating transparency in the path agreed upon and why. Such

TABLE 4.2 ■ Possible Questions for the First Stakeholder Meeting of the Evaluation

Questions	Why Ask?
What achievements are you most proud of in this program?	This is an easier place to start than discussing shortcomings, and you will learn a lot about how the program is relevant to key stakeholders, even if it is in a few instances. You will learn some history and about how people spend their time, make decisions, interact, and think—all in the context of discussing achievements.
What do you value about your own part of this program?	This question is different from achievements. People may value the goals of the program even if they have not been achieved, or they may value a side benefit that is less visible in the core description of the program. The discussion on values will also inform the criteria for the evaluation.
What does excellence look like for you in the program—if things were going great, what would that look like?	This asks participants to describe the standards they would use to judge how they are doing and can be translated into a rubric for how the evaluation report might present progress toward excellence. It is also useful in hinting at what is a desirable direction for the program, so that the evaluation can prioritize learning about those things that are most relevant for the client.
What are your three wishes for making this program or service the best it can be?	This question speaks to priorities and possible gaps and problems to be explored.
Who is missing? Who has important information for the evaluation? Who has to live with the evaluation results?	These questions inform who should be involved in the evaluation and asks those at the table to pause and consider whose perspective is important who might be excluded.
Given all that we have talked about, what are the most important questions this evaluation should answer?	Although the contract typically has the overall evaluation questions, this is an opportunity to verify that those questions are still relevant and to add sub-questions that inform the larger questions.

documentation is, in fact, in the interest of the ECM as well. In one of Tessie's early evaluations, the ECM did not secure the required contract approval for a modification in the timeline that she approved. The EIM, however, wrote a memo to the ECM for files documenting this agreement. When Tessie's company sent in the final invoice, the contracts officer refused to pay it because the timeline had not been followed. The EIM's memo saved the day and resulted in receiving full payment for the work.

PRACTICE

You are the EIM of a new evaluation. You reach out to your ECM, who tells you that he does not like many meetings because he believes in efficiency. What are the top three reasons to insist on start-up meetings? Make a convincing case about why a more collaborative start-up process is critical. (Hint: Reread this chapter for specific ideas.)

5 MANAGING THE EVALUATION TEAM

WHO SHOULD USE THIS CHAPTER

This chapter focuses on an evaluation implementing manager (EIM) who is working with an evaluation team (external or internal). Evaluation commissioning managers (ECMs) may have a role in team selection, determining changes and influencing the functioning of an evaluation even if they are not the formal team manager; they may also manage an evaluation steering committee or group of evaluation stakeholders.

Managing teams is a major field in itself and not one typically included in evaluation curricula. Yet, when an evaluation is implemented by two or more people, someone must make role assignments, provide direction, and ensure productive collaboration among evaluation implementers. In fact, although managing teams might seem to be a secondary skill area for evaluation managers in general, in some evaluations, it might determine the success of an evaluation. Although EIMs are typically more involved in team management, ECMs have some responsibilities in managing the teams or groups from their side as they oversee and provide guidance to the evaluation process, especially when commissioners hire several consultants rather than a consulting firm to implement the evaluation.

Configuring and managing evaluation teams is one of the most important skills for an EIM. The conflicts and stress experienced by evaluation stakeholders tend to map into and get played out in the evaluation team. An EIM who is unskilled in team management will continue to be surprised by the conflict and arguments within the evaluation team and the level of emotion or disengagement that might result. In addition, personal working styles and competence levels of each team member will further complicate the task.

This chapter explores the different configurations of evaluation teams, team composition, assignments, issues that may arise in team management, and strategies for managing evaluation teams effectively toward the completion of a high-quality, useful evaluation—an evaluation that matters.

5.1 GOALS OF TEAM MANAGEMENT IN EVALUATION

Let us step back and consider the job of team management within evaluation management. Frequently, evaluation managers are trained in evaluation—maybe even in project management—but not in team management. Managing evaluation teams is critical to the success of evaluation. The evaluation manager's goal is to enable team members to be productive individually and collectively, completing the evaluation to a high standard in a timely fashion. The tasks involved in team management include the following:

- Select qualified individuals to perform evaluation tasks (a responsibility that may rest with a commissioner, internal or external evaluator, or firm) and endeavor to identify and leverage the strengths of each evaluation team member so that collectively the qualifications are available.
- Clarify the role of each team member in the evaluation, provide guidance and feedback to each team member on the expectations and quality of the evaluation tasks they are responsible for, and monitor their performance on tasks.
- Orient the team on the purpose, parameters, and plans for managing the evaluation; establish ground rules for the team and collective responsibility for smooth implementation of the evaluation.
- Communicate with the team with updates and relevant information on the evaluation.
- Ensure good teamwork among members by addressing any issues among team members that get in the way of completing a good quality evaluation.

5.2 CONFIGURATIONS OF EVALUATION TEAMS

As discussed in Chapter 2, there is a wide variation in evaluation team configuration related to the competencies required for an evaluation. Both ECMs and EIMs may have teams they represent. For example, even when commissioners are not in charge of the evaluation team, they may be appointed to represent a group of commissioner staff who have an interest in being involved in the evaluation and may even join some of the evaluation activities. This is frequently the case when a commissioner has a strong evaluation office, which may make it difficult for the ECM to stay in their lane of management. These individuals may have strong points of view on points of methodology, process, analysis, and so on. In that case, these two must clarify their team roles in evaluation management and work closely together.

There are several important dimensions to consider in looking at evaluation team management.

- <u>Familiarity of team members.</u> One question is whether and for how long team members have worked with each other. In some cases (e.g., in evaluation consulting firms), evaluation teams have worked together on different evaluations and have already developed a rhythm of collaboration and a level of trust; in other cases, teams may be formed ad hoc by people who have never worked together before and may not work together again after the completion of the evaluation. Why does this matter? Whether long-term colleagues or strangers, evaluation team members must come together quickly, form a team, and establish sufficient trust and efficient ways to collaborate for the successful completion of the evaluation. The EIM will have to manage the team differently depending on the starting point of the team's configuration.

- Authority of the EIM. The EIM may have different levels of authority in directing the evaluation team. For internal evaluations, the team leader may be a senior internal evaluator supervising an internal team or a staff member managing colleagues at the same level as the team leader; sometimes, an internal evaluation team might include representatives of the programs being evaluated, over whom the team leader has little authority. In the case of a consulting firm, the team leader may be supervising a team of staff who are direct reports or peers; team members may also include external consultants who are experienced at working with this firm or totally new to the firm. A consulting firm may have hired an external consultant to lead the team. Some evaluation commissioners opt to hire consultants for the different roles they have identified in the terms of reference of an evaluation, thus everyone on the team is a newly contracted consultant including the team leader, who may have a harder task in forming and leading a team over which they have little authority.
- Team member competencies. Team members might identify as evaluation experts, subject matter experts, or context/program/evaluand experts. Each of these team members bring different assets to the team: Evaluation experts will drive for the implementation of a professionally informed evaluation process; subject matter experts offer benchmarking expertise of what other programs like this one need to succeed and how to understand different aspects of a program in line with their field of expertise; program/evaluand experts provide important information on the context, including strategies for access and inclusion, increased culture competence of the whole team, and political as well as historical information. These different perspectives can both enrich and create conflict within the team; a skilled team leader will turn this diversity into valuable information for the evaluation, while a less skilled one will be unable to contain the conflict that may arise.
- Commissioners as team members. In some cases, evaluation team roles create delicate situations; for example, when evaluation commissioners designate one or more of their own staff to participate in the evaluation team. In the case of corporate (global) evaluations that are managed by independent evaluation offices of United Nations organizations, the ECM may also act as a team member for some activities, participating in site visits and accompanying some of the data collection. In those cases, as an outside consultant, the EIM is supervising a team member who is both a client and team member (i.e., the EIM must oversee the activities of their "supervisor" and then turn around and report to that person in their role as client). In government-commissioned evaluations, sometimes the ECM designates a senior staff member from the commissioning office or a stakeholder office to be part of the evaluation team (e.g., to conduct site visits); during the site visit, the commissioner staff member may sometimes slip into an auditing role, checking on how programs are performing. It is certainly understandable why United Nations independent evaluation offices or government agencies might wish to do this: organizational

learning, quality control of evaluations, facilitating access, interpreting organizational culture to strengthen the design of the evaluation, and so forth. Nonetheless, this configuration is difficult for the EIM, as Tessie can attest to from her experience in several cases.

- Community members as team members. In many cases, it will be critical to the success of the evaluation and in line with values of equity and respect for diversity to include those affected by the program directly in the evaluation team for their perspectives, knowledge, and insights. In these cases, the EIM may have to manage a team that includes a stakeholder representative and/or an evaluand/team member. In the case of the standards of the Aotearoa New Zealand Evaluation Association (ANZEA), the team leader of an evaluation in Maori communities must be of the Maori ethnicity, and relationships and agreements established at the outset are an integral part of the evaluation and govern how the evaluation will be shaped, the access that the evaluation team will have, how findings will be vetted, and so forth. In fact, this type of embedded respect for culture, ethnicity, and sovereignty for Indigenous people has emerged as best practice worldwide. This expanded notion of who is part of the evaluation team has important implications for the way the EIM leader will manage the evaluation.

Such complex compositions of evaluation teams can offer an opportunity to gain valuable insights, open doors for the evaluation, and make evaluations more relevant and useful to the issues decision makers are facing. At the same time, the inherent conflict of interest of team members because of their multiple roles also creates a special challenge for the EIM who oversees the evaluation team and who must manage a client/team member or an evaluand/team member who represents an important agenda within the evaluation team. Identity diversity and power inequities may make it difficult for all evaluation team members to share issues they perceive as contrary to the perspective of those with strong agendas and more power. In such cases, the EIM must recognize and manage perceived conflicts of interest and create safe spaces for discussing issues, all the while addressing power inequities that may undermine the EIM's authority. A skilled evaluation manager can turn these potentially challenging relationships into assets, although we must recognize the difficulty they pose. Therefore, awareness and professional competence in managing the identities and power inequities of evaluation team members can make a critical difference in the success of an evaluation.

5.2.1 Issues That Arise from Evaluation Team Composition

Evaluation team composition may raise major challenges for the EIM because it complicates some of the requirements for a good and even ethical evaluation. An EIM might be tempted to ignore these challenges and hope they will not get noticed, but we assure our readers that it is preferable to address these issues promptly and directly with the ECM, within the team, and in the structure of the evaluation process.

- Confidentiality. When an evaluation team member is part of the evaluand, how can you ensure confidentiality and read a confidentiality statement with confidence and integrity during data collection? What if a team member represents the very group from which the information must be kept confidential?

- Impartiality. How can you enact impartiality when some members of the evaluation team are perceived as already having agendas?
- Who is in charge? When an evaluation commissioning organization's staff member acts as a team member and that team member disagrees with the EIM's decisions, this can undermine the EIM's authority both in the eyes of the team and in the eyes of the ECM. Tessie had an experience where the client/team member advocated for changing the evaluation's data collection methods during the first site visit because he did not have expertise in those methods and did not see how the methods would produce useful findings. Tessie had to divide her attention between holding her ground with the client/team member while continuing to guide the team and keep the evaluation on course.
- Difference of opinion. When an client/team member expresses strong views about what can be included or not included in an evaluation, team members might become intimidated into agreeing. Any expression of a strong view from this more powerful team member can compromise the independence of the evaluation team. When an evaluand/team member expresses strong views, they can push the whole evaluand community to their side, thus intimidating the evaluation team into silence about any offending finding.

5.2.2 Selecting the Evaluation Team

In many cases, evaluation managers do not select their evaluation teams; however, in some larger, multiyear evaluations, they must select or replace team members. In selecting evaluation team members, the primary goal is to select people with the required skills and experience in evaluation, the context, and the relevant subject matter expertise. In terms of evaluation methodology and logistics management, we might further specify the need for qualitative and quantitative analysis, field visit management, survey design and analysis, and so on. It is also helpful to look at the team as a whole and seek a mix of higher-cost (generally more experienced or with specialized expertise) and lower-cost people to use evaluation budget resources more effectively. Finally, it is important to line up the staff needed for the right time in the evaluation process (e.g., editors for the report writing phase, etc.).

5.3 MANAGING TEAM PERFORMANCE

Given the timeline and pressure on team members to perform different evaluation tasks, the EIM needs to work with each member to understand that member's strengths, communicate the role of that team member, and clarify the expectations for different tasks assigned to that person. In general, this is a time when the evaluation manager should communicate expectations clearly and be direct. If you as an EIM, for example, expect to use certain types of tracking forms or you have certain formats for how to present findings, this is a great time to put all that on the table. Giving people examples from other evaluations that demonstrate what you consider excellence is helpful not only for teaching less experienced people but also for managing expectations and ensuring quality for all team members, regardless of experience.

In cases where a team member's tasks are under their control, it may be more efficient to work one-on-one with that person and reserve team sessions for when teamwork is required to get the evaluation done. For example, designing and administering a survey and then writing a report with survey findings might be a solo task for someone, involving collaboration only in the design phase. Input from the team might be most helpful in reviewing or testing the survey, but really, that person can get this task done only under the guidance of the EIM.

In cases where people must collaborate, the EIM will work with them to help get them organized and make sure their tasks are clear. For example, an evaluation might require five simultaneous or overlapping site visits in which core evaluation data collectors visit sites and pair up with local data collectors. Such an activity will require standardized data collection tools and orientation or training on the use of those tools. Such evaluations require management skills for sub-activities—you may need a site visit manager under the EIM's direction.

Finally, the EIM will also monitor performance, provide feedback, and intervene and provide direct assistance, if needed. The EIM needs to be sufficiently knowledgeable and comfortable with the intermediate evaluation products so that if they need to be shared with the ECM or other stakeholders, the EIM can comfortably explain and defend them. In other words, you can delegate the work but will remain accountable for the outcome.

5.3.1 Orientation and Team Planning

As part of evaluation start-up, the EIM will convene and orient the evaluation team. Team planning is a key component of a good start-up when a team is involved. When resources allow, an in-person team planning meeting can be most helpful, although even when resources are scarce, a form of planning interaction is needed—for example, by email, telephone, or videoconference.

The agenda for a planning meeting might include the following:

- introducing team members
- briefing on the evaluation's scope (sharing the scope of work) and any updates
- developing a common vision of success for the evaluation and building a commitment to work together toward that vision
- reviewing everyone's roles
- presenting and discussing the workplan and key dates
- establishing rules and expectations for communication and meetings

The experiential goals of the meeting are to ensure that everyone on the team feels valued and sees how they can contribute as well as to develop and commit to a shared vision and to the team's success. If resources are available, and for larger evaluations, it is helpful to facilitate this meeting. In some cases, the whole team receives an orientation from the ECM, and in those cases, it is important that team members be on the same page prior to being in front of the ECM.

5.3.2 Communication

Clear and regular communication is paramount in all projects, especially in the fast-moving and frequently politically sensitive job of conducting an evaluation. Work plans must be revised regularly, and when a team is involved, this means renegotiating tasks and deadlines with several people. For example, one of the most unglamorous but critical tasks in team management and evaluation management more broadly is scheduling. Claiming space in the evaluation team's calendar to prioritize the evaluation tasks is critical, and yet the workplan may have to remain fluid and flexible.

EIMs also must decide on how much to share in writing and how much to meet and discuss. Meetings cost money, so they are best reserved for occasions where facilitated thinking and consensus building might be important. Regular emails such as a weekly email summarizing any updates and changes might be more cost effective and will create a track record that team members can refer back to. The EIM will still need to be in touch by phone or in person with individual team members to check in, provide feedback, and encourage good performance in their evaluation tasks.

In addition to the efficiency and completeness of communication, it is also important to pay attention to communication tone. This may seem obvious, but the EIM's behavior influences team communication. So, the EIM should be mindful and deliberate in the content and style of communication with the team. A polite and respectful tone is a must, as is adopting a calm tone even when there are stressful developments, including inclusive language in praising the team, and always being clear on what is being communicated.

Sometimes keeping a professional and polite tone can be difficult, and it is then that the EIM must have fallback strategies. The hardest case to manage was in an evaluation of a complex international health project where Tessie was EIM leading an evaluation team of four and getting ready to organize site visits to different countries. The newly appointed ECM viewed himself as the team leader and wanted senior members of the evaluand to lead these site visits; he said to Tessie, "Surely you agree that only health experts from our programs are qualified to lead each of these site visits to countries. How could evaluators ever hope to understand the complexity of these programs?" After a difficult and protracted negotiation, it was agreed that three health program experts from the evaluand would join a site visit to a different country from their own as team members. This turned out to be a great decision, as program implementers learned alongside the evaluation team, asked excellent questions, and strengthened the evaluation's ability to present data comparatively with attention to the importance of context in adapting health program strategies in different countries. The biggest lesson from this challenging experience was this: When you feel upset or irate at what a colleague with authority says, push yourself to a place of curiosity and ask them, "Tell me more about that." If you lead with your strong opinions and feelings, it will be hard to recover, and you will miss a chance to learn as well as manage the disagreement to a positive outcome. By hearing more from this ECM, Tessie heard his anxiety about managing this major investment in evaluation and his fear that the evaluation might misinterpret findings or miss important things. Once he felt heard, he as ECM and Tessie as EIM worked out a creative solution toward a common vision of success for the evaluation and increased the resources devoted to the evaluation as well as its visibility.

5.3.3 Assignments and Time Management

By the time the evaluation team is ready to get started on the evaluation tasks, there is probably already a budget allocation (level of effort) for evaluation staff and consultants, which may include the different anticipated roles and the time commitment expected for each role. If that is not available, the EIM must determine it and provide guidance to team members. Sometimes, the EIM may not have control over the selection of other team members—for example, some agencies hire independent consultants for different roles, including the EIM. The important thing is that no matter how the evaluation team is appointed, the EIM has a responsibility to organize and guide this team to implement the evaluation.

The approach and investment in good team management will differ depending on the size and duration of an evaluation and whether the evaluation team is temporarily convened to implement the evaluation or is a team that keeps working together to implement different evaluations (e.g., in evaluation units of a federal government agency or evaluation consulting firms). Yet, even when the team consists of only two people who will work together in a single evaluation, all rules of good team management apply. In fact, when managed well, an evaluation team can help increase the quality of the evaluation and be a fulfilling experience for all.

5.3.4 Issues That Arise Within the Evaluation Team

The following issues are ones EIMs should watch out for and try to address quickly so as to mitigate their impact on the team:

- Not vetting issues adequately. With their tight timelines and the defenses they stimulate, evaluations can sometimes be pressure cookers for the team. When team facilitation is not practiced, team members' perspectives might become marginalized or ignored. The EIM may get in a tug of war with that team member, and in the end, the EIM may say, "Just give me what you have, and I will write that section." Some marginalized team members might draft their own dissenting interpretation that is submitted along with the draft report or might become part of the draft report. As you can imagine, this may be confusing for the ECM who paid for a synthesis that takes all the findings and interpretations into account. In such cases, the evaluation will fail to benefit from all expertise in the team that might have helped the team reach a deeper understanding of all the issues. Or this conflict might be the result of a failure of the EIM to draw tighter boundaries around the scope of the evaluation.
- Not staying within the scope. In one of Tessie's evaluations of a health program, the health subject matter expert had special knowledge of the conditions of health worker unionization. Although the evaluation was to assess the effectiveness of a child survival program, this team member submitted a 30-page analysis and advocacy paper for unionization of the workforce while the work of writing the evaluation report fell to Tessie and the second team member.
- Mirroring a conflict experienced by the evaluand. In evaluations of programs surrounded with controversy, evaluation teams are likely to play out the evaluand conflict within the team. Rather than giving in to the strong feelings this may evoke, a good EIM will notice this conflict and turn it into an opportunity to empathize with and understand more deeply the different sides of the controversy. Rather than being feared, strong feelings should alert

the evaluation team that there is something valuable to explore in the topic of contention.

5.3.5 Teamwork

Managing teams is invisible when done well. Being inattentive to team management tasks is painfully visible to all and threatens the evaluation. Being good at managing teams requires attention throughout the life of the team. And even when teams have worked together in the past, it is important to recommit in the beginning of a new evaluation project.

In Bruce Tuckman's model of the lifecycle of a team (Tuckman, 1965; further operationalized in Egolf, 2011), teams go through four phases:

- forming—where team members are getting to know each other and are eager to figure out their place in the team and to be included
- storming—where team members experience conflict, question the rules of the team leader, and attempt to impose their own preferred way of working
- norming—where team members negotiate and agree to the way this particular team will work
- performing—where the team settles into productivity and gets its work done

Tuckman later added *adjourning* as a fifth stage; this fifth stage is certainly relevant in evaluation, which by its nature is a short-term (or at least a finite) endeavor. In this phase, the team leader needs to thank the team, approve final payments, and clarify any parting agreements about confidentiality, sharing the evaluation report, and so forth.

The EIM must facilitate team development through the different stages of a team's life and ensure a high-performing evaluation. Figure 5.1 summarizes the role and strategies of the evaluation manager at each stage of the team's life.

Many times, the EIM will not need to invest so deeply in team development and management, but when challenges come up, the EIM will have to intervene, troubleshoot, and resolve issues. It is best to facilitate the evaluation team actively to avoid having to address problems later that may take a lot more time to solve.

FIGURE 5.1 ■ Evaluation Manager's Strategies at Each Phase in the Lifecycle of an Evaluation Team

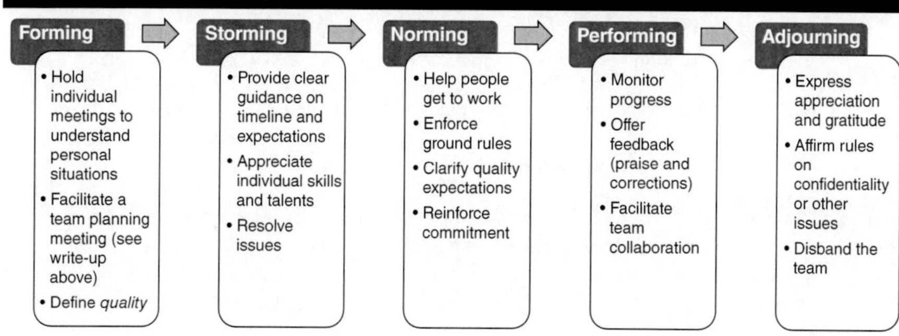

By reframing the model in Lencioni's (2002) book, *The Five Dysfunctions of a Team*, the EIM can promote good teamwork by focusing on and developing the following shared values and competencies within the team:

- Trust. Do we trust each other's competence and good intentions?
- Results. Are we focused on conducting a good evaluation as a whole?
- Commitment. Are we committed to the work and do we prioritize the evaluation in our professional lives?
- Quality. Do team members have high expectations for the quality of their own work?
- Managing conflict. Do team members have honest communication, including when they disagree? Can they handle that disagreement professionally while maintaining respect for each other?

These values and competencies need to be built under the leadership of the EIM among people who are coming together to work intensely on an evaluation. So, what might go wrong?

As we know, team dynamics are complex; team members bring their own personality and style as well as their habits and preferences.

Table 5.1 offers examples of challenges in evaluation teams that have confronted real-life EIMs and some suggested strategies to address these issues.

TABLE 5.1 ■ Challenges in Evaluation Teams and What Evaluators Can Do About Them

Characteristics of Excellent Teams	Examples of challenges include times when a team member . . .	The evaluation manager may . . .
Trust	does not feel valued by the team and wishes to write a separate evaluation report.	facilitate a team meeting to explore the possibilities of integrating the team member's perspective.
Results	takes weak notes related to a section that another team member is responsible for.	explore whether there is underlying hostility due to relational conflict. engage in team development to increase commitment to the whole evaluation.
Quality	is sloppy, does not submit products on time, shows up late for meetings, and submits poor writing.	provide direct and clear feedback for improvement. replace the team member and/or redistribute the work.
Commitment	prioritizes other commitments and has insufficient time to devote to the evaluation.	work with the team member; if more time cannot become available, replace the person.
Managing Conflict	lets the client know that they are upset with how this evaluation is implemented.	replace the individual, if possible. talk with the individual to understand the cause of their anger and address it, if possible.

The EIM needs to listen attentively to identify issues early and prevent them from blossoming into problems. Many times, personnel and team problems may manifest themselves as technical disagreements, but further probing may unearth issues of loss of face, feeling silenced or devalued, fear of failure, and other problems. Good facilitation processes can help teams work through issues, and sincere listening and relationship building on the part of the EIM are foundational to effective team management and strong team performance in evaluation.

5.4 MANAGING MULTIPLE EVALUATION TEAMS AT THE SAME TIME

Commissioners, internal evaluators, and evaluation consulting firms frequently have to manage several evaluations (and possibly evaluation teams) at the same time. The required skills and strategies are more broadly relevant to managing complex work and staff, but here are some tips specifically addressing evaluations:

- Plan to space the evaluations for adequate time and plan for contingencies.
- Use project planning software such as Trello or Asana to gain transparency on staff assignments by evaluation and by staff member overtime.
- Do not overburden program staff with evaluations that require their time for hosting site visits and providing data, participating in workshops and focus groups, and so on. (Do not underestimate the investment.)
- Be respectful to sites (in Zambia, one high-performing school had 20 site visits in one quarter). Consider not only your evaluation but evaluations from other funders (where relevant).
- Plan for adequate staff time to support, guide, and use evaluations.
- Prioritize, and do not be afraid to drop plans for an evaluation that will compromise the commissioner's ability to do a good job on its evaluation portfolio.
- Many commissioning organizations have limits on how many surveys staff receive per month, so find out the parameters and constraints for each evaluation and plan realistically.
- Ask if you need the information and what you will do with it.

CASE PRACTICE

Desmond, a senior partner in a Canadian evaluation firm, supervises Katrina, who is assigned as the EIM of an education program in a Latin American country. Katrina is working with a team of three—a junior colleague from the same firm; a regional consultant from Mexico; and Camilla, a consultant from the country where the evaluation is taking place.

Just after data analysis and before report writing, Katrina voices a worry to Desmond in their biweekly meeting: Camilla, the country consultant who brings special expertise in education workforce issues, is insisting on including an analysis of teacher's rights and unions as part of the evaluation. Katrina is concerned that this is outside the scope of the evaluation. Camilla is passionate about worker rights, however, and she refuses to pass up an opportunity to include it in the report. Katrina asks Desmond for advice on how to manage this team member who has many good contributions but will not budge on this topic.

If you were Desmond, what advice would you give Katrina? In giving this advice, consider the following:

- What might be Camilla's motivation?
- What diagnostic conversations are needed?
- To what extent should Katrina be firm, and what compromises should she consider?
- Is there a role for the evaluation funder in this issue (why or why not)?
- What are the options for how to handle Camilla's persistence?

6 MANAGING DATA COLLECTION

WHO SHOULD USE THIS CHAPTER

This chapter focuses on an evaluation implementing manager's (EIM's) role in facilitating access to data sources, monitoring the evaluation process, and intervening (when needed) to get things back on track. While much of this responsibility falls on the EIM, evaluation commissioning managers (ECMs) usually have a role in all these areas and certainly need to support the EIM. Internal evaluators will play a role as EIMs.

During evaluation start-up (see Chapter 4), the data collection and analysis plan has typically been finalized, which includes the drafts of all data collection instruments.

Depending on where they sit, different EIMs come to this point through different trajectories. External EIMs may have engaged in consultations to finalize the evaluation questions and data collection plan. EIMs of regularly performed, nationwide evaluations may be relying on an annual survey that they must launch within two weeks of contract award without consultation and without any modifications to the survey instrument. Internal EIMs may have engaged in few consultations because they are implementing agreed-upon evaluations following a standardized plan. ECMs may have approved a final evaluation design and are now stepping back from active engagement with the evaluation. Regardless of the position of the evaluation manager, the EIMs and ECMs need to communicate regularly and be ready to collaborate in resolving complex issues that may arise.

As seen in Figure 1.3, during the data collection phase, the ECM's role is to facilitate access to data sources, monitor the evaluation process, encourage the evaluation implementors (if separate from the manager), and intervene as needed to get things back on track. In Chapter 6, we will not review all that has to be done during data collection but will focus primarily on the specific responsibilities of the EIM—areas where they will have to actively monitor data collection, the types of issues that arise and how they may approach a resolution.

6.1 PRIOR TO INITIATING DATA COLLECTION

Let us begin with what is needed prior to initiating data collection. Data collection should not begin until data collection instruments are finalized, and it is the EIM's job to stay on top of the process and to make sure the piloting of instruments is completed swiftly. Having a clear plan and piloted data collection instruments will result in higher-quality data collection—more accurate data that we feel confident in interpreting. In the urgency to get data collection under way, it may be tempting to short shrift the piloting of data collection instruments, but this would be a mistake and would compromise the methods used and the evaluation as a whole because piloting allows us to identify a number of potential risks (e.g., questions that are not understandable to respondents, question flow that is confusing or inefficient, language that may give offense, long interview guides that take too long to administer, or questions that do not generate useful data).

A key management tool is the field guide or data collection/data management guide this guide explains expectations for communication with local authorities and respondents, data collection itself, file-naming conventions, review of data recording and storage, and quality control/supervision. This should be developed and shared before anyone starts data collection. Figure 6.1 suggests the timing of periodic monitoring using the field guide.

Preceding the launch of data collection, the ECM should provide an appropriate introduction of the evaluation and the team leader to respondents and local authorities.

Finally, throughout data collection, EIMs must keep their eyes on risk mitigation and management and on maintaining ethical standards during data collection. Risk management starts with a review of potential risks and possible plans to mitigate them and continues with risk monitoring to see what other risks are emerging so they can be addressed quickly. Maintaining ethical standards in data collection starts with an assessment of potential risks to respondents of participation on a physical, mental, and social dimension; determining the best ways to maintain respect, privacy, and confidentiality; and preparations for how to deal with adverse events during data collection (e.g., discovering abuse, trauma from topics of study, health events). In one case, the EIM received feedback that one of the data collection consultants violated confidentiality and referred to what he learned in a previous interview. The EIM immediately called this consultant and provided corrective guidance and then assigned this consultant only to paired interviews (where another data collector would be present).

6.2 EARLY IN DATA COLLECTION

For the EIM, the first weeks of data collection is an important time for a "pause point," where a check-in early in data collection can prevent small problems from becoming big ones. It is a great time to mid-course correct. Many issues may reveal themselves in a series of "firsts."

- Data collectors begin using an interview guide with a broad range of stakeholders.
- A survey is distributed and respondents try completing it for the first time.
- Analysts review the online data portal and see what data is there.
- Evaluators visit sites and begin understanding issues on the ground in comparison with assumptions made in the data collection guide or how several sites might be different from sites where pilot testing took place.
- The monitoring system is reviewed in depth and the quality of data is revealed.

FIGURE 6.1 ■ Monitoring Plan Overview

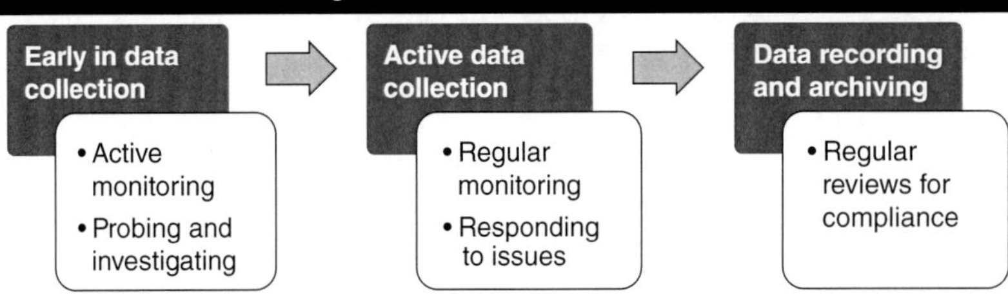

These first experiences may go smoothly, but there may also be many surprises that will require active engagement by the EIM and possibly the ECM. For example, sites may be sufficiently different from the pilot sites (e.g., following a different organizational structure, making the categorization of roles inapplicable). Respondents may drop off after completing three-fourths of the survey. The online portal may have significant gaps in the data included. The people being interviewed may have no exposure to key elements of the program about which they are being asked. These and other such surprises are not infrequent, and in these early days, the EIM needs to probe persistently to surface and learn what is really happening. Even in cases when an evaluation is conducted by internal evaluators who already know the context or when evaluation is based on a standardized annual survey, there may still be an unforeseen or unexpected change in the context that needs attention. Given the strict timelines of evaluation, and to avoid wasting efforts in data collection and compromising the evaluation, these types of issues require prompt and decisive action by the EIM.

Early in data collection is a time to ensure that data collection is off to a good start and to address any challenges that may compromise it. Quality control from Day 1 ensures you can identify where data collectors or supervisors may not have fully understood the process or expectations and address these with corrections before they have a larger impact on data quality. Figure 6.2 provides some guidelines for when to do this early quality control, depending on the data collection method(s) you are using.

In early data collection, EIMs need to check on every data collection sub-activity including, checking with

- data collectors to see how the interview guide is working and how the evaluand is responding to data collectors,
- survey managers on the response and completion rates of the survey, and
- analysts on the availability and quality of the data available through the monitoring system.

Here are some questions the EIM might check on in these monitoring calls:

- Are site visits taking place according to plan? Are there any surprises? What kinds of issues are we running into? How can these be mitigated?
- Do team members have access to the promised/expected data? If not, what solutions can we try?
- What is the response rate on the survey? Is this what we expected? What can we do to improve it?

FIGURE 6.2 ■ Timing for Checking on Data Collection by Data Collection Method

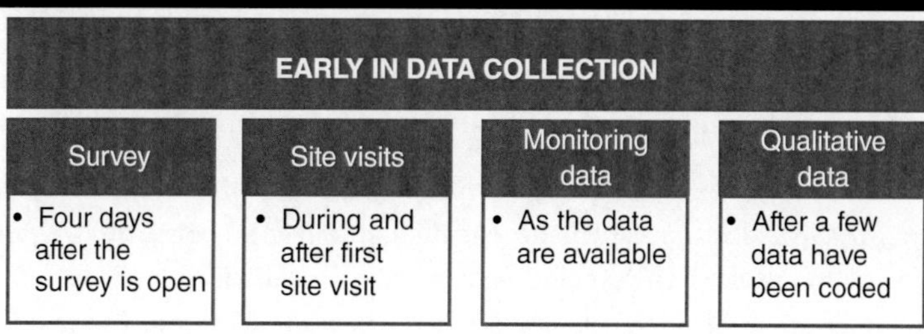

- How well are team members documenting their site visits and interviews? What do supervisors need to be doing differently?
- Are team members following ethical protocols (e.g., ensuring confidentiality and privacy, following protocols for protecting personal identification information, and treating respondents with respect)? If not, what solutions can we try?
- How well are reviewed documents summarized? What feedback does the team need?
- How well is data being coded (when that begins)? What changes can we implement?
- What are team members' early impressions?

In addition, the EIM should check with some evaluation participants in different sites to seek early feedback on their experience with the evaluation team.

6.3 ACTIVE DATA COLLECTION

During active data collection, the EIM engages in regular monitoring driven by the evaluation plan (as adjusted repeatedly during implementation), keeps lines of communication open with the evaluation team and stakeholders, ensures and conducts quality control, and troubleshoots issues as they arise. Many issues can arise during data collection: unforeseen events that lead to delays or scope creep, changes in expectations around the goals of the evaluation, turnover, adverse reactions to the evaluation process or early findings, and new insights from early findings that may require mid-course correction in the evaluation plan.

EIMs need to address issues systematically using the following strategies (this is not a series of sequential steps; these actions may overlap):

- <u>Prevention</u>: Keep considering the implications of every change, anticipate issues, alert colleagues, agree on responses, look out for early evidence, and act quickly.
- <u>Rapid assessment</u>: When an issue arises, review evidence, consult relevant parties, and assess the type of issue, its severity, and the possible paths to resolution.
- <u>Analysis</u>: When an issue is complex, it may require further analysis beyond the rapid assessment (e.g., a reexamination of data, more extensive consultations with relevant stakeholders, financial analysis, etc.).
- <u>Reflection</u>: Create time and space to assess the ethics, political charge, methodological soundness, interpersonal issues, and practical feasibility of any situation. This is a great opportunity for EIMs and ECMs to collaborate.
- <u>Communication</u>: Decide on the most constructive way to frame an issue and keep everyone informed appropriately until the issue is resolved.
- <u>Negotiation</u>: Enter discussions with interested parties with some clarity on the perspectives and needs of those parties, listen attentively, present issues clearly and without blame (as much as possible), present options (if possible), and leave room to step back and reconsider.
- <u>Action</u>: Once decisions are made, ensure required approvals and then put solutions in place swiftly, including contract modifications, memos to document mutual agreements, separations, new site selection, and so on.

Data collection issues can be difficult both to identify and to address. In preventing and resolving issues, EIMs must manage a polarity: On the one hand, they must act decisively to resolve issues rapidly; on the other hand, they must create calm space to engage in consultation and reflection, inviting collaborative problem solving. It is important for the EIMs (and ECMs) to be prepared and ready for unexpected issues and to address issues decisively but in a calm and considerate manner. For external evaluators, a thorough understanding of the evaluation contract and any follow-up amendments and documented agreements are key. Discussing potential risks in the management plan and having clear ethical standards helps lay a foundation for finding solutions.

6.4 MANAGING AND ARCHIVING DATA

Recording and storing the data collected begins as soon as the first data come in and takes place in parallel with active data collection. This is a less visible part of data collection, but a vital one. If it is not done well, important insights and data will not be available to the evaluator(s) for data analysis and report writing. The EIM needs to have full visibility into the data recording and archival process because this process is a critical part of evaluation quality.

The complexity of the recording and archival system will depend on the size of the evaluation, but being systematic and vigilant will help smaller evaluations as well. Some evaluators (both internal and external) have well-organized and clear processes for handling data, and larger evaluations may require data collector training. In such cases, the existing data collection system is clear, and the EIM needs to make sure it is followed.

For smaller evaluations, the evaluation manager should develop a clear path for data recording and archiving, as this is the only way to implement triangulation in data analysis and to make the logic of evaluation findings and conclusions transparent. Leaving the organization of data for later is a recipe for disaster—or, at least, for lower-quality data analysis. Such a data recording and archival system should include the following:

- a clear folder architecture for computer- or cloud-based storage of data (see Figure 6.3)
- file-naming protocols, including version control and archiving past versions (to be included in the data collection guide)
- data collection tools that provide for recording collected data and tracking data collection activities (see Tables 6.1 and 6.2)

FIGURE 6.3 ■ Possible File Structure for Saving Documents from Your Evaluation

ORGANIZING YOUR FILES

Archive

Background Documents

Data Analysis

Data Collection

- Folders by method

Deliverables

Meetings—Agendas and Notes

- Internal team meetings
- Client meetings

Proposal

Travel

Work Plan

TABLE 6.1 ■ Tracker for Scheduling and Completing Qualitative Data Collection

		Name of Organization (if Person/People Are Associated with an Organization)	Contact Information			Interview Details			0 of 0 Complete (0%)	
Name	Role/Title of Participant	Organization Name	Email	Phone	Status of Scheduling Activities	Date of Interview/ Focus Group Discussion	Location of Interview (If in Person)	Data Collector	Interview Complete? (Yes/No)	Comments
1										
2										
3										
4										
5										
6										

(Continued)

7										
8										
9										
10										
11										
12										
13										
14										
15										
16										
17										
18										
19										

TABLE 6.2 ■ Tracker for Preparing Qualitative Data for Analysis (Cleaning and Coding)

This is the ID that will link the transcript to the identifying information in this spreadsheet	Names of All Participants in the Data Collection Event	Roles of all participants in the data collection event	Name of Organization (If Person/People Are Associated with an Organization)		Type of Data Collection (Interview, Focus Group Discussion)		This Field Will Display the Name of the Month as Text. It Can Be Entered as a Number or Text, as the User Prefers	The Transcript Name Is Automatically Generated as Follows: Country ISO Code + Data Type Abbreviation + Stakeholder Group Abbreviation + Date (e.g., ZMB_INT_Gov_1-21-2017 is interview data from government stakeholder(s) in Zambia on January 21, 2017)	# of People in Data Collection Session				0 of 0 Complete (0%)	0 of 0 Complete (0%)		0 of 0 Complete (0%)	
Transcript ID	Name(s) of Participant(s)	Role(s) of Participant(s)	Organization Name	Country	Data Collection Type	Stakeholder Type	Date of Interview	Transcript Name	N-Female	N-Male	N-Total	Transcript Cleaner (Name)	Cleaned (Yes, No, N/A)	Uploaded to Coding Software? (Yes/No)	Coder (Name)	Coding Complete? (Yes/No)	Comments
1																	
2																	
3																	
4																	

(Continued)

5																	
6																	
7																	
8																	
9																	
10																	
11																	
12																	
13																	
14																	
15																	
16																	
17																	
18																	

- guidance for who is responsible for filling out data collection forms, uploading data, and monitoring compliance with the data collection plan

6.4.1 File-Naming Protocols

The issue of naming data files may seem too minor for the EIM, but if neglected, it can wreak havoc later on. For example, evaluation team members may use the wrong version of an interview transcript or be unable to find records that need to be included in an analysis, and this might not be found out until after a lot of work has relied on that incorrect or incomplete file. Essentially, if the data is not properly named, it may become inaccessible to the evaluators and will not inform the evaluation; all the effort that went into collecting it would then be wasted.

Monitoring data recording and archival files involves asking for reports by those in charge of populating the data archival system and verifying that these reports are accurate. Where possible, the EIM should conduct a physical inspection—go in the system and see that the data are actually there. Sometimes announcing such a check or asking for a tour of the data stimulates improvements in compliance with the existing data archival system. In any case, the EIM needs an accurate picture of where the data are and should conduct periodic checks to ensure that procedures are followed.

6.5 COMMUNICATION

In addition to tracking data collection efforts, the EIM must also keep many parties informed. This may include confirming changes in plans, facilitating sharing of emerging findings among members of the evaluation team, and providing direction and encouragement. It will make the EIM's job easier to anticipate required communication as much as possible and plan it on a calendar as a companion to the data collection plan. An additional good practice is to develop standardized communication formats; for example, for the weekly client update, the weekly team update, the communication for new evaluation sites, and so on. EIMs may also need to provide progress reports to higher-level managers, ECMs, and/or other stakeholders.

6.6 GOOD MONITORING PRACTICES

The biggest secret to monitoring is being clear on what you need to monitor and communicate with the team what you intend to do with the information. (See Figure 6.4.)

Here are some good practices in monitoring:

- <u>Dashboards</u>. Create a dashboard on key metrics that help you check whether progress is keeping up to pace, agreements have been obtained, and the evaluation is on track. Use your planning tools as a foundation for developing your monitoring tools to track progress and identify early signs of deviation from the plan.
- <u>Sharing</u>. Be clear on who has key input for the monitoring responsibility. Ask team members to report on progress and deviations from the plan in meetings and help people appreciate the interdependence of tasks. Seek feedback from

FIGURE 6.4 ■ Things to Monitor and Consider in Data Collection

OTHER THINGS TO MONITOR

Methods	Progress	Quality
Surveys (in person or online)	Reaching sample needed • Response rate • Refusals Need for coding of "other" responses	Completeness Coherence
Monitoring system data	Availability	Quality or missing data
Qualitative interviews	Reaching sample needed • Response rate • Refusals Transcript cleaning Coding	Completeness Coherence Coding
Document review	Documents coded Documents still needed	Completeness Coherence Coding

evaluation participants. Finally, keep the ECM up to date on high-level progress and challenges, presenting possible solutions to address issues. Engage the ECM in joint problem solving (where appropriate) and decision making when evaluation parameters might need to be renegotiated. It is never a good idea to let your ECM be surprised by a challenging issue that is brewing.

- Reflection. An evaluation moves fast, so you need to create some quiet time to think about what is going on. Designate "pause points" in your timeline. Then use them to pause and reflect. Think about what you know and try to anticipate issues that may come up in this evaluation going forward.

6.7 ADDRESSING THE UNEXPECTED

Even with all the best intentions and good planning, EIMs may find themselves in challenging situations during data collection (Bamberger et al., 2012).

6.7.1 False Data

The cornerstone of evaluation is having good data—data that we believe to be trustworthy. Discovering that the evaluation has used false data, especially when you discover it late in the process, is a terrible feeling with costly consequences. EIMs need to check often and be ready to address issues of data quality at any time during an evaluation. Here are some examples of how ECMs and EIMs have addressed the problem of false data.

An ECM shared with Tessie that they quietly stopped working with a well-known evaluation firm and began working with a different firm in an African country when they discovered that the cell phone data analyzed in their evaluation was all made up while the company's in-country data manager pocketed the fee meant to reimburse evaluation participants' time. This ECM wanted to avoid compromising the credibility of the evaluation as well as the cost and time of an official investigation, so they quietly redid the data collection and moved on with the evaluation.

In the case of a large evaluation in another country, the evaluation team was puzzled in a review of the data by an unexpectedly high number of children represented in the data. Further investigation uncovered that a data coder added nonexistent children to the data set because he was paid by the number of records entered. The team had to accommodate the additional cost of correcting this problem. Luckily, the team had done two things: (1) kept the original data collection forms and (2) checked early in data entry and caught the error (as suggested in the pause points discussion). If this had been identified later, this would have translated into a significant monetary loss for the evaluation team/firm.

In the case of a large, multicountry evaluation, Tessie's team had had trouble getting access to important data from the organization's monitoring system. (That might have been a hint of what was to come.) Immediately upon getting access to the monitoring data, Tessie's team completed the analysis needed, only to be told the next day by the ECM that the data they analyzed was made-up data used to test the organization's relatively new monitoring system. After a momentary and understandable panic, Tessie worked with a very contrite ECM to agree on a plan for how to get real monitoring data directly from the source: from headquarters and country offices. The ECM made a herculean effort to reach out to commissioner managers and was able to deliver data that was triple checked and cross-referenced, at which point, Tessie's team redid the analysis. The effort paid off in findings that were interesting and credible; the EIM–ECM goodwill that was built in resolving this data crisis translated into additional confidence in the evaluation.

6.7.2 Incomplete Data

We decided to devote a whole chapter on evaluation start-up (Chapter 4) because so many decisions taken during that time can be very costly to undo or fix later. One such example is when you are nearing the end of data collection and realize that you forgot to ask some important questions and do not have adequate data to answer the large evaluation questions in the evaluation terms of reference. What would you do if you found yourself in a situation where you need new data to be collected late in the evaluation?

In one case, an evaluation provider organization that occasionally worked with Tessie's company approached Tessie for help on a challenging evaluation that had become more complicated due to turnover. A one-year evaluation of a foundation's economic development program in the United States was nearing completion. The data had been collected from twenty or so sites and dozens of interviews had been completed and were ready to be analyzed. Unfortunately, the evaluation firm implementing the evaluation was on its third EIM who had also just given notice. At the request of the departing EIM, Tessie's organization joined the team and took over the completion of the evaluation. It is hard to analyze qualitative data someone else collected, but the foundation was unwilling to approve additional data collection. Tessie slipped in a little additional data collection in the form of interviews for composing case studies. This enabled verification and completion of data.

CASE STUDY

One of the evaluations where Mary was EIM included several site visits, a survey, and an analysis of the client's own monitoring data; the client did not like the survey design. Pedro (the ECM) thought the survey was too short, too superficial, and a missed opportunity to get a lot of data. Mary countered that the survey was well-targeted to assessing how widespread the issues were that they had identified in the early interviews and site visits and that a long survey would get a low response rate. Pedro insisted. In fact, Pedro considered this a great opportunity to ask about some other things the commissioning organization wanted to find out about. Mary countered that this was not relevant to the evaluation. Back and forth they went for a few turns. In the end, however, as Pedro would not give his approval, Mary agreed to lengthen the survey and add the questions submitted by Pedro. The mistake of that choice was felt immediately: (a) The response rate was very low, with most respondents dropping off after the first five questions (out of 30 total); (b) Pedro as ECM was called to the carpet for sending out a survey with questions that staff did not understand or could not respond to; and (c) Mary was asked to remove the survey from the data analysis process.

- What would you have done if you were in Mary's shoes?
- What advice do you have for Pedro?

7 MANAGING DATA ANALYSIS

WHO SHOULD USE THIS CHAPTER

This chapter focuses on an evaluation implementing manager's (EIM's) role in creating space for this activity, ensuring quality control, monitoring the analysis process, intervening as needed to ensure findings and conclusions are clearly supported by the evidence, and maintaining evaluation independence. While much of this responsibility falls on the EIM, evaluation commissioning managers (ECMs) may also have a role in all these areas. Internal evaluators acting as EIMs will play this role as well.

Data analysis is wedged between data collection and report writing and is the least visible part of evaluation. In fact, some evaluation guides do not list data analysis as a separate step, sometimes merging it with data collection ("data collection and analysis") and other times merging it with report writing ("data analysis and report writing"). The invisibility of data analysis is exacerbated because ECMs or other evaluation stakeholders usually have limited or no visibility into the data analysis process. So where does data analysis fit, and what is the responsibility of the EIM related to data analysis?

This chapter will help demystify the role and nature of the data analysis process in evaluation and clarify the different roles EIMs and ECMs play in this important phase of the evaluation.

An ECM

- monitors any issues around emerging findings and
- supports the evaluation team by protecting time and space for this task.

An EIM as team lead

- develops data analysis plans and provides analysis guidance for team members,
- provides quality control for data analysis,
- facilitates or arranges for facilitation of data analysis session and triangulation of data types, sources, and evaluators, and
- facilitates a session with the reference group or other client representatives to discuss the interpretation of findings and preliminary recommendations.

A solo evaluator (as EIM)

- develops data analysis plans,
- protects space for data analysis and triangulation, and
- may engage a peer in a data analysis session.

An internal evaluator (as EIM)

- develops data analysis plans,
- conducts data analysis, and
- protects space for data analysis and triangulation.

7.1 ROLE AND SCOPE OF DATA ANALYSIS IN AN EVALUATION

In some evaluation books, authors clearly call for data analysis as a distinct step in evaluation requiring its own plan, relevant analytical processes, software to support it, and methods to clean data and triangulate findings. Mertens (2020) links data analysis to report writing, while Morra Imas and Rist (2009) have a separate section on planning and conducting data analysis. In other texts, authors have data analysis embedded throughout their narrative. For example, Davidson (2005) has elements of data analysis in chapters such as "Dealing with the Causation Issue," "The Merit Determination Step," and "Synthesis Methodology"; while Bamberger, Mabry, and Rugh (2006) have data analysis sections embedded under different methodologies and call it out in separate sections under quantitative and qualitative analysis. Regardless of where they describe it, clearly evaluation scholars see a key role for data analysis in the evaluation process.

> As more and more evaluation terms of reference require mixed methods approaches (using several methods), data analysis is becoming essential for triangulating or integrating meaning across different methods, bringing data from different sources together to ensure that conclusions are more complete and are based on evidence. This triangulation is more than harmonization—it allows for exploring possible contradictions as data from different methods could "expand, diffract, tell different stories, or contradict" each other (Fetter & Molina-Azorin, 2017) as well as confirm or provide nuance across methods.

Data collection is incomplete without data analysis, because until we analyze the data, we do not know what it really means. Thomas Schwandt (2015) underscores the centrality of exercising judgment in the professional practice in evaluation and anticipates that "countless deliberations" will be involved in arriving at answers to evaluation questions throughout the evaluation. Unfortunately, in practice, data analysis is frequently underbudgeted, and with inevitable delays in the start-up and data collection phases, it is sometimes squeezed right out of the evaluation process. This is a major loss for the evaluation, as no evaluation method is complete only with its data collection component—every method has a data analysis component that enables the evaluation team to interpret and synthesize the findings. Thus, having spent significant resources and attention to strong data collection, evaluators allow the data analysis process to be compromised, largely due to time and resource management challenges.

We cannot stress enough the importance of the data analysis process for doing justice to the evaluation and showing respect to all those who engaged in data collection.

7.2 IMPORTANT QUESTIONS IN DATA ANALYSIS

What takes place in data analysis? Data analysis is the time when evaluators consider the data in its totality. This is the meaning-making phase of the evaluation where we ask such questions as

- What are the findings from different data collection methods (e.g., the survey, interviews, site visits, past evaluations, monitoring data, etc.)? Which evaluation findings are supported by data from different methods, and where are there contradictions?

- What key perspectives emerge from the findings? What characterizes different stakeholder perspectives?
- What issues emerge from the evaluation? Which ones seem clear and which ones seem contradictory? What polarities is the organization/program holding?
- What are the most important achievements for this organization/program? What are the biggest challenges? Which values are most important for different stakeholders?
- What remains unclear? What additional queries do we need to make of the data? What do we need to clarify with evaluation stakeholders? What additional data collection do we need to conduct?
- What are our areas of consensus in the evaluation team? Where do our perspectives differ? Why?

Open, interpretive questions such as the ones above will help the evaluation team go deeper and produce a stronger and more thoughtful evaluation. Data analysis is also a time to step back and consider the seriousness of making evaluative judgment based on the data collected by deliberating on the context, culture, history, intended use, controversy, and ethical issues in the evaluation (Schwandt, 2015).

7.3 THE COST OF SKIPPING DATA ANALYSIS

Evaluators form impressions about a program well before the completion of data collection and must work at remaining open to new findings that might contradict what they have seen so far. Let us demonstrate how much this matters. The impetus of one of the evaluations Tessie led was a recommendation from a larger organizational review to discontinue a particular program because it was deemed "not a good investment for the organization, and too expensive anyway." Internal rules of the organization mandated that an evaluation be conducted prior to discontinuing that program. You might think that the evaluation conclusions were preordained. Vowing to remain open and conduct this evaluation as any other, Tessie as EIM told the evaluation team to remain open to being surprised, including during the data analysis process. The data analysis uncovered many challenges (which was expected) but also revealed consistent use and satisfaction from 20 of the least wealthy countries that were involved as participants and beneficiaries of this program. Fueled by these conclusions, the evaluation team conducted additional data collection comparing this program with other similar programs and found it to be significantly less expensive. Presenting these findings and conclusions to all participants enabled the organization to grapple with the bigger question of their role in such programs and helped them develop a phased plan of disengaging from the program while providing time for participating countries to seek new funding elsewhere. Had the evaluation team been swept up by client expectations and had the EIM allowed the team to leapfrog over the data analysis process, the evaluation's conclusions would have failed to convey the complexity of the issues.

The authors of this book contend that the lack of a strong data analysis process is one of the causes of dissenting opinions in evaluation reports. When evaluation team members are encouraged to have their voice heard, the whole team grapples with conflicting findings and polarities and is given time and space to come up with a more comprehensive evaluation that reflects the totality of findings.

7.4 THE ROLE OF THE EVALUATION MANAGER IN DATA ANALYSIS

EIMs and ECMs have five important roles related to data analysis and interpretation:

- Protect the time and budget for the data analysis phase, including the funds and space for the data analysis meeting.
- Ensure the evaluation team has a strong data analysis plan and guidance and monitor progress and quality of analysis.
- Manage different data streams by pushing to identify findings supported directly by each one.
- Pay attention to the framing language of the findings, conclusions, and recommendations, and the logical connection among them, thinking about how to use constructive language even when giving bad news and flagging areas of controversy or contradictory findings.
- Protect the independence of the evaluation, even if there is pushback by the client or other stakeholders in the preliminary sharing of selected findings, conclusions, and recommendations.

Let us examine each of these roles.

7.4.1 Protect Time and Budget for Data Analysis

The client or the evaluation team members may be in a hurry to finish the evaluation, but the EIM and the ECM must stand firm on the need for taking the data analysis phase seriously. Data analysis starts early in the evaluation process and runs through to reporting (see Figure 7.1).

FIGURE 7.1 ■ ECM/EIM Roles for Data Analysis Across the Evaluation Process

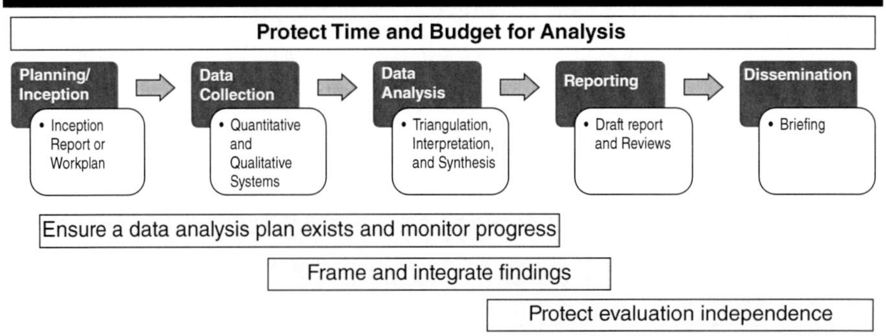

As the EIM, it is critical to ensure you have the time and resources needed to do the data analysis. As mentioned in Chapter 3 and Chapter 4, the budget and workplan must include time and funds to hold a data analysis meeting and any follow-up data collection or verification needed.

7.4.2 Ensure a Data Analysis Plan Exists and Monitor Progress

Ensure that during the evaluation planning, the analysis plan is sketched out—how all the data collected will be compiled, cleaned and prepared for analysis, and analyzed to answer evaluation questions about specific analytical processes, methods, and workplan. Analysis processes for qualitative data include developing coding strategies and code books, while for quantitative data, this involves the process of checking for errors in the dataset and determining what kinds of statistical analysis will be used (descriptive, inferential). Check on data collection progress and quality. Get started early with data cleaning and coding. Schedule and prepare for a data analysis, integration, and synthesis (DAIS) session, and create a standard for summarizing emerging themes from analyses of the various data streams (data from various methods) that can be shared and easily absorbed by others on the evaluation team.

7.4.3 Managing Different Data Streams

Evaluators already know they are responsible for keeping track of different data streams separately. The EIM is responsible for making sure data directories and processes are tracking, archiving, and analyzing data streams separately before the final synthesis. These data streams may include sections for secondary data (e.g., existing evaluations and other documents, monitoring systems, program records) and primary data (all data collected directly by the evaluation data collectors from evaluation participants through individual and group interviews, observation, etc.). This data should also be tracked by source. Big data systems are considered secondary data for these purposes, and their use should follow careful review of the assumptions and potential biases embedded in them.

7.4.4 Framing and Integrating Findings—the Data Analysis, Integration, and Synthesis Session

For a multi-person team, a good practice is to hold a facilitated data analysis meeting with all members of the evaluation team. This meeting should take place at a time when each data stream has been analyzed and emerging findings have been identified but with enough time after the meeting for additional data collection, analysis, or clarification.

In this meeting, evaluators should be tasked with reviewing data from each data collection method and presenting the key findings from each of these methods to colleagues. Color coding findings from each method on separate cards is a good way to keep track of findings from methods more easily.

Once all findings are presented, the team then groups method findings that support the same overall or synthesized finding. Visually, the more colors of method findings that support each synthesized finding, the stronger the evidence behind our synthesized finding.

Where there are contradictory findings, the team discusses what might be behind the apparent contradiction. During this process, the team keeps a running list of questions raised by the data and additional analyses or clarifications that are needed.

It is important to create a logical connection among data, findings, conclusions, and recommendations. Once "synthesized findings" are developed, the team can articulate conclusions, being clear on which synthesized findings support each one. Finally, at the end of the data analysis meeting, the team can articulate recommendations for each conclusion or for clusters of conclusions. Mapping findings to conclusions and recommendations ensures that these are grounded in the evaluation data.

A major contribution of the data analysis meeting is that it makes how the data are linked with what will be included in the report transparent for the EIM and the evaluation team. Then, if there are questions and pushback from evaluation stakeholders, the EIM will not have to scramble to find the information but will have it readily available.

Even when the team is small or the evaluation is conducted by one person, it is important to preserve the space for stepping back and reviewing all the data. Without such a step, the triangulation of data sources and methods that evaluators promise in every proposal is not possible, nor will evaluators be able to clearly outline the story the evaluation is telling.

After the data analysis meeting, there is often some follow-up data collection to clarify the questions raised during the meeting. In addition, this is an opportunity to engage with the ECM on any important, exciting, or controversial findings. It is a golden rule not to surprise the ECM in the draft report. It is not necessary to review all the findings and conclusions before the draft report, but any findings or conclusions that will surprise the ECM should be shared as well as all the recommendations.

7.4.5 Protect Evaluation Independence

The role of the EIM is critical in the moment when evaluation results are presented. We have experienced pushback on challenging recommendations even from the most collaborative ECMs. About a fourth of our ECMs have gently asked us if we can rephrase, make milder, or remove altogether a challenging finding. Sometimes the ECM or a stakeholder provides some additional information the evaluation team did not have, and the team feels comfortable adjusting the finding to reflect this information. In many cases, however, this was more a desire to soften the results. In this case, it is usually sufficient to respond, "I am sorry, we cannot do that because we need to be true to the data," but sometimes the pushback is escalated. In one case, the line manager whose unit's performance was found wanting by the evaluation called for a special report to justify the conclusions; in that case, this systematic data analysis process was extremely valuable and allowed the team to pull together quickly all the relevant detailed data behind the finding. Another client response when the news is bad is an attack on the evaluation methodology. No matter what, the EIM must remain calm, listen attentively, respond respectfully, and stand up for the team. Modifications to include new data or to provide additional explanations may be included, but the line between that and modifying the findings is thin, and the EIM must be vigilant.

PRACTICE: REFRAMING

For EIMs who wish to remain open to seeing all the evaluation's data, here are some mental exercises to keep your reframing muscles supple:

- Recall a program, organization, or service that has many problems. Ask yourself what would be lost and who would not be served if that organization was not there.

- Recall a program that was seen as successful. Ask yourself who does not have access to it, and then imagine what they would say if they were asked to assess it. A state health commissioner whom Tessie knows went further: She would sometimes dress as a homeless person and seek services in the agency she led, which motivated her to institute many reforms.
- Any time you are tempted to villainize one side, imagine that they have a good point and try to understand it instead. A good facilitator of a data analysis meeting does this for the team.

When the EIM's reframing muscles are exercised, it helps the evaluation team to reflect on the totality of data, explore different possible explanations, and look at issues from different vantage points. There are many choices the team can make in framing findings, so do not rush to a conclusion until you have engaged in healthy debate, even if you alone must debate all the different sides.

8 MANAGING EVALUATION REPORTING

WHO SHOULD USE THIS CHAPTER

This chapter focuses on an evaluation implementing manager's (EIM's) role in facilitating the development of an evaluation report and any required briefing and follow-up discussions that use evaluation findings. The EIM is generally responsible for ensuring the preparation and submission of the evaluation report and possibly facilitating a briefing session, while the evaluation commissioning manager (ECM) is responsible for providing feedback on the evaluation report (including facilitation of any internal process required) as well as organizing and participating in briefings. Internal evaluators will play both the EIM and the ECM roles.

Some of us came into the evaluation profession via graduate school, where we were trained mostly by people who had chosen an academic career. So, it is not surprising that many early evaluation reports looked like academic journal articles or master's theses—long literature reviews, detailed methodology sections, results sections with the findings laid out separately by evidence type (qualitative, quantitative) and source (secondary datasets, surveys, interviews, observation, documents).

Great evaluation reporting requires some serious "unlearning" of habits picked up in graduate school (Davidson, 2007). In this chapter, we distill our multiple decades of collective wisdom on what makes for awesome evaluation reporting. There is no one-size-fits-all for this, but there are some principles and practices that can lift your reporting game to a whole new level.

One thing to note in this chapter is that we are very deliberately referring to *reporting* (the verb) rather than *reports* (the noun). This is to help remind us that reporting is a knowledge-sharing interaction, a process you engage in with your primary intended users and not merely a product or output. This chapter focuses on the role of the EIM in developing a strong evaluation report while keeping in mind the responsibility for the broader function of reporting.

8.1 PRINCIPLES AND PRACTICES OF GOOD REPORTING

Academic articles must be written following very clear rules. These articles start with the literature review to lay out the theoretical and empirical landscape; then, we identify the question(s) we will be seeking to answer in the study, followed by the methodology and the measures we will use. Then we reveal the data and our analyses—always dispassionately and without leaping to interpretation too soon—and finally, right down at the tail end of the report or paper, we dare to offer tentative conclusions, along with the obligatory disclaimers about study limitations and, of course, "further research is required."

Evaluators trained in such academic writing found out the hard way that our clients and stakeholders were not quite as enamored with this approach as our professors were. Not only were these kinds of reports boring, impenetrable, and painful to read, but they also only ever appeared at the very end of the research or evaluation process, sometimes dropped like a bomb on unsuspecting stakeholders. Worse, they frequently included some unpleasant revelations that (given the lack of timeliness) were too late to fix. No wonder evaluation has had a negative reputation for so long!

Fast forward to the 2020s and, thankfully, we have figured out some better ways to share insights with our stakeholders. Here are eight principles that we both use in our evaluation reporting:

1. You have questions; we have answers.
2. Weave the evidence and values into a coherent performance story.
3. No surprises.
4. Reporting is a process, not a product.
5. No one should feel stupid when they read, watch, or listen to an evaluation report.
6. Structure reports for actionable answers.
7. One size does not fit all.
8. Co-constructed next steps are better than recommendations from afar.

8.1.1 You Have Questions; We Have Answers

It never ceases to amaze us how many evaluations we see *without* a set of high-level questions to guide the entire effort. We discussed this at some length in Chapter 2, along with some tips for how to get the key evaluation questions (KEQs) right.

There is another evaluation reporting miss that astonishes us: the lack of *actual answers* to the evaluation questions posed. What on earth could we mean by this: an evaluation with questions but no answers? Is that even a thing? Sadly, yes! Probably the most common version of the answerless evaluation is the one with KEQs that are trotted out at the beginning and then left dangling; we never see them again! Another common pattern is this: The evaluation is laid out as if the questions are going to be answered, but what follows instead is a summary of the evidence as if that, by itself, constitutes an answer . . . but it does not.

Evaluation needs to deliver evaluative answers to evaluative questions. In fact, evaluation has the word *value* in it, which means that evaluation actually *values* something—determines its value, makes a judgment on something, and determines its merit and worth. That is one thing that distinguishes evaluation from research. Any good set of evaluative questions would include some version of the following question: How equitable and substantial are the outcomes and impacts on people/groups/communities/organizations and the natural environments on which they (and we all) depend? Evaluation reporting needs to directly answer such questions, not merely "free associate" to them with relevant evidence.

For this outcome or impact question, that means not simply reporting on the size of any shifts, including the breakdown for particular subgroups—these are purely descriptive answers, not evaluative ones—but providing an explicitly evaluative assessment of how equitable and substantial those shifts are: Were the needed outcomes experienced by those who most needed them? Were they strong enough? Did they happen fast enough? How well has the initiative influenced the systemic and structural inequities that had been causing or exacerbating adverse outcomes and/or inequality?

Evaluation that stops short of speaking to the value, merit, and worth of something is incomplete. It is the EIM's job to encourage the evaluation team to complete the evaluation and ensure that the report responds to the evaluation questions. It is also the job of the EIM and the ECM to protect evaluators from pressure to make their evaluation value neutral.

8.1.2 Weave the Evidence and Values into a Coherent Performance Story

ECMs and EIMs need to urge evaluation teams to deliver reports with a few key messages that we want everyone to walk away from the evaluation with and with a narrative arc (story) that helps guide them there. The report should not present disparate evidence and leave it to the reader to process and interpret it—that interpretation is the job of those doing the reporting.

Great evaluation does much more than simply answer the specific questions posed. It also tells a clear and compelling story about whatever is being evaluated (the evaluand), the communities it affects (or should have affected), and the systems on which they depend. This broader story requires us to weave together relevant information about the context (historical, geographic, cultural, economic, social, and so on) and its people, the evaluand, and the evidence about the difference it has made.

What connects all of these elements and helps us tie them together into a coherent whole? Values—values tell us what is important to the people and their natural environment, which of their challenges the evaluand most urgently needs to address, what kinds of outcomes and impacts would be valuable or problematic for whom and why, which of them are particularly important, and which would be nice to see but are less crucial.

Great evaluation reporting brings the audience along on this journey of understanding. We do not merely describe the realities; we help our audience to understand the importance and relevance of each element and how they combine to create something that is better or worse than what was (or what would have been). This includes showing how different values and perspectives converge or diverge and how well the evaluand trades off or finds win–win solutions that address disparate values. Examples might include subsistence farmers' need to earn a decent living alongside the need for natural resources such as land and water to be farmed sustainably so that future generations do not lose access to them or business owners' need to remain viable despite price fluctuations alongside workers' need for a stable income and safe working conditions.

8.1.3 No Surprises

If your ECM cracks open your written report and sees even one major finding—especially if it's negative—that comes as a surprise, that is a fail for the EIM. Sorry, but it is!

No client or stakeholder likes to be blindsided by unexpected findings, especially when they turn up in a final report rather than a draft. When that happens, pushback or even outright rejection of the report becomes much more likely. That is not a mere emotional reaction to something unexpected; there are often major validity concerns with drawing sweeping conclusions without input from those who are closest to the action.

In our own work, we make it a practice to use real-time reporting to share emerging insights as they come to hand. This enables us to check our preliminary interpretations and allows decision makers to start making improvements immediately, which can often be captured as such before the evaluation is wrapped up. These real-time feedback loops are better for the organization and for those who are impacted by the policy, program, or change effort because improvements are made in a much timelier way. For leaders and staff, there is also no risk of a major flaw being exposed that is not already being addressed by the time the final report is written. The evaluation team looks (and is!) more helpful because we are delivering the insights people need in a timely way, not sneaking up on people with bombshell revelations. On top of that, people are more likely to believe, own, and take seriously conclusions that they were involved in drawing.

So, EIMs, here is a useful tip: If you are feeling nervous about how a finding is going to be received by your stakeholders, do not hold it back for a final report. Share it with them as a learning conversation within a sensemaking session or "data party" (BetterEvaluation, 2021; Hutchinson, 2017). These are collaborative meetings where the evaluation team brings evidence to share with an audience of stakeholders, who will then be engaged in making sense of it with you.

Data parties, also known as *participatory data analysis*, are particularly useful when you have contradictory, controversial, or concerning results or if your conclusions present a fundamental challenge to the current system. In these cases, the stakes are high for everyone, not only program staff. These are the findings that stakeholders will be motivated to jump all over if there are even slight weaknesses in our reasoning or evidence. These participatory data analysis sessions are really part of data collection, and what was learned can then be reviewed in a data analysis session that involves only evaluators, who will then feel free to speak their minds.

The "no surprises" principle is particularly important for findings that emerged during the evaluation but may have been thought to be outside its scope or highly unlikely. Examples include unanticipated problems with design or implementation, unexpected side effects, inequitable or environmentally damaging outcomes and impacts, or conclusions that challenge the overall system within which a policy or program operates.

So, what is the right move here? Well, it depends on how radically your scope might depart from the original plan. If the unexpected findings are side effects or unexpected negative results, the best advice is generally to pressure-test your findings with a live audience of stakeholders, get their reactions and feedback, and let them help you understand the nuances surrounding the findings. This deeper, co-created understanding will help you explain what you found in ways that are credible, valid, and thoughtful in the eyes of your audiences.

If your inquiry has revealed an important critique of the wider system within which the policy or program sits—something that was not expected to be questioned—things may not be quite so straightforward. Ideally, you could meet with the ECM and get permission to have the evaluation report investigate and present the issues you have identified. This will be essential if it is going to require additional resources. However, it is quite possible that you will be stopped in your tracks, so what is the appropriate response in that case?

There is an ethical dilemma here, and it is one that we have faced in our own careers as evaluators. Jane once raised an issue in an evaluation report that was a critical part of the overall picture and that it would have been remiss and invalid to edit out. Unfortunately, the client, which was a government agency, did not want this point made public in a report that could be subject to an official information request. Their response was to close the project off while the report was still in the draft stage so that they would not have a final (non-draft) report they would be required to make public.

A career in evaluation is probably going to encounter a moment like this at some point. So, what was the solution? Fundamentally, this was an impasse. If the issue was included, the report was buried. If it was not, the report would have been missing a crucial finding that had implications for validity, credibility, and ethics. Jane recalls that she was thinking about *the report* (the noun) at the time rather than *reporting* (the verb). In hindsight, one option might have been to report on the issue in a live discussion with the client and then negotiate whether and how the issue might be addressed in the written report. Even this solution does not completely resolve the issue, though; if the client refuses to allow the finding to be included in the written report, that report is still incomplete, which compromises validity as well as professional ethics.

EIMs need to explore all the options available to them for how to manage such an impasse or what to do to prevent it. Is there dialogue to be done up front? Are there ways to put information in front of policymakers through memos? Is there a venue for a discussion of the perceived threat of making information public? Is there a place for the client to state their interpretation or differences of opinion? In the United States, the General Accountability Office is such a place.

8.1.4 Reporting Is a Process, Not a Product

How do we deliver a written report with no surprises? As mentioned above, the main way we do this is by treating the reporting process as just that—a process. Put another way, it is a journey of discovery *with* our stakeholders, not something we drop into their laps. As such, we need to bring our audience along with us, ensuring that we all understand what we are seeing and that it is being reported in ways that are illuminating and helpful.

As we have stated before, 100% of the value of an evaluation is in its eventual use. That includes not only instrumental use (using the evaluation to inform specific decisions and actions) but also conceptual use (building understanding and insight, often for broader purposes) and process use (using the evaluation process to build capacity and shared understanding).

When we consider the wide range of uses we are trying to influence or enable, it becomes clear that dropping a paper report on someone's desk is not going to make that happen. The real benefit in utilization-focused evaluation is in how it actively engages stakeholders and uses their expertise to arrive at conclusions that make sense from their perspective and are clearly valid, credible, and useful.

8.1.5 No One Should Feel Stupid When They Read, Watch, or Listen to an Evaluation Report

The ultimate user of an evaluation report is its reader. This may sound obvious, but we have been surprised by how often it is forgotten. When put to practice, reader-focused writing can be compelling both in terms of accessible language and in terms of structure to make it easy for a reader to understand the main points and story of the evaluation.

A few years ago, Jane was commissioned to lead a review of the methodology used by a major international development agency in some of its biggest and most comprehensive evaluation synthesis reports. The client was concerned that the agency needed to kick things up a notch by adding some cutting-edge methodologies to the mix, so they were looking for suggestions about what to add and where the existing methodologies needed to be improved or better applied.

Unfortunately, the terms of reference did not exactly nail identifying the real problem. As Jane delved deeper into the project, it became clear that significant time and energy were being plunged into these reports, but hardly anyone was actually reading them. Why? Well, for starters, the reports were long . . . very long—175 pages was typical. That length of report is not ideal, but for these very expansive reports that were synthesizing findings from multiple evaluations, there was a lot to cover. The bigger and more glaring issue was that the reports themselves were completely impenetrable—painfully difficult to read, full of big words and very long sentences, and heavy going for even the most sophisticated reader. Jane's team even quantified its assessment of report readability by running the abstracts (which were the most readable sections of each report) through a Gunning Fog Index readability calculator. The most readable reports were at the level of peer-reviewed academic journal articles; the least readable were about as intelligible as United States tax legislation.

This low level of readability—where even an advanced reader would have trouble comprehending the report—was highly problematic. Yet the client was adamant that any attempt to use more straightforward language would be "dumbing down" the reports, which they were certain would impact their credibility.

This reminds us of a great quote from Peterson and Park (2010), who were not evaluators but rather psychological researchers seeking to understand what characterized the most highly influential pieces of research in their field. Their conclusion is a quote well worth pinning to your wall as a reminder:

> The evidence of history is clear that the research studies with the greatest impact in psychology are breathtakingly simple in terms of the questions posed, the methods and designs used, the statistics brought to bear on the data, and the take-home messages.
>
> Simple does not mean simplistic. Nor does it mean easy or quick. Rather, simple means elegant, clear and accessible, not just to other researchers but to the general public. No one's eyes glaze over when hearing about a high-impact study. No one feels stupid. No one asks, "And your point is?" (p. 398)

As evaluators, we should probably take issue with Peterson and Park's suggestion that we should keep our evaluation questions simple. But this quote is still valid for complex evaluations as well—the more complicated the language in the question, the more difficult it is to convey the story. We would say that "simple, but not simplistic" works for evaluation questions as well. Commit to delivering what one of our clients gratefully coined the "no head-scratching" evaluation.

Remember, too, that clarity is what makes your reporting accessible to a wider audience, including those who are most affected by the evaluand. Academic and technical language is sometimes used as a smoke screen to obscure findings that powerful stakeholders do not want shared or that evaluators are too nervous to state clearly. Language can also serve as an elitist wall that prevents those without specialist knowledge from being able to engage effectively with and critique your work. Clarity is an important way to shift that power imbalance in the right direction.

8.1.6 Structure Reports for Actionable Answers

One thing that can dramatically improve the clarity of evaluation reporting is to throw out the master's thesis structure we were taught in graduate school. That is where you report your quantitative and qualitative findings in different sections, which you break up further into subsections that cover each different source of data (e.g., interviews with community members, interviews with program staff, and so on).

Instead, try framing the entire report—especially the findings—around the KEQs and use these as the headings for your sections. That will force you to present all of the evidence pertaining to a particular question in the same section so that it can be considered together as a set, not kept divided off into its methodological silos. This simple structural move will not solve all of your clarity challenges, but our experience is that it makes a huge difference. Stand by for some more detailed guidance on written reports later in this chapter to help you synthesize your findings so the reader does not have to and writing findings statements that quickly and easily capture the key messages related to answering each evaluation question.

8.1.7 One Size Does Not Fit All

Every evaluation has a range of different audiences. Each audience has a stronger interest in some findings over others, requires a greater or lesser level of detail, and may or may not possess the expertise to understand some of the nuances or technical details. As a result, a one-size-fits-all approach to reporting will fail to meet the information and learning needs of all important stakeholder groups.

Having said that, there is a flipside to differentiated reporting that evaluation teams should be aware of. We have seen and heard of situations where the existence of different versions of a report intended for different audiences can create suspicion among some that they are not being provided with the whole truth. For this reason, it is advisable to make the various versions of an evaluation report, particularly a written or recorded version, available to all audiences. This way, people can choose to view the kind of report that will be most useful to them while not feeling that something is being hidden.

8.1.8 Co-Constructed Next Steps Are Better Than Recommendations from Afar

There is a pervasive assumption, particularly among client organizations, that a useful and actionable evaluation report is one with concrete recommendations about how to improve the policy, program, or change effort being evaluated. Many monitoring and evaluation professionals we speak with accept this view. However, in our experience, this is often *not* the best way to ensure that evaluation is useful, practical, and actionable. Let us explain why.

When evaluation teams cross over into the recommendations space, they are implicitly claiming expertise as program or policy designers, which not all evaluators have. Not only that, but there is *no way* that an external evaluation team could possibly be privy to the full range of budgetary, logistical, and political (either party politics or organizational politics) implications of the changes they suggest. Wading into the fray and making recommendations anyway can be a reputation-damaging move for an evaluation team. It is quite common for evaluation recommendations to be completely unfeasible, which instantly kills the credibility of the report, no matter how strong the rest of it is.

What is the alternative, then? Earlier, we mentioned the value of sensemaking meetings or data parties to engage key stakeholders in the collaborative interpretation of findings, particularly anything that is controversial, surprising, or negative. It is a natural extension to incorporate into these meetings a process whereby stakeholders work together on developing a set of action points or next steps based on the evaluative evidence they have now had the time to come to understand in some detail.

There are several advantages to bringing stakeholders, including program designers, policymakers, and other key decision makers, into the action planning process. First, these are the people who, unlike most evaluators, *do* have policymaking and program design expertise; therefore, they are better equipped to know how best to address an identified flaw or weakness. Second, the right stakeholders will also have a very clear grasp of the budgetary, logistical, and political implications of any proposed changes, which means that any action points they suggest are far more likely to be feasible. The third reason is psychological and motivational. It is a well-established fact that people tend to be far more committed to a course of action they were part of devising themselves. These action steps are "theirs" now, not an evaluation team's ideas to be accepted or rejected. Recommendations and action plans that were co-created with those responsible for implementing them are far more likely to happen—and to be implemented well. As EIMs, our role is to ensure that the conclusions and recommendations are grounded in the evidence, and we are responsible for ensuring that in the co-creation process, what emerges is linked to that evidence and does not go beyond it.

8.2 WRITTEN REPORTS

What does it mean to "structure reports for actionable answers"? We have learned the hard way that our clients are not enamored with the typical master's thesis structures we had been trained to use.

What is the alternative, then? Here are some of the good practices we have developed over the years for creating written reports that have our clients breathing huge sighs of relief—and sometimes even delight! We also encourage you to take a look at some innovative suggestions from other colleagues we know and love; for example, Kylie Hutchinson's (2017) *A Short Primer on Innovative Evaluation Reporting* is a gold mine of fun ideas that is sure to inspire!

8.2.1 Reporting Structures That Work

A piece of advice that Jane heard early on in her career was this: If you are writing something for managers, give them a two-page bullet point summary. For senior managers, make it a one-page bullet point summary. And for the CEO? A cartoon.

OK, that might be a slight exaggeration, but the overall message is on target. An important starting point for written reports is being very clear about the realities of our clients' and stakeholders' work lives and the massive information overload experienced by pretty much everyone. There is no point in getting offended when busy, overwhelmed people do not make it all the way through a long report. Our job is to design reporting that fits into their reality, not to try and force them to bend to our preferences.

It is important to remember that only a handful of people will read your evaluation report from cover to cover. Typically, the only people who do are (i) the main internal person who has been overseeing your work and is responsible for assuring its quality, (ii) a worker who has been told to summarize the findings for busy executives (red flag alert: they should not need to!), and (iii) someone who might want to take issue with the conclusions and recommendations.

Every reader only has so much time; they will pick up your report and start reading it, but they will stop when they run out of time or lose interest. Your job is to ensure that wherever they stop reading, whether that is after two pages or 10, they will have read the most important things you want them to understand. This is why we never *ever* make the reader wait until the very end of the report to see the most important findings and conclusions; we will lose them long before they get there!

Begin with some expectations of percentages of real estate for each section—we have seen so many evaluation reports where bullet point #3 is 25 pages long! Here is a structure you can try:

- a one-page summary infographic that highlights the key points in the story the evaluation tells
- executive summary: the shorter the better, and only go beyond two to three pages if you are including infographics, graphs, or pictures so it does not feel as dense. Anything over five or six pages is too long. Contents include one or two introductory paragraphs explaining what is being evaluated and why, followed by 7 (+/-2) headings, one for each KEQ; under each heading should be a direct answer to the question along with a brief summary of the evidence supporting that answer
- introduction, background, context, and description: what is being evaluated; which issues it was intended to address; the relevant historical, political, and cultural context; the purposes and audiences for the evaluation
- KEQs and values: a set of 7 (+/-2) high-level KEQs that the evaluation seeks to answer and an overview of the relevant values to be applied when answering those questions
- findings: 7 (+/-2) headings, one for each KEQ. Under each heading, provide a direct and explicitly evaluative answer to the KEQ along with a brief summary of the evidence supporting it (similar to the contents of the executive summary), followed by a clear, coherent, and well-reasoned presentation of the evidence relative to the values. This should be sufficiently transparent so that the reader can follow the reasoning used to reach the evaluative conclusions (i.e., the answers to the evaluative questions)
- conclusions: a summary of stakeholder reflections on the findings, including how it has influenced their thinking

- recommendations: a list of co-constructed next steps to address any identified issues
- appendixes or annexes: details about evidence, more details about the methodology, etc.

An improved report structure may seem like an overly simple solution that will not solve much. However, we have both been quite amazed at how it has disciplined and challenged us and our colleagues to deliver dramatically clearer and more coherent evaluation reports that get to the point faster and give much more direct answers to the KEQs. As EIM, you will have to push a bit, but it is worth it. Give it a try!

8.2.2 Creating a Skeleton Report Early On

Early in our evaluation careers, both of us recall writing evaluation reports and finding ourselves with a lot of leftover evidence. All of that survey and other data that we gathered certainly seemed relevant at the time, but somehow a lot of it ended up being surplus to our requirements. Worse, we found that we had collected a lot of evidence pertaining to some evaluation questions and far too little for others.

As EIM, one great way to avoid this embarrassing and wasteful occurrence is to push the team to create a skeleton report very early on, ideally before designing your data collection protocols or collecting evidence. Use the headings suggested in the section above, and under each one, sketch out which pieces of evidence will be presented where in the report and think through how it will be synthesized to generate clear answers to the KEQs. This way, every piece of evidence you gather will have a home in your evaluation report (no more leftover data). You will also be able to check that your evidence-gathering efforts have been spread roughly evenly across the KEQs, or at least evenly enough that you will not have any gaping holes in your evidence.

8.2.3 Reviewing and Revising the Report Outline

The report outline or skeleton report represents your initial ideas for how the evaluation report should be laid out. As the evaluation progresses, as evidence starts being dropped into the report, and as stakeholders provide their feedback, it is typical to adjust the report structure so that the ordering and layout make better sense to the various audiences. This iterative process continues right up until the report is finalized.

As discussed in Chapter 7, the EIM should insist on a data analysis and synthesis session when most of the data have been collected prior to commencing report writing. By then, each data stream will have been analyzed and emerging themes identified, but there will be enough time after the meeting for any final additional data collection, analysis, or clarification.

When you have finished the analysis, it is time to review the overall key messages, summary answers to the evaluation questions, key findings, conclusions, and recommendations and then revise the outline to best tell the story and help the reader process the information.

8.2.4 Planning and Making Assignments

Most evaluation reports are quite substantial undertakings, with more than one or two people involved in the write-up—sometimes many more. For the largest evaluations, you may not be writing one report but rather a series of reports that feed into one overarching one. For example, you might need a monitoring data report, a survey report, case study reports, an equity report, an environmental sustainability report, and/or a value-for-investment report.

Prior to assigning report writing responsibilities, a first step is to ensure that the whole team has agreed on the findings, conclusions, recommendations, and narrative arc or major messages of the evaluation. It is not the job of evaluation writers to draw conclusions on their own but to make sure these conclusions, recommendations, and major messages are well known to the writers.

For the EIM overseeing the report writing, whether internal or external, what are the best ways to assign responsibilities for the different pieces of writing and how do you ensure that all pieces come together in a seamless, coherent whole? First, identify your best writers and assign one or two of them to the final evaluation report. They should not simply be great writers; they should have strong skills in interdisciplinary boundary spanning because their task is to weave together multiple specialized elements into a coherent whole that will make sense to a lay audience. Consider any key areas of expertise that are pivotal for the entire project. For example, if the major overarching themes for the evaluation are equity and environmental sustainability, it will be important that your lead writer(s) have expertise in these areas. If the evaluation is being conducted in a very specific community, culture, or context, it is important that your lead writer(s) have a deep understanding (and, ideally, lived experience of their own) that will allow them to write credibly and authentically about the effects on that community, culture, and context.

For each of the auxiliary reports and for each section within the main report, it is important for the writing to be led by someone who was close to the evidence and was involved in conducting the analyses and making sense of the findings. If this is not possible, it should be someone familiar with the content area and the methodology who will be able to communicate with the analysts and understand the nuances well enough to convey them clearly.

8.2.5 Substantive Reviews and Collaboration

With multiple reports and/or report sections being written by different people, it is important to put in place a few measures that will help ensure that the structures, points covered, and writing styles are reasonably consistent. This helps make the task of stitching them all together less onerous.

Take case studies, for example. Some major evaluations will include in-depth case studies of specific program sites, organizations, or communities. To help ensure that these are written in a consistent way, you will need to create a coherent parallel structure so that each one covers the same general points and is laid out in the same consistent way. This not only makes it easier to extract the themes and lessons from across the case studies, but it also makes them easier for readers to navigate and understand. Just like the report outline, the outline for the case studies should be developed before data collection and then revised once you know what data are available and again after analysis.

These various chunks of the evaluation will cover different sources of evidence that may need to be analyzed separately but ultimately need to be synthesized together into a coherent whole. The process for reviewing these various elements needs to incorporate cross-checking and triangulation of the evidence from different sources to check whether they are telling a consistent or divergent story. A disciplined data analysis process (as described in Chapter 7) will help with the consistency and coherence of the reporting.

8.2.6 Data Visualization

Ensuring that your team delivers high-value, high-utility evaluations requires more than capturing the essence of what is important and answering the KEQs; it is also about conveying these insights and answers simply and elegantly in ways that your audience can easily grasp. Although a great reporting structure and clear writing will take you a long way toward this goal, you should not forget the visual aspects of the work.

Each potential reader of a written evaluation report will have a preference for certain kinds of data, analyses, and presentation styles. For all of us, however, our eyes are naturally drawn to tables, figures, photographs, illustrations, and infographics. In the written word, we are drawn to text boxes and to text that stands out from the rest, whether from bolding, italics, or a different size or color of text.

Rather than fighting this natural human cognitive wiring, it is important to use it to our advantage. Figures, tables, and other visual representations need to be clearly described and explained directly in the figure or table, without the need to sift through the text to understand them. Bold, italics, and colors should be used sparingly and should make it easy to skim the report and quickly find things of interest to the reader.

They say a picture is worth a thousand words, but that is only true if we get the picture right. Thankfully, the evaluation profession has been blessed with many stellar developments in data visualization over the past several years, so we have a lot of great ideas to draw from now. Gone are the days of pasting a default graph from SPSS or Excel into our reports, which is not only visually unappealing but also frequently fails to clearly convey what the findings are.

We will not reiterate all the good advice we have heard over the years, but here is one that we thought was a game changer and definitely worth highlighting: When titling a graph or table, do not simply state what the variables are (as is the default in academic writing) and leave the reader to figure out what it all means. Instead, think of your title as a newspaper headline. Use it to succinctly convey what exactly your reader should be seeing in or inferring from the graph or table.

Your goal with data visualization, as with your writing, is to make it as easy as possible for your reader to understand the most important insights without having to figure anything out for themselves. If there is a pattern in the data that seems obvious to you, do not assume that it will jump out for a reader. Help them out: Say directly what the pattern is, what it means, how important it is, and why.

8.2.7 Synthesizing, Editing, and Quality Management

Considerable care needs to be taken when bringing together a large written report where multiple authors have been working on different sections. Each writer will inevitably have their own style, yet the report needs to feel as though it has been written by the same person.

One good strategy for achieving coherence is having a clear structure and process for how these building blocks go together. As we advised earlier, structure your findings section using the KEQs as the framework. Then, sketch out the general ordering you will use under each KEQ to lay out the relevant values, the various pieces of evidence that are relevant to the question, and the evaluative reasoning you use to interpret and synthesize it all.

Overall, your report should lay out the following:

- the *what*: findings and the evidence supporting them, organized around evaluation questions
- the *so what* (conclusions): what do these findings mean as a whole, in context, and in relation to a broader field
- the *now what* (recommendations or considerations): what should happen because of these findings and conclusions grounded in the evidence

The following are some suggestions for using a reporting structure for your findings based on the KEQs. Start the section by listing the KEQ in full, followed by any brief explanation that might be needed by the audience. That could be as simple as restating the question in lay terms, it might be laying out the main sub-questions, or it could be a few sentences explaining the significance of this question to the overarching purposes of the evaluation.

Next, provide a succinct answer to the KEQ, including rubric-based ratings if you used rubrics to guide your evaluative reasoning. This should be followed by a couple of paragraphs briefly explaining the main issues considered when drawing the conclusion as well as the most important evidence that supports it.

Following these first few paragraphs succinctly laying out the question, answer, evidence, and reasoning, use the next few pages to provide an expanded summary that walks the reader through what you found and what it means. As you explain your conclusions and what led to them, keep the reader engaged by offering evaluative interpretations, not only descriptive ones. In other words, go beyond describing results or strengths and weaknesses to comment on how good, valuable, and important they are. For example, if you have found something that was not right or did not work well, decision makers need to know whether this is a major issue that they need to address immediately or a minor flaw that should be addressed the next time they are refreshing the design.

An important priority for overseeing evaluation report writing is ensuring good coherence and consistency among sections contributed by different team members. A good reporting structure will help, but you will still need your lead writers to synthesize evidence from multiple sources (as described in Chapter 7) and apply the evaluative reasoning in a broadly consistent way across all of your evaluation questions.

Once the report is drafted, each section needs to be reviewed by those who are most familiar with those particular pieces of evidence and analysis. It is their job to ensure that the findings they uncovered are represented accurately.

Finally, the entire report—along with any annexes or sub-reports—needs to be carefully reviewed for clarity, validity, and coherence. This quality assurance process should include several pairs of eyes from outside the evaluation team, including a meta-evaluator, if possible. Even if the EIM was not involved in the writing, this is a good time to step in as a quality control measure.

Reviewers should conduct the technical review first to identify any errors in the evaluative reasoning before it goes to those running the program. We have both seen cases where program managers or staff were given a draft report to review but then a technical review found that the draft conclusions were far too positive, given the evidence, or that a section did not consider the full range of evidence sufficiently. Not surprisingly, program staff may be extremely upset to see previously glowing conclusions being downgraded to something more modest in the final version.

8.3 THE DEBRIEFING MEETING

It may be tempting to breathe a sigh of relief once the evaluation report is written and you consider the project complete. But with all the effort you have put into crafting a truly insightful and useful evaluation, as the EIM, you should consider how to help stakeholders engage with and understand the findings and be part of figuring out what to do with them.

Some like to call this the *recommendations meeting*; we refer to it as a *debrief* or a *learning session*. People are much more likely to use the insights from an evaluation if they have been involved in drawing the conclusions—this is what we were aiming for in the sensemaking meetings mentioned earlier. But even if they have not, it is still extremely important to walk them through the findings and involve them in deciding next steps. That way, the action plan that emerges at the end of the meeting will be theirs, not only the evaluation team's.

If you have managed your stakeholder engagement processes well, the debrief meetings should be unsurprising events. Any controversial findings should have already been explored, discussed, and (ideally) agreed upon in earlier sensemaking meetings. The debrief is an opportunity to step back and reflect on the evaluation findings and explore their implications for future thinking and action. Who should be there, what should you cover, and how should you structure the meeting?

Depending on the size and scope of the evaluation, you may need more than one debriefing meeting to cover all the bases. It probably makes sense to start with one general meeting where you share and discuss the findings of the entire evaluation, followed by additional deep-dive meetings that explore particular elements in depth.

Who should attend? Two broad categories of people should be included: those who will need to act on the findings and those whose expertise will be needed to understand the implications of those actions.

Let us start with those who need to act on the findings. Bring in the relevant budget holders and decision makers as well as the designers, architects, or policymakers who would be involved in designing improvements or using the insights to design future policy or programming. In other words, include those people who will be charged with acting on the findings, either directly or by authorizing budget approval or work plans to do so. Do not limit this list to people who can take immediate action but include the people whose thinking feeds into policy and program design on an ongoing basis.

Good reflection and action planning also requires a clear understanding of how possible changes could affect people and the natural environment. We have all seen examples of decisions being made with good intentions by people who are sadly out of touch with the reality on the ground. Wherever possible, solutions should be co-designed with the individuals, families, and communities that would be affected by them so that they can bring their expertise and influence to crafting locally responsive solutions. There are times when that simply is not possible due to the large number of stakeholders or the geographic reach of the policy or program being evaluated, the logistics of making direct contact with numerous geographically dispersed groups, and/or because the primary impactees are unable to speak for themselves (e.g., very young children, those with intellectual disabilities, people living with dementia). If that is the case, look for creative ways to bring in that expertise anyway, even if your solution is not ideal. For example, you might invite advocacy groups, community or social workers who work closely with the affected communities, Indigenous elders (for their expertise on their natural environment and on their own people), experts in equity and inclusion, or environmental scientists (when looking at potential impacts on natural systems).

Now that you have the right people in the room, plan to facilitate a meeting that will be maximally engaging and useful. For starters, you will need to cover the main evaluation findings (i.e., the answers to the KEQs), focusing in particular on anything puzzling or controversial as well as any results that were identified as particularly important (whether positive or negative). Prepare a few questions that will help people dive deeper than a surface understanding; this is the depth needed to craft solid actions. Use breakout groups to have participants discuss what they are seeing, what it means, and what should be done to address any issues.

As facilitators say, people will do what they are ready, willing, and able to do, so do not expect this evaluation to result in full action planning. In some cases, the debriefing or learning session will allow for greater clarification of perspectives and issues that require further deliberation. In cases of greater readiness, the outputs of the debriefing meeting might be (i) a set of agreed-upon action points, (ii) clarity about who will be leading each one, (iii) a time frame for checking in on progress, and (iv) a shared understanding of what success should look like as well as any risks or warning signs to monitor for. In the end, you are not there to make decisions or supplant program managers and organizational leaders; you are there to facilitate deeper thinking about the evaluation's findings, conclusions, and recommendations.

8.4 REVIEWS AND APPROVAL

Reviews and approvals inevitably take a long time—longer than budgeted—and it is important to negotiate and push back on the ECM if they keep asking for more revisions. It is a good practice to negotiate the number of revisions in the beginning (see Chapter 4) based on what the budget allows, and again ensure the ECM is clear when you submit the report. The problems occur when the ECM cannot ensure timely feedback or keeps asking to let one more person review until the process of revision is inefficient. For ECMs, this is a time to engage in active management of gathering feedback and facilitating agreement on that feedback, as many times, evaluators are given contradictory feedback. We strongly suggest that ECMs appoint someone who reviews and makes decisions about where there are conflicting pieces of feedback—the evaluation team should not have to figure this out.

To manage feedback, we generally use a simple tool: an Excel spreadsheet with columns for Report Section, Page, Comment/Feedback, any Coding/Categorization of Feedback (to help determine who will address it), and Response. In this way, those commenting can see exactly what was done with their feedback or what was already addressed in the report. While start-up is an engaging, flexible process, we recommend that the report feedback process be more formal and documented in this explicit way because you are trying to wrap things up, place final touches, and ensure everyone is comfortable (or at least clear about the output of the evaluation).

CASE STUDY

To increase understanding and promote use, the UN Women Independent Evaluation Office began publishing *TRANSFORM*, a magazine that turned the findings and recommendations of corporate, global evaluations into accessible and well-laid out text. Take a look at how this 2017 report (https://www.unwomen.org/en/digital-library/publications/2017/1/transform-issue-9) made a complex review of UN Women's organizational structure in countries into interesting and engaging articles.

In your review, consider the following:

1. What stands out to you about this type of layout?
2. What do you think works particularly well?
3. Consider the competencies and resources you need to produce such an evaluation output and think about what might be feasible in the evaluations you work on.
4. What if you do not have the resources for such a publication—what other, less expensive strategies might you use?

9 MANAGING EVALUATION USE AND INFLUENCE

WHO SHOULD USE THIS CHAPTER

This chapter focuses on the shared responsibility of the evaluation implementing manager (EIM) and the evaluation commissioning manager (ECM) in facilitating evaluation use and influence. The ECM is generally better placed to manage evaluation use and influence, because the ECM's responsibility begins prior to and extends beyond the completion of the evaluation contract. Internal evaluators share the responsibility for evaluation use and influence with program managers and senior leaders.

No matter the *quality* of an evaluation, if it is not used or influential, it literally has zero *value*. (If the evaluation is not of good quality, however, and we could not stop it or make it better, we should consider the investment in it as sunk cost and be happy it is not used in misinforming decisions and possibly causing damage.)

Why does any organization invest in evaluation? For the same reason they invest in anything—because what they get out of it is worth the investment . . . or, at least, it should be. Good evaluation management includes making sure the evaluation delivers that value.

An organization's investment in evaluation includes more than the money paid to a contractor evaluation team or the time and resources used by the internal evaluation team and other participating stakeholders to get the job done. It incurs opportunity costs: The time, money, and other resources that are spent on doing evaluation might otherwise have been spent on enhancing or expanding the program or developing something new.

What makes an evaluation valuable? What makes it matter? No, it is not how technically sound it is or how valid its conclusions are. The bottom line is this: All of an evaluation's value lies in its eventual use and influence.

The good news is that the ECM and EIM have responsibility for managing the use and influence of evaluation, which is an important and visible job; EIMs and ECMs have an opportunity to guide evaluation in a way that makes the investment in evaluation worthwhile. The bad news is that EIMs and ECMs have little control over use and influence, where other discernible and indiscernible forces are at play—forces that are in no one person's control. If the evaluation is perceived as useful and influential, the ECM and/or EIM will get some of the credit. If the evaluation is perceived as a wasted investment or not used—or worse, misused—EIMs and ECMs will be the first to be blamed.

In this chapter, we answer several questions and share some real-life examples of evaluations and client organizations concerning the following questions:

- What does it mean for an evaluation to be used and influential?
- How can ECMs prime and enable organizations for better evaluation uptake, learning, and evaluation-informed decision making?
- What factors contribute to evaluations that are widely used and highly influential?
- How can we manage evaluations and evaluation processes to be maximally useful and influential while guarding against misuse?

9.1 NO, EVALUATION USE AND INFLUENCE IS NOT ONLY ABOUT IMPLEMENTING RECOMMENDATIONS!

When we think about evaluation being used, what may immediately come to mind is using the evaluation findings to inform decision making about the program, policy, or whatever is being evaluated (instrumental use). In fact, there is a great deal more to it, which led evaluation scholars to move to the concepts of *evaluation use* and *influence*, recognizing the complexity, context, and principles in considering evaluation use and influence (Herbert, 2014). Here are three dimensions all evaluation managers should consider about use and influence (Henry & Mark, 2003; Johnson et al., 2009; Kirkhart, 2000; Patton & Cambell-Patton, 2021; Weiss, 1998):

- *Type of use*. To inform decisions (*instrumental use*), increase learning and understanding (*conceptual use*), and advocate (*persuasive use*) as well as pause, consider, engage in dialogue, and build relationships (*process use*). Most evaluations aim to produce several kinds of use and influence (not only one), and they may end up resulting in some unintended uses as well, including well after the end of an evaluation. ECMs and EIMs cannot know the full extent of possible uses and influence of evaluation, and probably no one person ever can.
- *Perspectives*. Who is trying to influence whom and with what intention? Is management trying to find an "impartial" reason to close down a program? Is a government agency's policy unit trying to learn about how to improve public awareness of its increasingly decentralized services? Is an environmental group trying to raise awareness and activate funders to accelerate climate protection action? Is a coalition of organizations trying to build alignment of vision and improve collaboration? All these types of intended influences by different stakeholder groups might be going on at the same time.
- *When*. Different types of uses may take place at different times, starting with initial discussions about an evaluation and ending well after the completion of an evaluation contract. Conversations between partners that help align their interest and fortify their resolve may happen right at the start, when discussing the evaluation questions and other specifications to be included in a request-for-proposal document. Decisions may be informed by the evaluation at an

intermediate debriefing after a site visit. And evaluation findings can find their way into shaping program direction and strategy a year after the evaluation is completed because a change in leadership may make people more receptive to the evaluation's messages.

We add to these three dimensions of use and influence two additional possibilities:

- *Nonuse*. Nonuse might result from a failure to disseminate appropriately, deliberate neglect because of disinterest or resistance to the evaluation content, an intention to suppress the findings of an evaluation, or a strong disagreement or concern about the evaluation's quality and honesty. *Symbolic use* of evaluation also belongs here, where an evaluation is required so we tick the box and are done or where management is required to provide a response to evaluation and offers some diplomatic words to signal the end of the conversation.
- *Misuse*. Misuse may be unintentional where the evaluation is misinterpreted—perhaps because it is not written clearly, overstates a finding, fails to cover an important dimension, or uses inaccurate data or faulty analysis. Misuse may also be intentional; for example, where a finding or sentence out of context is used to support a conclusion that was not made by the evaluation.

Thus, adoption of recommendations is only one signal of evaluation use; evaluation can be used even if it didn't provide recommendations at all or when its recommendations are not adopted, or if it did not include recommendations at all. It can inform decisions invisibly, create awareness and highlight issues, provide a new lens for understanding a program or intervention, catalyze relationships, stimulate the establishment of networks and coalitions, and provide fodder for different parties to lobby for their positions on an issue. ECMs and EIMs should understand the range of possibilities in evaluation use and influence, plan accordingly, and protect against nonuse and misuse to the best of their abilities.

9.2 WHAT IS THE EVALUATION MANAGER'S JOB IN EVALUATION USE AND INFLUENCE?

At a personal level, this chapter should really come with a warning: ECMs and EIMs, beware! Evaluation is an opportunity for influence. Yet, the same controversial issues that the evaluation is working to uncover and explain are at play, influencing the evaluation. If the evaluation is visible, influential people may try to guide it, suppress it, or misinterpret it to serve particular interests. The ECM or the EIM may be trying to make the evaluation visible only to be subjected to political winds that may lead to misuse and even be detrimental for any evaluation manager's career. Nonetheless, it is still ECM and EIM's job to manage the use and influence of the evaluation.

We started this chapter with the assertion that use and influence are the yardstick with which we can judge whether our investment in an evaluation was worth it; if you agree with us, then ECMs and EIMs need to place it squarely in their list of responsibilities. This may be worrisome. Evaluation is a political endeavor and is frequently a controversial intervention, raising expectations and causing stress to intended participants;

if ECMs and EIMs are not attentive, it can get derailed, sidelined, misrepresented and misused, or become so controversial that it is terminated. Evaluation is also an opportunity to uphold values and criteria that help organizations and communities to build better programs and shape a better future, and all evaluation managers have a responsibility to enable these types of uses. The bottom line is that good ECMs and EIMs must make evaluation use and influence a priority from the beginning of an evaluation.

The first question is this: Are you part of the evaluation's life at the terms of reference (TOR) stage, during the evaluation, or after the evaluation contract is completed? Are you coming into the evaluation mid-stream to replace someone who came before you? Whenever you step into your role, ask yourself, "What purpose does this evaluation serve, and how do I envision it being used?"

From the beginning, it is important for the ECM and EIM to be clear about where overall direction and authority come from in managing use and influence. Who is in charge? In what forums should the ECM or EIM raise the question of intended use and influence in order to get guidance? Sometimes, there is a senior manager or committee that will provide that guidance, but other times, this may not be so clear. Even when there is an evaluation steering committee, the represented stakeholders may be interested in different types of use and influence, which may be aligned, totally independent of each other, or in conflict.

It is a good idea, especially if there is little guidance on use and influence, for ECMs to raise the question with their own senior management, for EIMs to raise it with their ECM client, and for internal evaluators to raise it with the leaders of the programs they are evaluating. Additionally, all evaluation managers may reach out for feedback from other stakeholders and document the final guidance received on the issue. ECMs especially might still be called on to explain things later when the political evaluation winds are at their peak, but they will at least have this early confirmation of their understanding.

In some cases, ECMs might be asked to drive a particular use of evaluation. ECMs may then be conflicted and feel like impostors: On the one hand, they are responsible for managing an independent and impartial evaluation and staying out of the way of the evaluation team's deliberations; on the other hand, they are told by their senior managers that they must intervene and make sure to highlight critical information about a program. In one of Tessie's evaluations, the ECM did not agree with a directive from senior management to prioritize negative information about a program, so they informed Tessie confidentially about this hidden directive and encouraged her to share her independent findings. As EIM, Tessie now had to manage senior management's expectations about an intended use that was not fully supported by her findings. She maintained the evaluation's independence but invested significant time in making the link with evidence crystal clear and led her briefing to a multistakeholder group with a question: "Here is where the data took us. Look at what we found—what do you think it means?"

This type of intended use is one that presents (or should present) an important ethical challenge for ECMs and EIMs. How do you perform your job ethically without compromising your career? If you get such a directive (sometimes hidden in diplomatic language), a possible strategy is to involve other senior or independent stakeholders in carrying the burden of opposition. We know this is hard and that you are asked to walk the cross-section of being impartial while aligned with the evaluation values, and you must remain committed to telling the evaluation story without glossing over nuances and being clear about what you know and being honest about what you do not know.

9.3 WHAT DRIVES EVALUATION USE AND INFLUENCE

There are four areas that all evaluation managers, whether ECMs or EIMs, must pay attention to in promoting evaluation use and influence in their evaluations (Asian Development Bank, 2022; Patton & Cambell-Patton, 2021; The UNICEF Evaluation Office et al., 2020):

1. context and politics: being contextually knowledgeable, strategic, and politically savvy as well as being able to adapt to changing contexts
2. strategic intent and influencers: aligning method choices with intent to influence and engaging influencers throughout the evaluation process, what Patton and Cambell-Patton (2021) refer to as the "full journey stance."
3. process and stakeholder engagement: engaging intended users and building trust
4. evaluation culture and capacity: promoting organizational and institutional readiness to use evaluation and creating trust in evaluators and data

As we reflect on this list, we can see that some of these factors are better managed by ECMs (e.g., context and capacity) while others are driven by EIMs (e.g., process and stakeholder engagement) and supported by ECMs. But really, both ECMs and EIMs will do better in every one of these areas of responsibility in collaboration.

Finally, we have a disclaimer: In performing well in these areas of use and influence, we intend to equip all evaluation managers to lean into the responsibility for use and influence and manage risks of lost opportunities or misuse. However, nothing can guarantee maximal use and influence or prevent nonuse and misuse of evaluation. We suggest stepping into this part of evaluation management by being fully attentive and vigilant rather than using the directive management suggested in earlier chapters of this book.

9.4 MANAGING CONTEXT AND POLITICS

All evaluation managers work within a political context and must be able to read the subtext and interpret the explicit and tacit goals of the evaluation. Even when there is widespread agreement among evaluation stakeholders, evaluation is an intervention that has a political dimension that all evaluation managers need to navigate. Carol Weiss (1993) was an early pioneer on this topic, contributing important insights into the deeply political nature of evaluation use and influence:

> The assumption is that by providing "the facts," evaluation assists decision-makers to make wise choices among future courses of action. . . . But evaluation is a rational enterprise that takes place in a political context. . . .
>
> Knowing that political constraints and resistances exist is not a reason for abandoning evaluation research; rather it is a precondition for usable evaluation research. Only when the evaluator has insight into the interests and motivations of other actors in the system, into the roles that he himself [sic] is consciously or inadvertently playing, the obstacles and opportunities that impinge upon the evaluative effort, and the limitations and possibilities for putting the results of evaluation

> to work—only with sensitivity to the politics of evaluation research—can the evaluator be as creative and strategically useful as he should be. (pp. 93–94)

This early advice has never been more important. We are now deep into an era where technology and social media amplify the viral propagation of information, misinformation, and disinformation within and among organizations and social networks. The social media whirlwind dramatically intensifies political forces, which can often derail good, evidence-informed decision making. And yet, these fast-moving and far-reaching information channels and social networks can also be used to our advantage. That is easier said than done, but a good starting point is some strategic forethought and a good understanding of how persuasion and social influence work. ECMs need to liaise with communication and knowledge management professionals appropriately to select the right channels of communication and media.

Most ECMs and EIMs are not in a position to decide what types of use and influence to prioritize. It might be tempting to avoid the question of use and influence by thinking, "This is above my pay grade," but as we discussed above, this may result in missed opportunities for greater value-for-money evaluation. It might also be tempting to decide on evaluation use and influence goals based on what the ECM or EIM deems appropriate. The risk here is that an individual evaluation manager's understanding will inevitably be partial and have significant blind spots. So, it is best to get input from senior managers and other stakeholders by enabling conversations among them. This facilitated transparency will help ECMs and EIMs identify areas of agreement and areas of potential conflict, which will inform their use and influence strategy.

Through engagement and listening, evaluation managers aim to understand what drives evaluation use and influence in their evaluation or evaluative endeavor. A useful activity would be to map the different perspectives on evaluation use and influence by stakeholder group and then identify what might be most controversial and what possibilities of misuse might need to be avoided. Then, ECMs and EIMs can settle on a common use and influence strategy, and EIMs should advise the evaluation team accordingly.

9.5 MANAGING THE PROCESS AND STAKEHOLDER ENGAGEMENT

The way the ECM or EIM drives use and influence is through attention to and intentionality in the process of evaluation. This is different from process use (learning and clarity that evaluation actors derive from participating in evaluation); it is about actively making choices with the intent to set up an evaluation to be used and influential. We have emphasized managing the process in every chapter in this book so far, including in developing the TOR in commissioning organizations (Chapter 2); managing each part of the evaluation start-up process (Chapter 4); the way we establish the roles, relationships, and communication between evaluation actors (Chapters 4 and 5); team planning and management (Chapter 5), and monitoring and communication throughout the evaluation (Chapters 6, 7, and 8).

With engagement and judicious transparency, ECMs and EIMs aim to make evaluation use and influence a *joint responsibility*. For external evaluations, this is the joint responsibility of the ECM and EIM; for internal evaluations, it is the joint responsibility of internal evaluators and program leaders. Neither side can make it happen on its own, but together, they can excel at it. When all evaluation managers and program leaders recognize their interdependence and work together on the evaluation process, we believe that evaluations' chances of being useful increase significantly (Forss et al., 2002). And, by making evaluation use a joint endeavor, the evaluation manager will be sharing the credit and will avoid being left holding the bag if things go wrong.

Optimizing evaluation use and influence starts well before a particular evaluation is even conceptualized, then starts again when the TOR is put together, then starts yet again on the first day the EIM and evaluation team begin their work. ECMs and EIMs have many opportunities to promote use and drive influence over the course of the evaluation process: when the TOR is organized by the ECM, when the proposal is being developed by the proposal writer, in the start-up of the evaluation contract, in the convening of stakeholders during a site visit, at the outset of a data analysis and synthesis meeting, and so on. This does not mean that the evaluation will be modified constantly; it means that the ECM or EIM will keep an open mind about what might emerge that informs evaluation use. As a result of this heightened awareness of use, evaluation managers will be alert to a deepening nuanced understanding of the different perspectives on evaluation use and the factors that influence the ability of the evaluation to communicate its intentions, findings, and recommendations clearly.

An important first step for any evaluation—which typically occurs during but is not limited to the inception phase—is a series of meetings with stakeholders to discuss the purposes of the evaluation. Ensuring the right people attend is the responsibility of both the ECM and the EIM. Be sure to include not only those holding the purse strings (i.e., the budget holders who have commissioned the evaluation) and those in positions of power. It is important to proactively seek out all important groups of potential evaluation users, especially those who have been sidelined in the past. Communities and others who would be potentially impacted by the evaluation are often left out of these discussions because they do not have influence over decisions about the policy or program. But in a vibrant, democratic society, evaluation can provide a great opportunity to shift that power imbalance and bring in some much-needed expertise about how well things are working on the ground.

As with any part of the evaluation, this early engagement is not about gathering stakeholder views and doing exactly as they ask. The expertise of the EIM and the evaluation team, particularly their understanding of evaluation use and influence, can help them read between the lines and identify opportunities and priorities for use and influence that ECMs and other evaluation participants may not have considered. This type of stakeholder engagement facilitates instrumental, process, and conceptual use.

An important outcome of early stakeholder meetings is to get organizational and community stakeholders to take the lead on evaluation use in collaboration with the evaluation team (whether they are internal, external, or a hybrid). That leadership needs to be proactive and happen throughout the evaluation; it is not something we tack on the end.

Discussions about evaluation use and influence are not a one-off "done and dusted" series of meetings at the front end. Rather, they will be part of an iterative check-in process that helps keep the evaluation relevant and useful throughout its course.

9.6 DEVELOPING AN EVALUATION USE AND INFLUENCE STRATEGY

Evaluation use and influence does not magically happen, as we all know from experience. If we truly need evaluation to be both used and influential—which, of course we do—it is important to think through exactly what kinds of use and influence we need and how we are going to make that happen. Thinking strategically and being intentional is another strategy to facilitate instrumental, process, and conceptual use.

Although most clients and evaluation teams will ideally have done some thinking about use and influence while scoping and commissioning the evaluation and writing proposals, the real core of this thinking happens during and after the early meetings with stakeholders, some of which take place with the ECM in developing and determining the evaluation scope, and others in discussions about the evaluation design with the EIM and evaluation team.

Here are a few high-level questions[1] to help ECMs and EIMs figure out what is needed:

1. *What kinds of use and influence* are needed from this evaluation, and why?
2. Ultimately, *who needs to use the evaluation* insights or be influenced and in what ways?
3. What is the *time frame* for any needed use and influence?
4. What is most *important* among different kinds of use and influence? What are the priorities here?

What kinds of use and influence? As EIMs speak with stakeholders, review any relevant documentation and understand the background and context, observe, listen, and intuit which of the different kinds of use and influence are most needed. Zoom out and consider the political context (both in the larger social environment and in organizations), which can be a major factor in evaluation use. Remember, not all these use and influence needs will be top-of-mind for stakeholders. In some cases, the evaluation makes clear the values that need to be upheld in the evaluation and that must drive evaluation use. For example, in UN Women's evaluations, a common evaluation use and influence goal is the inclusion of most marginalized women's groups.

So, what types of use and influence should evaluation managers target? In Patton and Campbell-Patton (2021), the utilization-focused evaluation framework tackles a higher-level use: the realm of evaluation's relevance to global social and environmental issues—equity, climate change, and social justice deliberately leading with principles-focused evaluation to drive positive change as its utilization goal. Evaluation managers who are clear on the principles and values prioritized in the evaluation should consider how to drive use and influence accordingly.

Who needs to use the evaluation? Patton (2008) articulated the concept of *primary intended users*—the specific subgroup of stakeholders who will potentially use the evaluation to inform decisions, thinking, design, and/or action. This is the nub of the "Who needs to use the evaluation insights or be influenced by the evaluation?" question. Remember to think through each different kind of use and influence and add a "by whom" to it. Use systems thinking to identify potential unintended consequences

[1] Adaptation of a set of questions is from a United Kingdom Department for International Development (DFID) learning module on evaluation use and influence, developed by Jane Davidson. Used with permission.

within and outside a program's boundaries and encourage the evaluation to create room for a more holistic understanding of impact (remember Figure 1.1). For example, if a program funds road building that might divert economic activity away from nonprogram communities to program communities, involving nonprogram community representatives in the evaluation will help explore possible unintended, harmful consequences.

What is the time frame for use and influence? A common barrier to evaluation use is that the evaluation process (from conception to reporting) often takes too long, and the insights are not available in time to feed into key decision points or discussions. To avoid this problem, ask specifically about any upcoming decisions, meetings, or policy development processes that are looming on the horizon. Find out what kinds of insights might usefully feed into those, in what form (to make the best sense to the audience), and on what timeline.

What is most important? It is easy to create a massive evaluation use and influence laundry list. Indeed, wouldn't it be great if the evaluation was useful and influential in *all* of those ways? In fact, aiming for everything will likely spread resources too thin. The smart move is to figure out which of those uses (and for whom) are most important and should therefore be prioritized. This can be hard when goals are unclear or there are too many of them—and pursuing too many things with limited resources means none will be achieved. Thus, based on input from organizational leadership and early stakeholder engagement, ECMs should map stakeholder perspectives on use and influence and do their best to align the use strategy with a vision of positive change for different stakeholder groups and the planet. Then ECMs can reach out to those with the authority to help prioritize, approve, and support these goals.

Based on this map of stakeholder perspectives, the goals and values of the evaluation and the organization, and guidance from senior leaders, the ECM is now ready to articulate a use and influence strategy for the evaluation in relation to the program, organization, community, network, and the planet.

9.7 INVOLVING KEY INFLUENCERS IN EVALUATION

Central to any highly effective use and influence strategy is stakeholder involvement (Patton, 2008). There is no good substitute for being part of the evaluation process as a way of truly understanding the evidence and being motivated to act on the insights gained.

There are two real-world challenges for stakeholder involvement. The first is that very few evaluation commissioners, programs, and community organizations are willing to release leaders and staff for the very significant amount of time it would take to be involved in the entire evaluation process. Second, even if they could, the reality is that there are typically many more people who need to use and be influenced by the evaluation than can ever feasibly be directly involved.

So, what can we do instead?

Here is where we introduce the concept of *key influencers*.[2] This term has been used in marketing and communications to refer to people who already have the attention and trust of a business's target audience. When they speak, people listen and act.

We are not usually looking for charismatic personalities to influence evaluation stakeholders but rather people who have personal connections with those we are seeking to influence. This idea dates back to some seminal research on the role people play in the flow on mass communication that was made by Paul Lazarsfeld, the pioneering social researcher after whom the American Evaluation Association's most prestigious theory award is named (Katz & Lazarsfeld, 2017).

Let's apply the key influencer concept to evaluation involvement:

1. To help make the evaluation useful and influential, who needs to be directly involved in the evaluation? Who in our stakeholder networks do people really listen to and trust? [These are the key influencers.]
2. Key influencers are not only there to help us disseminate findings. They can also help enhance the evaluation's validity (with their expertise), its credibility (with their reputation), and its social justice (through their expertise, lived experience, and/or ability to represent the interests of marginalized groups).
3. Where and how should we involve these key influencers in the evaluation process? What is the most judicious use of each key influencer's time to make their involvement both worthwhile for them and valuable for the evaluation? Which of these will be most important, and why?

The fundamental idea here is this: People are most likely to believe and act on something when they hear it from a person they know and trust (as opposed to a distant source). Within any organization, community, or network, some people are more well-known and better trusted than others. They are the influencers in general. Involving key influencers facilitates persuasive and conceptual as well as process and instrumental use.

When we think specifically of our primary intended users and who most strongly influences them, that is our group of key influencers for that particular evaluation. If we need to be selective about who to involve directly in evaluation (because we cannot involve everyone), then involving those key influencers is going to give us the most powerful return on that investment.

9.7.1 How Do We Identify the Key Influencers?

To identify the key influencers, it helps to approach this task from several angles:

- *Who are the people you most need to influence with this evaluation?* These are the primary intended users. Who do these people listen to the most, especially when it comes to getting them on board with a new way of thinking or doing things? Consider not only influencers in formal positions of power but also those whose views hold sway around the water cooler.

[2] The next few sections draw on a piece of work Jane did with the UK Department for International Development, which included developing a learning module for their [non-evaluator] leaders on how to scope, commission, and support influential evaluation. Involvement of key influencers in evaluation was laid out in that module.

- *Who needs to be involved to ensure the evaluation is seen as credible and fair in the eyes of those who ultimately need to be influenced?* Answer this question from the perspective of each important audience for the evaluation.
- *Who is best placed to persuade the target audiences and to help disseminate evaluation insights and findings?* Again, do not think this is the job of the communications department and stop there; instead, think of those who have a platform for speaking with people about the kinds of issues this evaluation is likely to raise.
- *Who has the formal power and authority to change systems and processes, if needed?* Instrumental use in particular is more likely to happen in the hands of people who have the authority to make that change without first having to persuade several other people.

Now, before ECMs and EIMs begin engaging influencers, look at who is already present and vocal in this evaluation. It is much harder to engage a disinterested potential influencer than to enlist one who is already involved. Having said that, be sure not to fall into the trap of only thinking positively about influencers. Key influencers can be obstructive and destructive as well as constructive.

- Who are likely to be the most vocal and influential critics of the evaluation?
- Who could potentially derail or undermine any positive change if they were unconvinced about the validity or credibility of the evaluation?
- For those who are likely to be critical of the evaluation or any changes arising from it, whose expertise or perspective do they most trust and respect?

It is the ECM's and EIM's job not only to engage influencers but to manage them, to earn their respect and confidence in the evaluation, to manage their expectations, to enforce appropriate boundaries, to protect the independence of the evaluation team, and to respond to their feedback.

As we mentioned in Chapter 2, it is important to ensure that the group of people working on the evaluation will bring together expertise in evaluation, context, culture, and subject matter. At the same time, when putting together a credible team with the right expertise, consider which groups have a *right* to be involved in the evaluation not only because of the value of their expertise but also for reasons of social justice (Ghanbarpour et al., 2020). Which groups have a right to ensure their voices and values are privileged and heard and that their expertise and perspectives are acknowledged and used? Consider the following:

- *Indigenous peoples.* The United Nations Declaration on the Rights of Indigenous Peoples (United Nations, 2017) affirms Indigenous peoples' right to self-determination and to participating in decisions and actions that affect them.
- *Historically underserved and/or marginalized groups.* First and most obviously, an evaluation process that further marginalizes people would be an incredibly poor starting point for figuring out how a program, policy, or system should be better meeting their needs. Second, equitable outcomes cannot be achieved

without a deep understanding of why the current approaches have persistently failed the same groups of people, often for generations. Exclude that expertise from the table—or include it at token levels—and not only do you destroy validity, but credibility will be gone as well.

- *Advocacy groups for those with limited ability to speak for themselves* (e.g., children, frail elderly, people with severe illnesses or disabilities). In including these groups, make sure they have the support they need to fully participate in the evaluation.

9.7.2 Where and How Should We Involve Key Influencers?

Once the key influencers have been identified, the next step is to figure out where in the evaluation process to involve them. As we mentioned before, it is very unusual to be able to take a group of stakeholders through an entire evaluation process. When such high involvement is a requirement, it tends to rule out direct involvement of senior managers. However, with a more strategic approach, there are ways to involve different people in different parts of the evaluation. That way, many people get a taste of the evaluation, but no one has to commit to an unreasonable amount of time.

Figure 9.1 shows some of the many different places in the evaluation where we might wish to involve people.

Who might be considered for each of the above? While there's no cut-and-dried answer that will fit all evaluations, Table 9.1 should serve as a useful guide.

The final step is to figure out how best to involve the people selected. Do not assume. Ask people what they are most interested in, how much time they have to devote to the evaluation, and what kind of engagement process works best for them.

ECMs should ask, what is the most judicious use of each key influencer's time to make the evaluation experience worthwhile for them as well as making its insights

FIGURE 9.1 ■ Opportunities for Stakeholder Engagement in the Evaluation Process

TABLE 9.1 ■ Types of Stakeholders to Engage at Various Points in the Evaluation Process

Involvement Point	Stakeholders to Consider
Evaluation steering committee	Decision makers at strategic and operational levels, community leaders involved in the program, advocacy groups, evaluation and subject matter experts
Developing evaluation questions	Decision makers at strategic and operational levels, program staff, program participants, community members, policy and program designers, people potentially experiencing unintended positive or negative consequences
Developing a theory of change	Policy experts, local context and culture experts, subject matter experts, on-the-ground implementers, program participants, people potentially experiencing unintended positive or negative consequences
Defining *quality, value*, and *success*	Policy and operational leaders, program participants, Indigenous groups, others familiar with the community context, culture, needs, and aspirations, program staff, policy and program designers, people potentially experiencing unintended positive or negative consequences
Developing evidence-capturing instruments	Monitoring staff, anyone skeptical about the program or the evaluation
Gathering evidence	Those who need to see for themselves to understand and believe, those in a good position to capture the evidence as part of their regular work, those who maintain monitoring databases that will be used in the evaluation
Evaluative sensemaking	Decision makers at strategic and operational levels, policy and program designers, program staff, program participants (or those close to them), people potentially experiencing unintended positive or negative consequences, internal evaluators
Co-presenting and sharing findings	Senior leaders, excellent presenters and persuaders, whoever you will need to engage to be most influential with each audience
Action planning and developing recommendations	Those who will lead and implement subsequent change [They know what's feasible, helping design the change will ensure they will own it.]

credible, valid, reflective of all relevant voices, and maximally influential? How will you know if you got this wrong? Important people will either not show up to the meetings at all, or if they do, they'll have their laptops out, going through emails while supposedly listening to you in the background. How will you know you got this right? Important people will participate, ask hard questions, and open doors. ECMs and EIMs need to work together to make sure key influencers are involved strategically so that the evaluation benefits from their engagement. Caution: Important people may also try to take the evaluation in places that were not intended, so do not get caught in between formal organizational leaders and powerful influencers.

A final note: Engaging people takes time, including the time of the evaluation team, so budget for it, prioritize, and be strategic.

9.8 STRENGTHENING EVALUATION CULTURE AND CAPACITY WHILE FACILITATING EVALUATION USE

We have devoted a whole chapter on evaluation culture and capacity (Chapter 10). Of particular importance to ECMs is the recognition that evaluation use and influence continues well after the completion of evaluation. Even when other evaluation management tasks end at the end of a specific evaluation, the ECM's job may continue with not only report dissemination but also briefings, facilitated conversations, blog writing, participation in meetings about new strategies, and so on. The ECM will need to become a voice for that evaluation, so if you are in that role, use intentional language, do not use hyperbole, tell the evaluation story and make room for the many stories it contains, convey nuance and uncertainty, and if you are not sure, say so.

Long-term efforts to ensure evaluation use also reinforce the culture of evaluation and build evaluation capacity among others in the organization. Here are four examples of practices that build evaluation culture and capacity (in order of from least to most investment required), while facilitating evaluation use.

1. *A follow-up meeting six months later*. An activity that encourages evaluation use and influence is to place the topic of a past evaluation on a regular meeting about six months after its completion and see what has happened since then and how it relates to the evaluation's content. Even as an EIM, Tessie has frequently asked for 30-minute structured calls with past evaluation clients between six months to a year after an evaluation. These calls always resulted in learning for the evaluation teams, and evaluation clients also appreciated them.

   There are many ways to think about and design a post evaluation follow-up engagement, some of which are quite pedestrian and not particularly useful. Do not default to simply checking whether recommendations were implemented. Instead, circle back to the various kinds of use that were identified earlier in the process—instrumental use, conceptual use, and process use—with questions such as the following (Patton & Cambell-Patton, 2021):

   - In what ways and how extensively were the evaluation findings used to improve or refine an existing policy or program; to decide whether to purchase, support, expand, continue, scale back, or close something down; and/or to inform the design and development of something as it was built?
   - How helpful was the evaluation in changing people's understandings by giving them new ideas or insights about the program/policy/project and/or the issues it addresses?
   - How effectively have the evaluation findings been used to legitimize and mobilize endorsement for a position or course of action and/or to delegitimize endorsement for an erroneous view that is clearly not supported by the evidence? (Alkin, 2017)
   - How helpful was participation in the evaluation process for building useful capacity for the individuals, groups, communities, and organizations that were involved?

2. *Formal procedures for follow-up after evaluations are submitted.* United Nations organizations require a formal management response in an Excel format by recommendation. This file is then used as a checklist and reviewed over the year

to see what actions have been taken. The executive management must give this to the board of directors. Although no formality will oblige resistant evaluation participants to do what they do not wish to do, the process gives the evaluation results added visibility and reinforces the importance of evaluation in the organization. It also gives an opportunity for proponents of change to keep insisting on recommended and agreed changes.

3. *Meta-evaluations and synthesis evaluations*. Some evaluation commissioners engage in meta-evaluations or in synthesis evaluations seeking to learn from evaluation, improve evaluation quality, and use evaluation to think more strategically. Tessie's company has been involved in such work, and it makes the investment in evaluation visibly useful to organizations. The United States Agency for International Development (USAID) disseminates its lessons from synthesis evaluations widely, and they have resulted in significant insights for program staff.

4. *Multiyear companion evaluations*. At a higher level of evaluation investment are multiyear evaluations with explicit learning, monitoring, and program improvement goals. These contracts are companions to funded initiatives and perform monitoring and evaluation activities that are used by those initiatives. Examples include the USAID's Monitoring, Learning and Evaluation five-year contracts (discussed in Chapter 10), the four-year contract of the African Science Academy Initiative that Tessie led for the National Academies of Medicine (then named Institute of Medicine), and the MacArthur Foundation's multiyear evaluation contract that accompanied their grantee funding in Nigeria. As we discuss in Chapter 10, this depends on the evaluation system of the commissioner. These long-term contracts facilitate evaluation use but also reinforce the role of evaluation in the organization and, with the ongoing collaboration, build evaluation capacity among program staff.

Ultimately, the degree and type of evaluation use determines the value-for-money of evaluation—whether the evaluation matters. Funders elected to invest in evaluation instead of adding funds to the project or supporting another initiative in the organization. This investment makes sense only if the evaluation produces useful knowledge, insights, clarity, new ways of perceiving the program and stakeholder roles, new networks and coalitions, and actions on recommendations with confidence about the way forward. Evaluation use is not only a desirable consideration for all evaluation managers but is also necessary for a successful evaluation.

PRACTICE

With an emphasis on evaluation use, some colleagues worry that evaluators are stepping into roles of facilitation, strategic planning, and communication that are not appropriate for them. What do you think? How can ECMs and EIMs lean toward being strategic and drive for influence, and at the same time defend the evaluation's independence and not taking one side? (Hint: Consider the evolution of evaluation competencies in your response.)

10 BUILDING EVALUATION MANAGEMENT CAPACITY FOR EVALUATION COMMISSIONERS

WHO SHOULD USE THIS CHAPTER

This chapter focuses on an evaluation commissioning manager's (ECM's) role to develop individual and organizational evaluation management capacity within their own organization, a role that, although less visible outside the organization, significantly influences that organization's success in commissioning and managing value-for-money evaluations. Evaluation implementing managers (EIMs) may also have a supporting role by conducting audits of evaluation units and facilitating evaluation capacity activities in organizations. The EIM's biggest contribution to organizational evaluation capacity, however, is in the way they engage organizational stakeholders during an evaluation, thus demonstrating the value of evaluation in real time.

How can an organization that commissions and uses evaluation excel in it? If the intention is to manage evaluation to enable learning from it, improve programming and organizational performance, make good decisions, and report effectively to stakeholders (including the public), then how can ECMs set things up for success? As we have mentioned before in this book, 100% of the value of an evaluation lies in how much it is used and influential. To that end, it matters a great deal where and how the evaluation is housed and where it lands—in fertile organizational soil where it can contribute to learning and growth or on a forgotten shelf?

In Chapter 2, we covered in some detail how to define and scope good evaluations, develop clear and complete terms of reference (TOR), and select strong evaluation teams. Looking beyond any specific evaluation, what generates a strong appetite for evaluation more generally? The answers lie in the systems, structures, leadership, know-how, and organizational culture that comprise an organization's evaluation and learning system. In this chapter, we review how ECMs can improve evaluation management at an organizational level so they can get the most out of their evaluation investment.

Looking at the organizational level, we pose the following four questions:

- What does a strong evaluation system look like?
- How do you build an evaluation culture?

- What evaluation competencies are needed at different levels of the organization (leadership, evaluation office, program managers, implementing partners and grantees)?
- At the operational level, how do you develop a strategic plan for evaluation, monitor quality, and strengthen the evaluation function?

10.1 BUILDING A STRONG EVALUATION SYSTEM

A useful way to think about organizational systems is by using the metaphor of an iceberg, divided into levels. This encourages us not only to think of the more obvious surface features, but also the less-tangible elements that lie deeper within the organizational culture.

At the top level, above the surface of the water, are the visible aspects of an evaluation and learning system. These include various artifacts that guide evaluation and organizational learning such as a vision statement for evaluation, a strategic evaluation plan, the positioning of evaluation units within or throughout the organizational structure, evaluation leadership, personnel, and resources to support them all (Preskill & Catsambas, 2006).

Below the water's surface and less visible is a strong evaluation system that will position the evaluation function strategically and close to the organization's leadership, particularly those leading organizational strategy. In addition, deep evaluation expertise, evaluation-savvy leadership, and robust resourcing of evaluation and learning sets the organization up for success and sends a clear message to its members that we truly care about how effectively we are making changes and that evaluation is essential to the success of the organization.

Too often, the evaluation function is tucked away in a "miscellaneous" section of the organization's structure alongside a mishmash of unrelated central functions. Worse, we have frequently seen it positioned several rungs down the organizational hierarchy. Not only does this send a message that evaluation is not that important, but it also means that evaluative input into strategic decisions needs to pass through multiple layers of bureaucracy, typically consisting of people who are not deeply familiar with evaluation and are weak advocates for it. Not surprisingly, in these cases, evaluative insights rarely feed into strategic thinking or strategy adaptation under such an organizational structure.

10.1.1 Where Should the Evaluation Function Be Positioned, Ideally?

The optimal positioning of the evaluation function differs by organization type and structure. Its positioning has implications for the types and number of evaluations undertaken and the relevance and return on investment of these evaluations to the organization. The overriding principle is that evaluation should be positioned as closely as possible to those making the key decisions it is expected to inform. Position it close to those responsible for implementation and it will primarily inform operational decisions. Place it close to a knowledge management and learning function and it will likely be driven by learning agendas. Locate it alongside those responsible for policy and strategy formulation and adaptation and you will see evaluative thinking more powerfully infused into strategic direction. If you want it to play all these roles and more, consider creative ways of planting evaluative expertise in multiple layers and functions of the organization.

Foundations and Nonprofit Organizations

In foundations and large nonprofit organizations, the best positioning we have seen is in top leadership: typically, a director of evaluation and learning (or similar job title) who reports directly to the chief executive officer (CEO), is a core member of the senior management team, and regularly interacts with governors and the board. The only downside of this strategic positioning is its possible distance from the operational side, including serving grantees and communities. Some organizations address this by assigning a member of the evaluation team to work closely with each of its programmatic or policy teams. This combination of strategic positioning and operational access and responsiveness can provide great opportunities for evaluation to be useful and influential in both spheres and for each to inform the other. In practice, we have seen organizations shift the positioning of evaluation with each new leader. In one of the larger foundations, we saw evaluation shift from reporting to the CEO to being tucked away seven layers below. Such dramatic sidelining of evaluation has huge symbolic implications in the message it sends leaders and staff about what really matters.

Sometimes, there is an advantage to locating the evaluation team alongside another centralized function. For example, a natural synergy can often be found with strategy, where evaluative thinking and frameworks can be incredibly powerful. When positioned alongside strategy, evaluation can help with strategic analysis and deepen an organization's understanding of the nature and severity of the baseline situation that the organization seeks to change. It can also help identify the deeper structural issues and root causes that must be addressed for change to succeed (e.g., structural racism or a policy environment and financial sector that permit and incentivize the plundering and destruction of natural resources). Other useful ways in which evaluation dovetails with strategy include helping to formulate a coherent organizational strategy grounded in a plausible theory of strategic change, conducting systems baselining to document the starting point for strategic change, and monitoring and learning from the change as it develops and unfolds.

Another frequent positioning of evaluation is in combination with the organizational learning function. Typically, when evaluation sits alongside organizational learning, commissioned evaluations include learning questions that feed into the broader learning agenda of the organization; for example, a foundation focused on building equity regularly includes in its evaluation learning questions about the factors and strategies that promote equity and lead to sustainable strengthening of more under-resourced grantees. Finally, evaluation might be positioned with knowledge management and communications, which has some similarities to positioning it with organizational learning and influences the organization's public brand, enhances staff recruitment, and increases the public influence of the organization.

United Nations (UN) Agencies

Most United Nations (UN) organizations have an evaluation office, but there are significant variations in the positioning and roles of those offices. Some evaluation offices are designated as "independent" evaluation offices that report to the board of governors such as the World Food Programme (WFP) and the United Nations Development Programme. In contrast, the United Nations Children's Fund (UNICEF) evaluation office does not include "independent" in its title, and the UNICEF executive director (i.e., the executive, not the board) appoints the director of evaluation.

In the case of UN Women, around 2013, its office of evaluation merged with the audit function into a new office called Independent Evaluation and Audit Services. This action seemed driven by resource limitations and had clear implications for the role of evaluation in the organization. The naming, reporting, and placement of the evaluation function in UN agencies has implications for the power, independence, resourcing, and role of evaluation. It could be a major problem to place evaluation together with audit, which implies that those making that decision see the two as more or less the same. The ECMs frequently answer to a manager whose expertise is in audit and who may subtly influence ECMs to narrow their scope to verification rather than evaluation. Audit findings are linear and clear, recommendations are typically nonnegotiable, and their adoption is enforced by regulation. In evaluation, we deal in complexity, polarities, perspectives, trade-offs, and the unknown. Typically, evaluation use is not mandated by law nor can it rely on compliance alone. In the end, evaluators who work under audit may end up giving up or leaving, and that would be a true loss to the organization.

Besides placement, another variation in UN evaluation offices is the role that evaluation staff play in commissioning and conducting evaluations. The WFP evaluation office, for example, has grown significantly over the years and is focused on commissioning (rather than conducting) evaluation. The office emphasizes and leads significant evaluation capacity-building efforts to enable countries to commission their own program evaluations while the evaluation office directly commissions larger, cross-country, impact evaluations with learning agendas informed by WFP's strategy. In contrast, the United Nations Population Fund (UNFPA) evaluation office does not commission others to do evaluations but is involved directly in leading, managing, and conducting evaluations from planning and design to data collection, analysis, and report writing. Members of the evaluation office are hands-on, acting as team leaders or team members in evaluations. UNFPA evaluations are also informed by organizational strategy, and the learning needs of programs (e.g., looking at areas that have not been evaluated in the last five years). The variation in evaluation staff roles demonstrates that one size does not fit all; choices in the role and operation of an evaluation office are driven by organization size, mandates, and history.

Government

Governments are major funders and commissioners of evaluation, so understanding and strengthening the housing and administration of evaluations in government and the way national and local systems value evaluation has important implications for society as well as how government evaluation agencies and ministries prioritize evaluations. Let us discuss these three aspects: positioning and structure, the way national and local systems value evaluation, and how evaluation units set evaluation priorities.

(a) Positioning of evaluation in government organizations. The positioning of evaluation in government agencies and ministries differs depending on the way current legislation supports or hinders transparency and freedom of speech, its strength in protecting civil rights, and its demand of accountability in government services. Here are some examples of the authorizing environment for evaluation in different national governments:

- In the U.S. federal government, evaluation is placed throughout government institutions: in independent agencies such as the General Accountability Office and within agencies such as the evaluation office in the Program, Policy and Learning Bureau of the U.S. Agency for International Development (USAID). In 2019, the U.S. government passed the 2018 Evidence Act, a law that requires all agencies to establish evaluation units and engage in more evaluation, increase the use of big data in evaluation, and build evaluation capacity across the public sector.
- In Canada, the treasury board secretariat establishes the evaluation policy (most recently in 2016), requiring a five-year departmental evaluation plan that covers, among other items, all programs of grants and contributions with annual average expenditures at or above $5M per year over five years.
- In Sri Lanka, evaluation has been positioned in the Department of Project Management and Monitoring under the Ministry of Finance. There are no Monitoring and Evaluation (M&E) units within ministries and departments, while planning units are tasked to handle M&E. These planning units are established in each ministry, department, province, and district and administered under the Department of Planning, which is also under the Ministry of Finance.
- In Brazil, the evaluation function is spread through several different government agencies at the federal level. A Policy Monitoring and Evaluation Council coordinates and approves resource allocation for evaluation, and the Secretary for Evaluation and Information Management coordinates M&E of public policies connected to the Ministry of Citizenship (formerly the Ministry of Social Development); some ministries have their own evaluation function (e.g., in education and health).
- In South Africa, evaluation at the national level is led by the national Department of Planning, Monitoring and Evaluation, which develops national policy and systems and leads on priority evaluations. It partners with sector departments that are also responsible for undertaking departmental evaluations within their sector.
- In Japan, evaluation has been positioned as a major policy support function for some decades, primarily to reduce unnecessary costs and work on administrative reform and to promote evidence-based policymaking, particularly in the last decade. The Ministry of Internal Affairs and Communications has a division tasked to work on government-wide evaluation standards, align evaluation practice in different ministries, hold expert committees, and run a web portal site (https://www.soumu.go.jp/main_sosiki/hyouka/seisaku_n/portal/index.html) to ensure transparency. The type of evaluation that is practiced is mostly performance measurement.

The placement of evaluation in the public sector and its emphasis has a major impact on the questions asked, the lessons learned, and the programs that are designed over time. In cases where evaluation is decentralized in different agencies and ministries, there might be variation in the standards for how evaluation is conducted—there might be more stability in ministry and agency evaluation units staffed by career civil servants, because those units are more protected from volatile national politics. In the end, however, no placement can protect evaluation from politics because evaluation is inherently a political activity.

What conclusions can we draw from reflecting on the placement of evaluation in national governments? In the United States (U.S.) and Canada, we see the important role of national legislation and requirements that have triggered significant investments in evaluation. In South Africa, we have seen provocative evaluations that have challenged the status quo, drawn national attention through the media, and informed future changes. In Sri Lanka, we have seen evaluation uses by parliament to advocate for change. In Japan, we see evaluation as a companion strategy to administrative reform. In Brazil, we have seen the evaluation coordinating agency increase or diminish its influence as a direct reflection of the elected government's views regarding the value of evaluation. For government agencies, drafting evaluation policy closely reflects the role, mission, and values of their organization while remaining consistent with existing legislation and any broader directives.

In the United States, where the evaluation function is well-embedded in government agencies, the placement of evaluation has tended to be more stable (i.e., its placement, staffing, and funding have changed gradually over the years, except for unusual circumstances). For example, in the early 2000s, the Centers for Disease Control increased its capacity in evaluation dramatically in response to the AIDS epidemic; it placed M&E advisers in country offices around the world to assess the AIDS epidemic, and it began to commission more sizable international evaluations. This coincided with the development and use of its "framework for program evaluation in public health" (Milstein & Wetterhall, 1999). In the United States, more recently, the 2018 Evidence Act that mandated evaluation offices be established in government agencies has stimulated the establishment of evaluation offices in agencies that had none.

(b) How national and local systems value evaluation. Let us now turn our attention to the second aspect: how national and local societies value evaluation. A legal framework that is positive toward evaluation is not enough.

In the United States, for example, we have seen a shift from valuing evaluation and scientific evidence to mistrusting it. In South Africa, we have seen examples of evaluations of national programs that created political pressure for change. And in Sri Lanka, we have seen the opposition government successfully use evaluation to advocate for their political position. How society views evaluation matters.

Tessie remembers a conversation with UN evaluators who ran a survey in their organization to see what made an evaluation most credible for their colleagues. The evaluation team fully expected that the response would be that a robust methodology is the most important factor for the credibility of evaluation; the resounding feedback from colleagues was, "I turn to the end of the report and see who was involved and who was consulted in the evaluation process, and that helps me decide if the evaluation was credible." Trust in the independence, impartiality, representation, and inclusive consultation of the evaluation is essential for evaluation to be used and, thus, useful. This public trust in the evaluation process is delicate and depends on the level of trust the public has in its political leadership and its public service. Government evaluation functions require a high level of transparency, protection of the politics of the day, avoiding sensationalism and the appearance of being partisan, and upholding of their reputation. Therefore, communicating effectively about their evaluation—its goals, process, and use—is an additional responsibility of government evaluation units.

(c) How evaluation units set evaluation priorities. A clear link between evaluation and strategy is mutually beneficial.

Earlier, we stated that it is best to have evaluation functions embedded in public institutions and invest authority in them to manage those functions. This delegation enables public institutions to pose and answer their own questions relevant to their programming. These evaluation units need to avoid getting stuck in quantification, alienation from program realities, or linear approaches that cannot support planning for what is needed beyond 12 months. There is sometimes a tendency to measure the things that can be measured rather than measuring what is important to the agency and the public. We recommend complementing training in quantitative methods with training in robust and inclusive qualitative evaluation to inform and be synthesized with larger quantitative analysis to ensure relevance, effective targeting, more accurate interpretation of findings, and inclusion of minority voices; for example, using rubrics (Davidson, 2005) enables contextually appropriate evidence to demonstrate they have achieved different levels of outcomes, using appreciative evaluation (Preskill & Catsambas, 2006) complements the problem analysis focus of many evaluations, and transformative evaluation (Mertens, 2008) prioritizes social justice. Analysis can focus on variation, positive deviance, and particular challenges and be flexible in pursuing emerging issues that need attention.

10.1.2 The Hybrid Decentralized Model of Evaluation

ECMs and their leaders must balance centrally placed evaluation capacity and leadership with evaluation that is embedded in different offices and programs. An organization may be allocating significant funds to evaluation but have a small evaluation office. To understand the true investment in evaluation of an organization, we need to look at both these aspects.

The Kellogg Foundation, for example, follows what it calls a hybrid model in which evaluation is "decentralized but not totally." The Kellogg Foundation has a central evaluation function, while program staff commission and manage evaluations for their programs at their level. The central evaluation function has some capacity to support these evaluations, while certain teams have funds to hire consultants who serve as evaluation liaisons with the central office and help manage the evaluation. The central evaluation office staff recommend evaluation scopes of work and approve the budget/contract amount for each evaluation, even though the program team does the management of the contract. Decentralizing program evaluations has allowed the director of evaluation to focus on cross-cutting evaluations. She also submits quarterly and annual reports to the board on the evidence of progress that is submitted in the director's performance review, which enables the board to monitor the "ends policies" (the long-term, visionary goals of the organization). The board uses this information to have in-depth conversations about the Kellogg Foundation's strategic choices.

The WFP evaluation system is also a hybrid decentralized model, in which country directors and staff are in charge of country-level evaluations (called *decentralized evaluations*), while the headquarters office in Rome manages corporate evaluations. For these decentralized (country) evaluations, the country director and staff decide which country programs to evaluate (in line with the stated requirements in each program), develop the TOR, and commission the evaluations. The WFP central office supports country-based evaluations through its regional evaluation advisers, who are placed in each region and support all countries in that region. The central WFP evaluation office manages corporate/global and regional or cross-country evaluations that are linked to the organization's knowledge management priorities and is also responsible for overall quality control of evaluations, evaluation capacity-building for the organization that includes evaluation training both online and in person, and the development and refinement of evaluation standards and guidelines.

As we reflect on the range of placement and structure of the evaluation function, these two hybrid models give us insight on some of the factors we should consider in placing evaluation. We urge evaluation commissioners to consider the following roles and tailor them to their own organizational context:

Headquarters/central evaluation office is responsible for the organization's evaluation policy, standards, philosophy, values, cross-cutting evaluations, corporate evaluations, facilitation of use by leadership, contributions to the learning agenda, quality control, encouragement, and evaluation capacity and for identifying and supporting evaluation champions.

Program offices are responsible for the evaluation of programs, stakeholder engagement, building evaluator networks, participating in learning agenda development and organizational learning, and being evaluation champions.

Knowledge management/communications/training divisions are facilitators/champions of learning and disseminate lessons from evaluation, provide input to evaluation priorities and evaluation questions, amplify messages from evaluation, and infuse evaluation conclusions into the narrative of the organization and the organizational brand.

Leadership sets goals and priorities for evaluation based on organizational strategy, uses evaluation results to inform strategy, engages key stakeholders in discussions using evidence from evaluation and through the evaluation process, and ensures the evaluation director is well informed and is a key supporter of learning and strategic positioning in the organization.

10.1.3 Evaluation Values, Vision, and Philosophy

You might find yourself wondering how important an evaluation vision and philosophy are to commissioning and delivering good evaluations. Could we not simply perform evaluations for important programs? The answer is this: An evaluation vision and philosophy influence the choices and investments in evaluation that organizations make. For example, if an organization's vision is to use evaluation for learning, it will prioritize learning questions and might develop good links between evaluation and knowledge management; if it values stakeholder involvement, it will engage evaluators most skilled in facilitation and collaborative evaluation; if it values efficiency, it will ask for methods that help illuminate resource use and value for money. Every question we ask costs money to answer, so although it would be great to have answers to all questions, that is not possible. The vision and philosophy clarify the role of evaluation and the questions the commissioning organization prioritizes.

Another question is how an organization sees those who implement its programs. Are implementers seen as partners, contractors, or vendors? Are implementers seen as inferior, vulnerable, and ignorant in relation to the commissioner or are they seen as smart, knowledgeable, and equal? One of Tessie's international clients did not include country office staff in a discussion on how to strengthen sharing evaluation knowledge across countries; when Tessie pointed this out, advocating for inclusion of country staff, she was told it was not convenient. When Tessie pressed the point again, she was given permission for pro forma and limited engagement. The rhetoric was inclusive, but the process was not. For those working with organizations to develop evaluation systems, it is critical to discuss organizational philosophy and values and to develop a vision for evaluation that aligns with them.

Another example of the importance of vision and philosophy can be seen in the evolution of USAID's evaluation policy from explicitly favoring randomized control trials (RCTs) as the gold standard to more wholistic language, asking for the selection of an appropriate method depending on the purpose of the evaluation. This language shift significantly influenced the type of evaluations undertaken by USAID and allowed them to answer evaluation questions that require methods other than RCTs.

10.2 EVALUATION CULTURE

How do you know that an organization has a strong evaluation culture? There are four things that all organizations with a strong evaluation culture have:

- commitment from the top
- transparency and shared meaning using evaluation
- a robust learning agenda
- learning about evaluation

10.2.1 Commitment from the Top

As explained above, leaders who support evaluation use it in developing strategy and making decisions. For important and complex decisions, these leaders choose not to guess or check with a few trusted advisers; instead, they commission evaluation—either internal or external—and use the evaluation process to engage stakeholders, listen to different inputs, and consider what different data sources and analyses reveal. They use evaluation to invite creative thinking and dialogue. When a decision has been reached, they use the data from evaluation to share and explain the merits of that decision to their organization and outside stakeholders.

Leaders who use evaluation appropriately carefully choose what to evaluate; they do not evaluate everything. Overusing evaluation might be a way to avoid or postpone making a decision. There should always be a balance between doing the work and evaluating it. So, the act of choosing what to evaluate is a key investment decision that needs deliberation and an explicit decision.

10.2.2 Transparency and Shared Meaning Using Evaluation

In organizations that use evaluation well, references to evaluation findings and conclusions are frequent. You will find them in strategies and reports, in presentations from different program units, and in operational support units. The plan for what will be evaluated is public, and evaluations are anticipated with some excitement. Jane and Tessie get very excited when clients urge us to accelerate our evaluation plan because it is needed to inform an upcoming decision; even when we argue against it, we are energized by this commitment to and visibility of evaluation in our client organization.

An example of transparency and shared meaning using evaluation can be found in USAID's Monitoring, Learning and Evaluation (MEL) contracts that are put in place to organize and administer all evaluation services for a USAID mission (or country office). The evaluation firms who are awarded a MEL contract work side-by-side with USAID's country leaders and program staff to embed evaluation throughout the country portfolio and to promote evaluation use throughout the program life cycle.

In a positive evaluation culture, the evaluation questions included in the TOR are ones that the organization is discussing. You hear it in planning or review meetings; staff have different points of view and concerns and colleagues anticipate the evaluation results to inform their conversation and decisions.

Organizations with a strong evaluation culture not only use evaluation but are more generally inclined to use data to inform and justify decisions.

10.2.3 A Robust Learning Agenda

A robust learning agenda is a more advanced element of an evaluation culture. Having a learning agenda means that an organization is not only using evaluation for programmatic decision making but also is thinking about the role of evaluation in long-term organizational learning. For example, the Ford Foundation's equity-focused programming included an investment in learning about what leads to effective and sustainable equity programming.

A robust learning agenda means that the organization is strategically identifying its knowledge gaps and planning on how to increase its effectiveness and efficiency in investing, programming, and organizational structure. Individual evaluations may be grouped into thematic areas or learning topics so they can benefit the organization over time. The organization then moves from doing individual evaluations to an evaluation strategy that looks at similar questions across projects and/or organizes its portfolio into clusters of similar projects that aim at systemic and sustainable impact. When organizations have a strong learning culture, this is usually coupled with a strong evaluation culture.

One of the best examples we have seen to date is the Laudes Foundation, which has developed an organizational learning agenda to focus its evaluative work. Each programmatic team developed its own learning questions, and then several others were added at the intervention, strategy, and mission levels. The learning agenda is driven by learning champions, one from each programmatic team and several from senior management. The learning champions are supported by a senior learning manager. Feeding into their work is an evidence synthesis and map that summarizes what is already known from both internal and external sources of evidence. The Laudes Foundation's organizational learning agenda is further informed by a systemwide theory of change as well as several sub-theories of change, which show how the Laudes Foundation seeks to effect change in different industries/sectors by influencing different system actors (policymakers; businesses; the financial sector; and workers, producers, and communities). A set of evaluative rubrics clarify what a successful system shift will look like on the key elements of the systemwide theory of change and are used to create a shared language across all evaluation work, which enables more productive cross-system learning conversations among the learning champions and with their colleagues and partner organizations. To support the learning process and to build organizational learning capacity, the Laudes Foundation commissioned a developmental evaluation to walk alongside the strategy and the work of the programmatic teams. It is rare to see such a thoughtful and comprehensive mix of organizational learning elements in the same organization. Thankfully, the Laudes Foundation is very generous in sharing what it has learned so that others seeking to effect change, especially in the same priority areas (equity and climate), can benefit from what it learns.

10.2.4 Learning About Evaluation

In organizations where leaders and staff rely on evaluation, it is clear that they need qualified evaluators—EIMs and ECMs—because they need good quality evaluations and evaluative thinking. These evaluators need to bring the best of the evaluation community to serve the organization, and this means engaging in professional organizations for evaluation, presenting and publishing about the organization's evaluation work, learning from others, and being part of networks of strong outside evaluators. If the investment in evaluation is serious, then learning about evaluation will be visible in the participation of the evaluation and program staff in evaluation conferences where they present their work and learn from experts and peers.

Being part of evaluation networks has the benefit of ongoing learning and enables the evaluation office to reach out to outside experts as needed for support in TOR development and evaluation implementation. When you consider the power of an outside evaluator to tell the story of your organization and programs, you can see how important it is to choose well.

10.3 EVALUATION COMPETENCIES FOR COMMISSIONERS OF EVALUATION

To enable wise allocation and management of evaluation funds, especially in a decentralized model, organizations need to develop capacity for evaluation management throughout the organization. Increased evaluation capacity in program staff will enable those staff to share in the management of evaluation; ideally, they will be strong partners to evaluation, asking good questions, providing sharp feedback, and using the evaluation process and report to catalyze positive change in their programs. Similarly, evaluation-competent leaders guide evaluation to support important priorities, build strategic partnership through the structured engagement and transparency enabled by evaluation, and develop credible evidence for organizational change.

The question is, how much do organizational leaders and program managers need to know? Here are some thoughts to consider for different levels of the organization.

10.3.1 Everyone in the Organization Needs to Understand Why an Evaluation Is Undertaken, What High-Level Questions It Is Asking, and What Decisions or Thinking It Will Inform

On the positive side, a shared understanding about evaluation creates visibility for organizational priorities and the organizational learning agenda. UN Women developed a practice of regularly publishing a colorful and well-laid-out magazine on the findings, conclusions, and recommendations from every central, organizational evaluation. UN Women staff began to look forward to the next positive evaluation story about their organization and saw how management incorporated what they read into its planning and strategies. This made it a lot easier for evaluators to get access and support in data collection when working with UN Women.

On the risk management side, opacity and ambiguity in evaluation can create mistrust and fear and can lead to uncooperative program staff. In one of Tessie's client organizations, educators were resistant to internal evaluation, refusing to share data from a learning program for people who were incarcerated because they feared that the data would be used against these people. Such fears are often well grounded in past experience, and there is no substitute for being open and transparent about the evaluation's purposes and intended uses. When Tessie went to speak with them, she learned that they had planned to walk out in the middle of the meeting. But when they were invited to speak about how they understood program excellence and how evaluation would help them toward their vision of success, they were willing to consider the importance of good data; data from their learning programs began to flow in after that. In one foundation, when the evaluation office sent out a survey for input on developing an organizational learning agenda, it was initially not well received. Staff worried, "We have enough work to do, and they now want us to learn on top of it—from whom, and how?" The evaluation office turned this negativity into an opportunity to meet with staff, clarify its intentions, and seek input. The result was greater understanding about the role of evaluation and the power of evaluative thinking in effective programming.

10.3.2 Evaluation-Competent Leadership Is a Must

Let us consider the question of how much evaluation knowledge is needed for leaders from the lens of the responsibilities of leadership. Good leaders and managers are responsible for the performance of their business units; this includes their outcomes and impact as well as their activities. To effectively manage for performance, they must understand their organizations within the economic, political, and social contexts where they operate; they must be aware of the perspectives of clients and staff, and communicate effectively about organizational performance and priorities; and they must use this deeper understanding to make good operational and investment decisions.

Evaluation is an important means of assessing and appreciating how well their unit is performing. Furthermore, there is an important investment decision: Resource allocation for evaluation should be made judiciously, and risks and opportunities must be considered and managed. If not designed and implemented well, evaluation can open a can of worms, hide problems, or exacerbate them. So, leaders need to be familiar with evaluation and guide it effectively so that it enables them to review strategic, programmatic, and organizational performance and to engage clients, stakeholders, and staff in understanding the past and building the future of their organizations.

Evaluation-competent leadership is about thinking clearly and critically, asking important questions, being mindful about assumptions and being willing to question them, approaching data and conclusions critically, and having the courage to see whatever the data tells you. Evaluation-competent leaders clearly appreciate the links between evaluation and strategy, evaluation and learning, and evaluation and communication; they also recognize the power of evaluation to engage staff and stakeholders in creative conversations that further the impact of the organization. Evaluative thinking is strategic thinking; it incorporates systems thinking and adaptive management principles, leading to process improvement. Evaluation findings and conclusions strengthen the credibility of communicated messages. Evaluation engagement increases staff learning and confidence about how to enhance the impact the organization is trying to achieve. And every evaluation is an opportunity to reaffirm organizational values and align the organization with its mission and vision.

Although leaders and managers do not need to know how to conduct evaluations themselves, all leaders would benefit from bringing evaluative thinking into their leadership practice. For example, leaders should be able to articulate a theory of change for their organization and programs and clarify the values and standards by which they and their colleagues should assess their success toward valued organizational outcomes. All leaders need to ask good clarification and follow-up questions when reading a report on programs managed or overseen by their organization. Evaluation-competent leaders review evaluation findings with eager curiosity to learn what the data tells them; they can guide investments in evaluation and insist that the way evaluation is implemented is consistent with organizational values. In UN agencies, for example, evaluations will typically identify one key value that must be visibly incorporated in the evaluation (gender equality, human rights, environmental sustainability, children's rights, etc.). More sophisticated approaches bring in a multiplicity of values that speak to the full range of impacted communities as well as those parts of the natural system that are potentially affected.

10.3.3 Program Staff Must Be Able to Articulate Their Program's Theory of Change, Standards of Program Excellence, and Assumptions and Risks

Training in evaluation hones your evaluative thinking, which is clear and critical thinking about what is likely to work, under what conditions, and why. When program staff understand the theory of change, they are clear about their role in bringing it to life and can question whether the cause-and-effect links they see are sufficient to bring about the desired change. Articulating standards of excellence makes it easier to check how well you are doing on an ongoing basis (in monitoring) and in evaluation. Articulating assumptions and risks enables staff to see the bigger picture and to get clearer on what is possible and what else outside their program may influence their ability to reach desired outcomes and fulfill stakeholder needs.

In the case of the WFP in 2018, the Independent Evaluation Office submitted a request to the human resources department to add evaluation competencies to the standard staff competencies used, pointing out that evaluation competencies are separate and distinct from the other general competencies. Requests for modification of standard competencies are rarely made and almost never accepted, so it is interesting to see how increased evaluation capacity in the WFP made this consideration possible.

10.3.4 Evaluation Competence in the Evaluation Unit

Depending on the size of the organization and the types of evaluations required, the evaluation unit will need a commensurate competency level. If the evaluation unit staff are conducting evaluations themselves, trained evaluators are necessary. If they are commissioning evaluations and overseeing them, some training is important, including short, deep-dive workshops relevant to the types of evaluations they are commissioning. In other words, they need enough to be able to make a wise selection of evaluators, to know how they need to engage their colleagues in the evaluation, to be competent in monitoring the progress of the evaluation and providing guidance as needed, and to manage evaluation use and dissemination of the final products of evaluation.

Driven by the American Evaluation Association competencies (2018), an evaluation unit must be able to do the following (in parentheses, we list the relevant competency domains):

- understand the organization's mission, vision, and values (context)
- understand the organization's learning priorities and needs for evaluative evidence (context, professional practice, methodology)
- determine the right pieces of evaluation work to meet those needs and priorities (context, professional practice)
- set evaluation priorities and plan for the evaluations that the organization will undertake (context, management)
- manage evaluation procurement (management)
- manage stakeholder engagement (interpersonal)
- guide the evaluation (management, methodology, interpersonal)
- ensure evaluation use (context, management, professional practice, interpersonal)

To be able to perform its role, an evaluation unit needs to have a clear understanding of the information and learning needs of the organization in the context of organizational programmatic strategy and which pieces of evaluation work would best meet those needs. It must have sufficient evaluation management expertise to select the right team and to guide the evaluation process all the way from inception to evaluation use and influence. That includes ensuring that the evaluation stays on the radar of the primary intended users and engaging them at the right times to provide them with the insights they need to inform their decisions or thinking. To do this effectively, the evaluation unit needs to have strong connections to and regular exchanges with leadership, program staff, and external key stakeholders.

Depending on the kinds of functions an evaluation unit can have, the evaluation unit should ideally include expertise in organizational learning and an understanding of how different pieces of evaluative work can help meet different informational and organizational learning needs. A strong evaluation unit needs the right mix of knowledge, skills, and attributes to engage effectively and credibly with a wide range of stakeholders, from the boardroom to grassroots groups—not only collecting data but also building high-trust relationships. They will need expertise in the formulation of evaluation questions and knowledge of how to scope and estimate a budget for evaluation so that the evaluation has a good chance of being able to answer those questions. Furthermore, the evaluation unit will need excellent interpersonal and project management skills, along with enough understanding of evaluation to be able to engage effectively with evaluation teams. Finally, some knowledge of how learning and influence occur within organizations will help ensure good evaluation uptake, influence, and use.

Evaluation as a field has been evolving rapidly over the last 20 years. We have moved from the linear debate of quantitative versus qualitative evaluation to the complicated space of mixed methods and a plethora of approaches to the complex space of social justice and environmental sustainability. We have traded paper surveys for mobile ones and stepped into the world of big data combined with Geographic Information System data mapping. Evaluation offices need to pay attention to these evolving trends in the practice of evaluation and keep developing evaluation capacity accordingly. To keep up, we recommend a review of the office structure and staffing every five years.

Additional capacities that are important for government evaluation units include the following:

- developing evaluation policies
- quality of evidence
- form, storage, and access of data (especially with the increased use of big data)
- data security
- investment in strong information technology systems
- moving from small-scale research methods to evaluation of large-scale projects
- formal and informal links and pause points with decision makers and the public

Prioritizing and planning for an evaluation unit's learning is covered in the next section on developing an evaluation strategic plan.

10.4 THE OPERATIONAL LEVEL OF EVALUATION

10.4.1 Developing an Evaluation Strategic Plan

An evaluation strategic plan for evaluation commissioners outlines the process for developing and using evaluation to support organizational and programmatic strategy. In fact, a good evaluation strategic plan is a key component of any good strategic plan. An evaluation strategic plan includes evaluation values, vision, and philosophy; a list of priority evaluation topics; assignment of responsibility for specific evaluations; and resources to achieve the goals of the evaluation strategic plan. Once the vision and broad organizational or programmatic outcomes are clear, evaluation can serve to assess the current situation, including strengths and assets, challenges and gaps, context, values, and broader systems issues. This assessment then helps organizations to identify what is already known and clear and what areas require further study and evaluation. To develop a relevant list of topics for evaluation, you might ask such questions as

- How do our investments and programs help us achieve our goals and desired outcomes?
- Is our selection of investments the best one to help us achieve our goals?
- In what ways are our programs relevant to the people we are serving?
- Who benefits from our investments, who is left out, and who is harmed?
- How can we improve the efficiency of our organizational and program operations?
- Where can we achieve economies of scale?

As discussed in Chapter 2, evaluation requires investment, so prioritizing the needs for evaluation every year and across years is important. In the same way that you cannot design and implement all the programs you might wish to undertake, you cannot evaluate everything that might be of interest. The evaluation plan must be aligned with the strategic plan and the decisions that need to be made in subsequent years. Larger, more complex evaluations may take a year or more to be commissioned and completed, so those need to be broader and more future oriented.

The evaluation strategic plan also needs to define the roles different departments and people will play in the evaluation. It should be clear which departments own the evaluation and are responsible for participation by relevant parties. Most importantly, it needs to be clear who is leading the charge of evaluation use. Evaluations with clear champions and high engagement have a higher chance of being both relevant and useful to the organization and key stakeholders.

The evaluation strategic plan should also define the values that underpin evaluation in the organization and that need to be reflected in evaluation questions as well as how evaluation is conducted. Clarity on values will help select evaluators who are the best fit for the organization and are most likely to have methods that are embraced by evaluation participants.

Finally, the plan must be clear on the resources that will be allocated for evaluation, including any additional evaluation capacities needed by the evaluation unit and program managers. Such a plan will enable the evaluation unit to accompany programmatic work, secure buy-in and collaboration, and do the necessary preparations and planning to ensure high-quality, relevant evaluations for the organization.

10.4.2 Monitoring Evaluation Quality

As with any investment of organizational resources, it is important to reflect both during and after the evaluation on how well it truly delivered value for the time, money, and other resources devoted to it. This ensures you use your experiences as a client—positive and negative—to learn how to get the most out of evaluation. This meta-evaluation reflection serves both to ensure adherence to the standards and guidelines and to improve the evaluation process and organizational systems that support it.

The meta-evaluative reflection process should be applied to the following:

- the commissioning process itself
- the choice of evaluation team

- the management of the evaluation contract from the client side
- how well you planned for the evaluation work to be influential and the extent to which that plan worked
- the value of the reporting (content, timing, delivery mode)

Here are some useful questions to ask about each evaluation:

- What were the most important contributions of this evaluation?
- How well did the request for proposal process work? Did we get a strong list of contenders? Who did not bid that we would have liked to bid? Why?
- In hindsight, how did the evaluation team perform? Did we choose the right evaluation team?
- How well did we support the evaluators in understanding the context and our needs and in filling any knowledge gaps?
- How well did the evaluation meet our information needs and others (e.g., learning, capacity building)?
- Did we get well-reasoned and well-evidenced answers to our most important questions?
- How did the evaluation prioritize our most important values (equity, gender equality, environmental sustainability, human rights, etc.)? What more could we have done?
- Were the evaluation and its findings actionable? Who has used them so far? Who has not used them, and why? What additional actions might we take to enhance evaluation use?
- What aspects of the evaluation disappointed us, and why?
- Do we have *aha* moments? Are we getting smarter?
- Are we getting high-quality evaluations? Are we using them?
- To what extent was the evaluation valuable?

10.4.3 Developing Evaluation Learning Plans

We have seen evaluation commissioning organizations that are serious about evaluation reach a point where they wonder,

- What evaluation training do we need for the continuing education of our evaluation unit?
- To what extent can we find the evaluation training we need in the marketplace, and in what areas should we build our own evaluation capacity-building offerings?

These are great questions, and several organizations are grappling with them. Here are some things to consider.

- *Your needs today and tomorrow.* To decide on the training evaluation staff needs, consider the functions they play today and look ahead—in what ways do you want to grow your evaluation function? Participate in evaluation conferences as well as conferences on statistics, social issues, big data, and public policy, and listen to what experts and colleagues are discussing.
- *Bring it back home.* Encourage colleagues who attend conferences or training to share soon after they attend. This will be stimulating and informative for everyone.
- *How deep to go?* Commissioners of evaluation need to understand evaluation methodology, but mostly, they will not know enough. Today, no evaluator knows about or can perform all methods and approaches that exist and keep emerging every day in evaluation. So, do not be upset when your team does not know how to conduct a social network analysis or how to work with a truncated distribution. You can always hire a consultant for a specialized requirement. Make sure, however, that you cover the basics: (1) Your team needs to take courses on evaluation management and know what a good evaluation plan looks like, how to develop a theory of change and strong evaluation questions, how to monitor evaluation, and what a good report layout looks like. (2) Next, you need to take some survey courses on quantitative and qualitative methods, survey design, focus group management, mixed methods, and using rubrics. (3) Take courses on stakeholder engagement and facilitation of evaluation (appreciative evaluation, collaborative, empowerment, etc.). (4) Take courses on how evaluation can prioritize the values important in your organization (e.g., gender transformative, environmentally sustainable, etc.), and courses on evaluation use and reporting. (5) Finally, take anything that inspires you and indulge your curiosity.
- *Buy or build?* Sending staff to training is much cheaper than building your own courses. Building and running courses is a different job than managing and conducting evaluations, so do not underestimate it; you would not want trainers to come over and do your evaluations in your place. If you build your own training, you will have to assign instructors or keep training new instructors in the content. With turnover and people getting pulled in different directions, the quality of instruction will vary, which will diminish satisfaction and learning. Or you may fail to adhere to the schedule, and colleagues will go without the needed training. Asynchronous training is great but needs some instructor involvement to get the most out of it. Furthermore, someone will need to keep up with the research and latest issues and update the curriculum. So here is our advice: Build your own training when it comes to walking people through your own processes and systems and complement that with training from the outside. Universities around the world offer quality evaluation training, and there are also training institutes and ad hoc training available. If you want something that is not offered, make an agreement with an outside consultant to offer it to your team. Of course, if you have a talented evaluation

trainer, then by all means, take advantage of it, but it is less expensive and more sustainable to rely on your academic and professional communities.

- *Prioritize the core.* Unless your evaluation unit conducts evaluations, prioritize evaluation management competencies. All evaluation skill building may contribute to making you a better manager, but there are some things you need to do well. You may love surveys and do them superbly, but if your job is to monitor evaluation quality and engage stakeholders, then that needs to come first. So, please, take another look at our suggested priorities, and make sure you have #1 covered before moving to #2 under the "How deep to go?" section above.
- *Individual evaluation journeys toward a collective purpose.* In her book, *Being an Evaluator: Your Practical Guide to Evaluation*, Donna Podems (2019) guides readers through an evaluation learning journey in a way that pushes for a deeper understanding of evaluation and is a good companion to the evaluation practitioner and to new evaluators. As we walk in our evaluation journeys, she reminds us that no matter what skill building your colleagues engage in, keep your collective sight on the purpose of evaluation because your work and the decisions informed by it will have an impact on people and the planet.

REFLECTIONS

Here are four prompts to guide reflection and learning for strengthening evaluation commissioner capacity.

1. Review the evaluation guidelines of your organization and those of an organization you consider to be a strong evaluation commissioner. How are they similar or different? What stands out to you about how guidelines can influence evaluation choices and evaluation quality?
2. Facilitate a conversation in your evaluation unit about what they most appreciate in the evaluation work they do and in what ways they see their evaluations making a positive difference in their organizations and for those their organization serves. Facilitate the same conversation with program staff (the ways in which evaluation makes a positive difference in their work). Facilitate the same conversation with a few program participants. Do this when an opportunity arises (you do not have to invest major resources). Share the content of these conversations with colleagues in the evaluation unit and reflect on the insights of program managers and participants (evaluation "clients"), and how you can continue to ensure that evaluation makes a positive difference for them.
3. Use the learning plan section of this chapter to review your evaluation learning plans for evaluation unit staff.
4. Think of all the things your evaluation unit's work contributes to your organization and the people it serves. Then, prioritize: If you had three wishes to strengthen your evaluation unit's contributions, what would they be? Pick one and develop a plan to make it happen.

REFERENCES

CHAPTER 1

American Evaluation Association (AEA). (2018). *AEA guiding principles (2018 update).* https://www.eval.org/p/cm/ld/fid=51

Aotearoa New Zealand Evaluation Association (ANZEA). (2015). *Evaluation standards for Aotearoa New Zealand* (April), 1–30. http://www.anzea.org.nz/evaluation/evaluation-standards/

Bamberger, M., Rugh, J., & Mabry, L. (2012). *RealWorld evaluation: Working under budget, time, data, and political constraints* (2nd ed.). SAGE.

Canadian Evaluation Society (CES). (2010). Competencies for Canadian evaluation practice. *Canadian Evaluation Society, 11*(4), 1–15. https://evaluationcanada.ca/txt/2_competencies_cdn_evaluation_practice.pdf

International Development Evaluation Association (IDEAS). (2012). *Competencies for development evaluation evaluators, managers, and commissioners.* https://ideas-global.org/the-competencies-framework/

Morra Imas, L. G., & Rist, R. C. (2009). *The road to results: Designing and conducting effective development evaluations.* The World Bank.

Patton, M. Q. (2011). *Developmental evaluation: Applying complexity concepts to enhance innovation and use.* Guilford Press.

United Nations Development Programme (UNDP). (2013). *Solutions related to challenges of independence, credibility and use of evaluation. Proceedings from the Third International Conference on National Evaluation Capacities* (October). http://web.undp.org/evaluation/documents/NEC/NEC-proceedings-2013.pdf

United Nations Evaluation Group (UNEG). (2016). *Evaluation competency framework.*

United States Government Accountability Office (GAO). (2018). *Goals and objectives for serving the congress and the nation: Strategic plan 2018–2023*, 1–68. https://www.gao.gov/assets/700/690260.pdf

World Food Programme (WFP). (2015). *Evaluation policy (2016–2021*). https://www.wfp.org/content/wfp-evaluation-policy-2016-2021

World Food Programme (WFP). (2016). *Evaluation brief—WFP's evaluation policy 2016–2021.* https://www.wfp.org/content/wfp-evaluation-policy-2016-2021

Yarbrough, D. B., Shulha, L. M., Hopson, R. K., & Caruthers, F. A. (2011). *The program evaluation standards: A guide for evaluators and evaluation users* (3rd ed.). SAGE.

CHAPTER 2

Davidson, E. J. (2010, June 9). 9 golden rules for commissioning a waste-of-money evaluation. *Active Learning Network for Accountability and Performance in Humanitarian Action* https://www.alnap.org/system/files/content/resource/files/main/9-golden-rules-for-commissioning-a-waste-of-money-evaluation-%C2%AB-genuine-evaluation.pdf

Dershem, L., Bishop, A., Kerner, B., Davidson, E. J., & Chianca, T. K. (2018). *Retrospective evaluation scoping guide.* Save the Children. https://resourcecentre.savethechildren.net/pdf/rie_scoping_guide_final.pdf/

Heider, C. (2014, October 28). *Value-for-money: Value-for-whom? IEG World Bank Group.* https://ieg.worldbankgroup.org/blog/value-money-value-whom

Morra Imas, L. G., & Rist, R. C. (2009). *The road to results: Designing and conducting effective development evaluations.* The World Bank.

Patton, M. Q. (2008). *Utilization-focused evaluation.* SAGE.

Patton, M. Q. (2011). *Developmental evaluation: Applying complexity concepts to enhance innovation and use.* Guilford Press.

Scriven, M. (1991). *Evaluation thesaurus.* SAGE.

Williams, B., & Hummelbrunner, R. (2010). *Systems concepts in action: A practitioner's toolkit.* Stanford Business Books.

Wholey, J. (1987). Evaluability assessment: Developing program theory. *New Directions in Evaluation, 33*, 77–92.

World Food Programme (WFP). (2021, April). *Decentralized evaluation: Guidance for process and content*. https://docs.wfp.org/api/documents/9f13fcec2d6f45f6915beade8e542024/download/

CHAPTER 4

Love, A. J. (1991). *Internal evaluation: Building organizations from within*. SAGE.

Morra Imas, L. G., & Rist, R. C. (2009). *The road to results: Designing and conducting effective development evaluations*. The World Bank.

Patton, M. Q. (2017). *Facilitating evaluation: Principles in practice*. SAGE.

Patton, M. Q., & Cambell-Patton, C.E. (2021). *Utilization-Focused Evaluation* (5th ed.). SAGE.

Preskill, H., & Catsambas, A. (2006). *Reframing evaluation through appreciative inquiry*. SAGE.

CHAPTER 5

Egolf, D. B. (2011). *Forming storming norming performing: Successful communication in groups and teams*. Writer's Club Press.

Lencioni, P. (2002). *The five dysfunctions of a team: A leadership fable*. Jossey-Bass.

Tuckman, B. W. (1965). Developmental sequence in small groups. *Psychological Bulletin*, *63*, 384–399.

CHAPTER 6

Bamberger, M., Rugh, J., & Mabry, L. (2012). *RealWorld evaluation: Working under budget, time, data, and political constraints* (2nd ed.). SAGE.

CHAPTER 7

Bamberger, M., Rugh, J., & Mabry, L. S. (2006). *Real-World evaluation: Working under budget, time, data, and political constraints* (1st ed.). SAGE.

Davidson, E. J. (2005). *Evaluation methodology basics: The nuts and bolts of sound evaluation*, (1st ed.). SAGE.

Fetters, M. D., & Molina-Azorin, J. F. (2017). The *Journal of Mixed Methods Research* starts a new decade: Principles for bringing in the new and divesting of the old language of the field. *Journal of Mixed Methods Research*, *11*(1), 3–10.

Mertens, D. M. (2020). *Research and evaluation in education and psychology: Integrating diversity with quantitative, qualitative, and mixed methods* (5th ed.). SAGE.

Morra Imas, L. G., & Rist, R. C. (2009). *The road to results: Designing and conducting effective development evaluations*. The World Bank.

Schwandt, T. A. (2015). *Evaluation foundations revisited: Cultivating a life of the mind for practice*. Stanford Business Books

Sligo, J. L., Nairn, K. M., & McGee, R. O. (2018). Rethinking integration in mixed methods research using data from different eras: Lessons from a project about teenage vocational behavior. *International Journal of Social Research Methodology*, *21*(1), 63–75.

CHAPTER 8

BetterEvaluation. (2021). *Data party*. https://www.betterevaluation.org/en/evaluation-options/data_party

Davidson, E. J. (2007). Unlearning some of our social scientist habits. *Journal of Multidisciplinary Evaluation*, *4*(8), iii–vi.

Hutchinson, K. S. (2017). *A short primer on innovative evaluation reporting*. Kylie Hutchinson.

Peterson, C., & Park, N. (2010). Keeping it simple. *The Psychologist*, *23*(5), 398–400.

United Nations Women. (2017, February). *TRANSFORM—The magazine for gender-responsive evaluation*. https://www.unwomen.org/en/digital-library/publications/2017/1/transform-issue-9

CHAPTER 9

Alkin, M. C., & King, J. A. (2017). Definitions of evaluation use and misuse, evaluation influence, and factors affecting use. *American Journal of Evaluation*, *38*(3), 434–450.

Asian Development Bank. (2022, March). *Evaluation, influence, action: How independent evaluation improves the Asian Development Bank's development effectiveness*. https://www.adb.org/documents/evaluation-influence-action-how-independent-evaluation-improves-asian-development-banks

Forss, K., Rebien, C. C., & Carlsson, J. (2002). Process use of evaluations: Types of use that precede lessons learned and feedback. *Evaluation, 8*(1) 29–45.

Ghanbarpour, S., Noguez Mercado, A. P., & Palotai, A. A. (2020). A language justice framework for culturally responsive and equitable evaluation. *New Directions in Evaluation, 2020*(166), 37–47.

Henry, G. T., & Mark, M. M. (2003). Beyond use: Understanding evaluation's influence on attitudes and actions. *American Journal of Evaluation, 24*(3), 293–314. https://doi.org/10.1177/109821400302400302.

Herbert, J. L. (2014). Researching evaluation influence. *Evaluation Review, 38*(5), 388–419.

Johnson, K., Greenseid, L. O., Toal, S. A., King, J. A., Lawrenz, F., & Volkov, B. (2009). Research on evaluation use: A review of the empirical literature from 1986–2005. *American Journal of Evaluation, 30*(3), 377–410.

Katz, E., & Lazarsfeld, P. F. (2017). *Personal influence: The part played by people in the flow of mass communication.* Routledge.

Kirkhart, K. (2000). Reconceptualizing evaluation use: An integrated theory of influence. *New Directions in Evaluation, 2000* (88), 5–23.

Patton, M. Q. (2008). *Utilization-Focused Evaluation.* (4th ed). SAGE.

Patton, M. Q., & Cambell-Patton, C. E. (2021). *Utilization-focused evaluation* (5th ed.). SAGE.

The UNICEF Evaluation Office, Ocampo, A., Shiva Kumar, A. K., & MacPherson, N. (2020). *Influencing for children: Evaluation matters.* United Nations Children's Fund. https://evaluationreports.unicef.org/GetDocument?fileID=15338

United Nations. (2017). *United Nations declaration on the rights of Indigenous peoples.* https://www.un.org/development/desa/indigenouspeoples/wp-content/uploads/sites/19/2018/11/UNDRIP_E_web.pdf

Weiss, C. H. (1993). Where politics and evaluation research meet. *Evaluation Practice, 14*(1), 93–106.

CHAPTER 10

American Evaluation Association. (2018). *AEA evaluator competencies.* https://www.eval.org/About/Competencies-Standards/AEA-Evaluator-Competencies

Davidson, E. J. (2005). *Evaluation methodology basics: The nuts and bolts of sound evaluation,* Thousand Oaks: SAGE.

Mertens, D. (2008). *Transformative research and evaluation.* Guilford Press.

Milstein, B., & Wetterhall, S. F. (1999, September 17). Framework for program evaluation in public health. *Morbidity and Mortality Weekly Report, 48*(RR-11). Centers for Disease Control and Prevention. https://www.cdc.gov/mmwr/preview/mmwrhtml/rr4811a1.htm

Podems, D. R. (2019). *Being an evaluator: Your practical guide to evaluation.* Guilford Press.

Preskill, H., & Catsambas, T. (2006). *Reframing evaluation through appreciative inquiry.* SAGE.

INDEX

Academic articles, 105–106
Active data collection, 86–87
Advocacy groups, 132
American Evaluation Association (AEA), 17
Aotearoa New Zealand Evaluation Association (ANZEA), 74
Approvals, 57, 119–120
Assignments, 77–78
Authority of EIM, 73

Bill and Melinda Gates Foundation, 6
Boilerplate problem, 29
Budget, 30, 52–53

Canadian Evaluation Society (CES), 17
Chief executive officer (CEO), 139
Commissioners, 9, 29, 40
  as team members, 73–74
Commissioning, 57
  building capacity in commissioning evaluation, 41
Communication, 77, 92
Competitive selection, 38–39
Confidentiality, 74–75
Context expertise, 36
Contractual accountability, 57
Corporate evaluations, 58
Countless deliberations, 98
Curriculum vitaes (CVs), 32, 43–44

Data analysis, 97
  cost of skipping, 99–100
  evaluation manager in, 100–103
  questions in, 98–99
  role and scope of, 98
Data analysis, integration, and synthesis (DAIS), 101
Data collection, 83
  active data collection, 86–87
  communication, 92
  early in, 84–86
  false data, 93–94
  file structure for saving documents, 87 (figure)
  file-naming protocols, 92
  good monitoring practices, 92–93
  guide or field guide, 84 (figure)
  incomplete data, 94–95
  managing and archiving data, 87–92
  things to monitor and consider in, 93 (figure)
  timing for checking on, 85 (figure)
  prior to initiating, 83–84
  tracker for preparing qualitative data for analysis, 90–91 (table)
  tracker for scheduling and completing qualitative data collection, 88–89 (table)
Data parties, 108
Data visualization, 116
Davidson, J., 19, 98, 110
Debriefing meeting, 118–119
Decentralized Evaluation Quality Assurance System (DEQAS), 24
Decentralized evaluations, 144
  recommended duration of, 41 (figure)
Department of Planning, Monitoring and Evaluation, 141
Diversity, 9

EnCompass Learning Center, 6
Evaluability assessment, 20
Evaluation commissioners
  evaluation competencies for, 147–151
  evaluation culture, 145–147
  evaluation function, 138–143
  evaluation values, vision, and philosophy, 144–145
  hybrid decentralized model of evaluation, 143–144
  operational level of evaluation, 151–155
  strong evaluation system, 138–145
Evaluation commissioning manager (ECM), 6–7, 67
Evaluation competencies, 34–35
  for commissioners of evaluation, 147
  evaluation competence in evaluation unit, 150–151
  evaluation-competent leadership, 148–149
  high-level questions, 148
  program staff, 149
Evaluation contracts, 21 (figure), 27
  award, 54
  evaluation management structure, 56–61
  evaluation requirements and preparation, 64–65
  key evaluation start-up tasks, 64–69
  kick-off meeting, 65–68
  questions for, 66 (table)
  reviewing evaluation contract, 64 (figure)
  stakeholder kick-off process, 68
  start-up, 55, 61–64
  submission and approval of evaluation plan, 68–69

tactical and strategic goals, 61 (figure)
Evaluation culture, 145
commitment from top, 145–146
learning about evaluation, 147
robust learning agenda, 146–147
transparency and shared meaning using evaluation, 146
Evaluation implementation manager (EIM), 5–8, 65–66
Evaluation implementor, 38
competitive selection, 38–39
preselected group, 39–41
Evaluation management, 1, 3–5
bodies, 58 (figure)
evaluation competency models, 17 (figure)
evaluation phases, 10–14 (table)
evaluation process, 9 (figure)
foundations, 59
investing in evaluation planning, 60–61
job, 5–14
key evaluation management competencies, 17–18
nonprofit organizations, 59–60
"project river" within complexity, 2 (figure)
roles, 6 (figure), 7–8
stakeholder engagement, 17 (figure)
structure, 56
tasks, 14–16
United Nations, 57–58
United States Federal Government, 58–59
Evaluation managers, 5, 8
in data analysis, 100
data streams, 101
ECM/EIM roles for, 100 (figure)
evaluation independence, 102
framing and integrating findings, 101–102
job in evaluation use and influence, 123–124
plan, 101
protect time and budget for data analysis, 100–101
Evaluation reporting, 5, 14, 105, 109–111
co-constructed next steps, 111–112
debriefing meeting, 118–119
evidence and values, 107
one-size-fits-all approach, 111
principles and practices of good reporting, 105–112
questions and answers, 106–107
reviews and approvals, 119–120
structure reports for actionable answers, 111
surprises, 107–109
written reports, 112–118
Evaluation team, 15, 71
challenges in, 80 (table)
configurations, 72–75
evaluation manager's strategies, 79 (figure)
goals of team management in evaluation, 71–72
issues, 74–75, 78–79
managing multiple evaluation teams at same time, 81–82
managing team performance, 75–81
selecting, 75
Evaluation use and influence, 121–122
drives, 125
evaluation manager's job in, 123–124
implementing recommendations, 122–123
key influencers in evaluation, 129–133
managing context and politics, 125–126
managing process and stakeholder engagement, 126–127
opportunities for stakeholder engagement in evaluation process, 132 (figure)
stakeholders to engage at points in evaluation process, 133 (table)
strategy, 127–129
strengthening evaluation culture and capacity, 134–135
Evaluations, 4–5, 20–23
boundaries, 23–24
budget, 52 (figure)
criteria and scoping, 23–27
function, 138–143
hiring researchers to conduct, 35
learning plans, 153–155
procurements, 31
quality, 152–153
stakeholders, 15
steering committee, 124
strategic plan, 151–152
values, vision, and philosophy, 144–145
Evaluative thinking, 149
Evaluators, 6, 9. *See also* Sole evaluators
External EIMs, 83
External evaluation, 27

False data, 93–94
Familiarity of team members, 72
File-naming protocols, 92
Fixed-price contract, 27
Ford Foundation, 146
Foundations, 6, 59, 139
Funding, 57

General Accountability Office (GAO), 18, 141
Good monitoring practices, 92–93
Governments, 6, 140
evaluation units set evaluation priorities, 143
national and local systems value evaluation, 142–143

positioning of evaluation in government organizations, 140–142

Graduate Evaluation Diversity Initiative (GEDI), 40

Headquarters/central evaluation office, 144
Heider, Caroline, 20
Historically underserved and/or marginalized groups, 131–132
Hutchinson, Kylie, 112
Hybrid decentralized model of evaluation, 143–144

Immediate/tactical goals, 61
Impartiality, 75
Inception phase of evaluation, 60
Inception report, 31, 60
Incomplete data, 94–95
Indefinite delivery indefinite quantity (IDIQ), 40
Indefinite quantity contract (IQC), 40
Independent Evaluation and Audit Services, 140
Independent Evaluation Office, 149
Indigenous peoples, 131
Internal contradiction problem, 30
Internal evaluation teams, 41
Internal evaluators, 8, 22–23, 67–68
International agencies, 6
International Development Evaluation Association (IDEAS), 17
Investing in evaluation planning, 60–61

Joint responsibility, 126

Kellogg Foundation, 143
Key evaluation questions (KEQs), 106, 116–117
Key influencers in evaluation, 129–133
Knowledge management/communications/training divisions, 144

Laudes Foundation, 146–147
Lazarsfeld, Paul, 130
Leadership, 144
Learning
  about evaluation, 147
  session, 118
Lencioni, P., 80

Mertens, D. M., 98
Meta-evaluative reflection process, 152–153
Methodology Directive Trap, 31–32
Ministry of Internal Affairs and Communications, 141
Monitoring, Learning and Evaluation (MEL), 146
Morra Imas, L. G., 4, 98

National and local systems value evaluation, 142–143
Natural systems, 1
"No surprises" principle, 108
Non-evaluators, 24
Nonprofit organizations, 6, 59–60, 139

One-size-fits-all approach, 111
Operational level of evaluation, 151
  evaluation learning plans, 153–155
  evaluation quality, 152–153
  evaluation strategic plan, 151–152
Orientation, 76
Overriding principle, 138

Park, N., 110
Participatory data analysis. *See* Data parties
Patton, Michael Quinn, 16
Peterson, C., 110
Podems, Donna, 155
Political forces, 126
Pre-proposal, 44–47
Prequalification process, 40
Preselected group, 39–41
Pre-start-up, 43
  clarifying, negotiating, and selection, 53–54
  evaluation contract award, 54
  pre-proposal, 44–47
  responding to terms of reference, 47–53
Primary intended users, 128–129
Procurement inflexibility, 30–31
Program offices, 144
Project management, 4–5
Proposals, 44
  process, 32
  writers, 44

Randomized control trials (RCTs), 145
Realistic budgets, 34
Recommendations meeting, 118
Reference group, 58
Reporting, 109
Request for application. *See* Request for proposal (RFP)
Request for proposal (RFP), 20, 21 (figure), 44
Request for quotation. *See* Request for proposal (RFP)
Reviews, 119–120
Rist, R., 4, 98
Robust learning agenda, 146–147

Save the Children, 6
Saving Newborn Lives (SNL) program, 6
Schwandt, Thomas, 98
Scope of work (SOW), 20, 21 (figure)
Selection committee, 38–39
Seven-step approach, 3
Shared meaning, 146
Social justice, 143
Sole evaluators, 35

pitfalls in evaluator competency specifications, 35–36
strategies for getting right competencies of evaluation team, 36–37
Staffing, 49–51
strategy, 51 (figure)
Stakeholders, 29
kick-off process, 68, 69 (table)
Start-up phase, 55
Steering committee, 58
Strategic goals, 61
Strategic lens, 44
Structure reports for actionable answers, 111
Subject matter expertise, 35–36
Submission and approval of evaluation plan, 68–69

Tactical lens, 44
Team member competencies, 73
Team planning, 76
Teamwork, 79–81
Technical advisory group (TAG), 59
Terms of reference (TOR), 20, 21 (figure), 44–47, 56, 124, 137
budget, 52–53
checklist form, 46 (figure)
content of evaluation, 28–29
good practices in writing evaluation, 32–35
guidance on evaluation, 28 (table)
key activities, tasks, and deliverables, 50 (table)
pitfalls to avoid in evaluation, 29–32
process of writing, 28–35
responding to, 47–53
shared responsibility table, 49 (table)
staffing, 49–51
timeline, 49, 50 (figure)
Time and materials contracts, 27
Time frame for use and influence, 129
Time management, 77–78
Timeline, 49, 50 (figure)
Transparency, 146
Tuckman, Bruce, 79
model of lifecycle of team, 79

U.S. Agency for International Development (USAID), 141
U.S. Agency for International Development's evaluation office in Policy, Planning, and Learning Bureau (USAID/PPL), 60
U.S. federal health agency, 30
United Nations (UN), 57–58, 139–140
United Nations Children's Fund (UNICEF), 140
United Nations Development Programme (UNDP), 15
United Nations Evaluation Group (UNEG), 5, 17
United Nations Population Fund (UNFPA), 140
United States (U.S.), 57–59, 142
United States Agency for International Development (USAID), 135

Value-for-money evaluation, 20
Value-free evaluators, 36
"Value-free" evaluation, 36
Values, 27, 33–34

Wholey, John, 20
World Food Programme (WFP), 5, 31–32, 60–61, 140
Written reports, 112
data visualization, 116
planning and making assignments, 114–115
report outline, 114
reporting structures, 112–114
skeleton report, 114
substantive reviews and collaboration, 115–116
synthesizing, editing, and quality management, 116–118

FSC
www.fsc.org
MIX
Papier | Fördert
gute Waldnutzung
FSC® C083411

Kolibri 360 GmbH
Ferdinand-Jühlke-Straße 7
99095 Erfurt, Deutschland
produktsicherheit@kolibri360.de